European Childhoods

European Childhoods

Cultures, Politics and Childhoods in Europe

Edited by

Allison James and Adrian L. James
University of Sheffield

First published in 2008 by
PALGRAVE MACMILLAN
Houndmills, Basingstoke, Hampshire RG21 6XS and
175 Fifth Avenue, New York, N.Y. 10010
Companies and representatives throughout the world.

PALGRAVE MACMILLAN is the global academic imprint of the Palgrave Macmillan division of St. Martin's Press, LLC and of Palgrave Macmillan Ltd. Macmillan® is a registered trademark in the United States, United Kingdom and other countries. Palgrave is a registered trademark in the European Union and other countries.

ISBN-13: 978-1-4039-9750-0 hardback
ISBN-10: 1-4039-9750-0 hardback

This book is printed on paper suitable for recycling and made from fully managed and sustained forest sources. Logging, pulping and manufacturing processes are expected to conform to the environmental regulations of the country of origin.

A catalogue record for this book is available from the British Library.

A catalog record for this book is available from the Library of Congress.

10 9 8 7 6 5 4 3 2 1
17 16 15 14 13 12 11 10 09 08

Transferred to Digital Printing 2008

Contents

Preface

In 2003, we had the pleasure of spending nearly two months working at the University of Trondheim in the Norwegian Centre for Child Research (*Norsk Senter for Barneforskning* – NOSEB), during which time we put the finishing touches to our book, *Constructing Childhood*. In the course of many discussions with our friends and colleagues at NOSEB, we tested out the soundness and applicability of our ideas and, in the process, refined our thinking about some of the main theoretical concepts that underpin the book, such as the notion of 'the cultural politics of childhood'.

Out of this dialogue came a conviction that if such analytical perspectives were indeed valid, they would be capable of shedding light on the social construction of childhood throughout Europe and from this conviction came the idea for this book. As editors, we would like to thank all of our friends and colleagues who have contributed to this volume, not only for writing their chapters, but being so accepting of our sometimes considerable demands as editors. The final collection is, we hope, one to which they are proud to have contributed and that will make a real contribution to the development of childhood studies within Europe and beyond.

ALLISON AND ADRIAN JAMES
Department of Sociological Studies, University of Sheffield and the Norwegian Centre for Child Research, University of Trondheim

Notes on the Contributors

Ferran Casas   is Senior Professor of Social Psychology in the Faculty of Education and Psychology at the University of Girona, Spain. He is the director of doctoral studies on Psychology and Quality of Life, and since May 1997 has been Director of the Research Institute on Quality of Life in the same university. He is also co-ordinator of the Catalan Interdisciplinary Network of Researchers on Children's Rights and Quality of Life. During the last ten years he has produced numerous articles and eight books, including *Psychosocial Perspectives on Childhood* (1998). His main topics of research are well-being and the quality of life, children's rights, adolescents and audiovisual media, families' quality of life in city environments and intergenerational relationships.

Dympna Devine   is a Senior Lecturer in the School of Education and Lifelong Learning, University College Dublin, Ireland. Her recent books include *Flexible Childhood? Exploring Children's Welfare in Time and Space* (co-edited with Helga Zeiher, Harriet Strandell and Annetrine Kjorholt, 2007); *Equality, Diversity and Childhood in Irish Primary Schools* (co-edited with Jim Deegan and Anne Lodge, 2004); and *Children, Power and Schooling – How Childhood is Structured in the Primary School* (2003). Other publications include chapters in edited collections and journal articles in *Childhood*; *Children and Society*; *International Studies in Sociology of Education*; and *Irish Educational Studies*.

Eva Gulløv   is a Senior Lecturer at the Department of Educational Anthropology at the Danish University of Education, Copenhagen, Denmark. She is the author and editor of numerous publications on children, childcare institutions and methodology in ethnographic child research, including the co-edited book *Children's Places: Cross-cultural Perspectives* (2003).

Heinz Hengst   was Professor of Social and Cultural Sciences, Hochschule Bremen, Department of Sozialwesen, Germany. His work has focused on childhood for more than 25 years, with his research interests mainly concerning questions of contemporary childhood, children's culture and changing generational relations. He is author, co-author, editor and co-editor of numerous articles and books on childhood, including *Kindheit als Fiktion* (1981), *Kindheit in Europa*

(1985), *Die Arbeit der Kinder* (2000), *Kinder, Körper, Identitäten* (2003), *Per una sociologia dell'infanzia* (2004) and *Kindheit soziologisch* (2005).

Michael-Sebastian Honig is Professor of Educational Science at the University of Trier, Germany, and was scientific assistant at the German Youth Institute (DJI), Munich from 1976 to 1997. In 1986 he became Dr. rer. soc., investigating violence within families. He qualified as a professor in educational science in 1996 with a discourse on the theory of childhood. He is co-editor of *Zeitschrift für Soziologie der Erziehung und Sozialisation (Journal for Sociology of Education and Socialization)*. His work and projects concentrate on the theory and history of social pedagogy, early childhood education, ethnography in educational settings and changes in generational ordering.

Adrian James has researched and published widely in the field of socio-legal studies, including the completion of two ESRC-funded projects on aspects of child welfare in divorce. He was a Special Adviser to the House of Commons Select Committee on the Lord Chancellor's Department for its scrutiny of the work of CAFCASS. Appointed as Professor of Applied Social Sciences at the University of Bradford in 1998, he became Professor of Social Work at the University of Sheffield, in September 2004. His latest book, co-authored with Allison James and published by Palgrave Macmillan, is *Constructing Childhood: Theory, Policy and Social Practice* (2004).

Allison James is Professor of Sociology at the University of Sheffield. As one of the pioneers of the new social studies of childhood she has carried out empirical and theoretical research into children's culture, children as social actors, child health, children's time use and the cultural politics of childhood. She also has research interests in identity, the life course and food. Her current research projects include children's perceptions of hospital space and children's perspectives on food. The author of numerous books and articles on childhood, her most recent work is *Constructing Childhood: Theory, Policy and Social Practice* (with Adrian James, 2004).

Anne Trine Kjørholt is Director and Associate Professor at the Norwegian Centre for Child Research, Trondheim, Norway. She has research interests in a number of areas, with publications relating to discourses on childhood, children's rights, childhood as a symbolic space, children's cultures and early childhood education and care. Her current research centres on the modern child and the flexible labour market, children as citizens, and children's and young people's local knowledge in Ethiopia and Zambia.

Randi Dyblie Nilsen is Professor at the Norwegian Centre for Child Research, Norwegian University of Science and Technology where she lectures on the international MA and PhD programmes. Her research interests in childhood studies are broad, and include a continuing interest in ethnographic approaches at day-care institutions together with theoretical and methodological issues. One of her latest articles in English is: Searching for Analytical Concepts in the Research Process: Learning from Children. *International Journal of Social Research Methodology* 8 (2005) 2: 117–35.

Jens Qvortrup is Magister and PhD in sociology at the University of Copenhagen, Denmark. His areas of interest include the sociology of generations, childhood, welfare research and comparative sociology and has published extensively in these fields. He was among the first to engage in the sociology of childhood and was founding president of ISA's Sociology of Childhood section (1988–98) and director of the pioneering study Childhood as a Social Phenomenon (1987–92). He is currently co-editor of the journal *Childhood*.

Spyros Spyrou is Director of the Centre for the Study of Childhood and Adolescence and Assistant Professor of Anthropology and Sociology at Cyprus College, Cyprus. His research interests include childhood, education and identity construction. He is particularly interested in the role of nationalism and racism in children's identity constructions. He has worked with and been a consultant to a number of international organizations, including the United Nations, the Sesame Workshop and Search for Common Ground. He is currently working on an EU-funded project on integrating into policy-making the perspectives of children from single parent families about poverty and social exclusion.

1
European Childhoods: An Overview

Adrian James and Allison James

The publication by UNICEF (2007) of a report comparing children's welfare in 21 Western states has triggered an important debate about children and their childhood in different countries. Whilst attracting some criticism as a consequence of the subjective nature of the data on which some of the judgements are made, the report nonetheless has enormous symbolic value, drawing attention as it does to apparently significant differences in the physical and emotional well-being of children. In making comparisons between the daily lives of children based on six dimensions of welfare, which highlight major disparities within Europe – with the Netherlands appearing at the top of the league (followed closely by Sweden, Denmark, Finland, Spain, Switzerland and Norway) and the UK at the bottom – it provides an important and timely context in which to begin to ask questions about the political, cultural and social factors that underpin the construction of such different childhoods within Europe.

With the growing global political awareness of the significance of children's rights and perspectives, following the almost unanimous acceptance and ratification of the United Nations Convention of the Rights of the Child (UNCRC), it is also important to explore the extent to which children's interests are, in practice, finding common expression in different societies, since this is arguably a profoundly important indicator of the way in which different societies understand and view children and childhood. This volume proposes to do this in the specific context of Western Europe: its aim is to compare the ways in which social and welfare policies on childhood are being framed within the social, political and legislative context of different European societies and being realized, for children, in and through forms of cultural practice. If, as is frequently argued, 'the child is a nation's future', such a comparative project is timely, not least because of the drive for a common European political identity. It is also the case, however, that the ambitions for achieving this identity have been frustrated, for the time being at least, by the recent failure of a number of Member States to endorse the proposed European Constitution, a failure that is perhaps, at least in part, a reflection of concerns about the potential impact of such a shared political identity on the different *social* and *cultural* identities of the peoples of Europe, some of which are reflected in the findings of the UNICEF report.

In drawing together perspectives from a number of European countries, this volume sets out to explore the ways in which 'culture' is produced and reproduced through policies for children and to identify any commonalities or differences among them, which might be relevant to the European debate. Drawing on a variety of empirical evidence, ranging from the analysis of policy documents in different European states to a consideration of the ways in which 'childhood' is constructed and represented through to the exploration of the local impact such policies have for children themselves, this book offers an analysis of the ways in which children are positioned by such policies in Member States and asks about the significance of these for childhood and for the adult citizens that today's children will become.

It is inevitable that a major contextual element of this analysis is provided by the UNCRC, given the impact this has had on the global discourse about children's rights. Part of the motivation for putting together this collection, therefore, was to consider whether there has been any harmonization of policies and practices across Europe as a result of the perceived universalizing of ideas of childhood or whether, as seems likely given the influence of the cultural politics of childhood in different countries (James and James 2004), there are still significant if subtle political and cultural differences that work against such a harmonization, despite the UNCRC.

A key feature of this volume is therefore a comparison between the social and welfare policies for children developed in avowedly child-centred states such as Norway and Denmark, and others such as England, Germany, Ireland, Spain and Cyprus, where children are positioned rather differently in their welfare politics. In each context, cultural ideas about what is a 'good' or 'proper' childhood are explored and the ways in which these are given effect through social and welfare practices that shape children's everyday lives are examined. In particular, a key focus is on the various ways in which the concept of 'the best interests of the child' are expressed and how Member States provide for the participation of children in determining this. As a result, comparisons can be drawn about the relationship between cultures, politics and childhoods in different European societies and the extent to which a European childhood is emerging. In the process, the chapters contribute, both individually and collectively, to wider theoretical debates about the globalization of childhood, children's needs and the universal rights of children.

A number of common themes and issues emerge. In asking the question 'What is a good or proper childhood?' the contributors reveal significant differences between the way in which childhood is understood in the context of child-centred states, such as Norway and Denmark, and those in other states. This comparison reveals, in particular, stark contrasts in the ways in which what is 'good' for children is framed and what a 'proper' childhood is thought to be like, framings that produce very different outcomes for children's everyday experiences. Importantly, what also emerge are the connections between how such ideas are framed and the growing awareness of concerns about, and the need to reinforce, more abstract notions of national identity through such (re)constructions of childhoods.

The chapters also reveal differences in the ways in which the future for children is envisaged and the impact of the pursuit of such futures on children in terms of their daily lives. Such differences are clearly reflected in the policy documents in which children's futures are articulated, highlighting the role of policy as discourse in the construction and reconstruction of childhood, and therefore in the production and reproduction of culture. Many of these differences centre on the distinctions between concepts such as 'pedagogy', 'socialization' and 'education' as different ways of teaching children, distinctions which produce different mechanisms for the transmission of cultural knowledge and which therefore lead to different outcomes for children's everyday experiences and their futures. The role of *schooling*, to use a more generic term – literally, the action of teaching – in the production of these futures is therefore crucial, the *nature* of this schooling providing a clear reflection of the different cultural politics of childhood in each country. The impact of such schooling also represents a powerful challenge to the intentions of the UNCRC, for if children's understanding of themselves in the context of their national identities is shaped so forcefully, it severely limits their ability to think freely about who they are and who they want to be, and thus their right to participate in decision-making about their future.

A further theme of the book is how different Member States[1] provide for the 'best interests' of children through different constructions of children's rights, and in particular of the right to be involved in decisions concerning their future (UNCRC Article 12), based on sometimes widely differing assumptions about children's competence and their roles as social actors in society. As each chapter illustrates, children's experiences are profoundly and differentially shaped by these framings of their 'best interests' and the assumptions on which these are based; and these are firmly rooted in adults' perspectives on and values in relation to children and childhood, which are, once again, a product of the cultural politics of childhood. In this context, the relationship between children, the family and the state emerges as being of critical importance in terms of the extent and ways in which the state is involved with families in the joint project of producing a 'good' childhood, through the provision of different kinds of institutional arrangements for children/childcare and welfare policies to support parents.

Such constructions provide us with important information about the way in which children's rights are perceived and therefore about the way in which their citizenship is understood. Not surprisingly, we can see that children are also differently positioned throughout Europe with regards to citizenship, their participation in decision-making and policy-making, and their involvement in shaping ideas of cultural belonging. Here a continuum can be seen between, at the one end, countries in which children are recognized as social actors, with their own 'children's culture' (e.g. Scandinavia) and as the carriers of national culture (e.g. Scandinavia and Cyprus) and, at the other, those in which children are increasingly seen primarily in terms of the reproduction of labour and the workforce of the future (e.g. the UK).

Crucially, this continuum serves to highlight the complex interrelationship between structure and agency in the context of childhood, by identifying the connections, made through the conduit of intergenerational relations, between the state and the family, the market and culture, and therefore between the reproduction of labour through institutional practices and the reproduction of culture through social practices. The growing perception and awareness of children as social property and as human capital that emerges in this context places renewed emphasis on children's futurity. Thus, whilst Qvortrup, argues persuasively in chapter 11 for the incorporation of childhood into thinking about and analysis of the role of the welfare state now that the 'new' social studies of childhood has established childhood in its own right, we must not lose sight of the powerful impact that such emerging perceptions can have on the lived experiences of children and on the struggle to establish them as bearers of rights, which is illustrated by the other chapters.

In chapter 2, Anne Trine Kjørholt explores the contrast between two very different experiences of childhood and children's participation in Norway – that of children in kindergartens compared to that of asylum-seeking children – and the dilemmas raised by trying to reconcile these two very different sets of experiences with ideals of what constitutes a 'good childhood'. In doing so, she implicitly identifies a number of issues that are faced by every country in Europe, revolving around the ever-present global problem of military conflict and the resulting displacement of civilian populations, which results in large numbers of people seeking asylum in the comparative peace and prosperity of EU Member States. In particular, she draws attention to the uncomfortable realities of life for asylum-seeking children and especially to the crucial question of the extent to which their rights under the UNCRC are guaranteed and protected, both in absolute terms and relative to the children of the states in which asylum-seekers hope to be granted residence.

For Norway, as the first country in Europe to incorporate the Convention into its domestic law, this is a particularly acute and sensitive issue, since the implications of every aspect of the Convention must now be considered in the light of its implications for Norwegian law. In addition, this process will necessarily raise important issues for every aspect of childhood in Norway, including the complex and difficult questions that arise from a consideration of the relationship between rights and citizenship. That Norway is in the vanguard in confronting the challenges raised by the incorporation of the UNCRC into its domestic legislation does not make these questions any less acute for other Member States, however, for as the other chapters in this volume reveal, the relationship between children's rights, children's citizenship and children's futures is fundamental to debates about childhood throughout the EU.

In an interesting and revealing chapter, Randi Dyblie Nilsen draws on data from her research to describe the Norwegian construction of a 'good' and 'proper' childhood, as evidenced in policy and practice, in the context of the fostering of a positive relationship between children and nature, through the expansion of nature day-care centres. Significantly, however, embedded in the experiences of such centres are important cultural values and expectations, including the child's right to participate and the encouragement of children to exercise their agency and their autonomy, issues which are also at the heart of Kjørholt's chapter.

More than this, Nilsen argues that this particularly Norwegian construction of childhood suggests that the construction of a national identity is at stake, with a particular emphasis on the independence of children. This contrasts sharply with current developments in England and Wales (see James and James, chapter 6), which seem to emphasize dependence on and control by adults. Indeed, it is difficult to envisage the events described by Nilsen occurring in England, let alone being encouraged by parents or politicians – the notion of young children being allowed and encouraged to use sheath knives would be almost certain to spark a public outcry and lead to yet another spate of health and safety legislation! Yet, as other chapters reveal, Norway is far from being the only European state that is currently engaged in the process of identifying and reinforcing a national identity through policies aimed at shaping children and childhood.

Turning to developments in southern Europe, Casas considers the importance attached in Spain to the notion of responsibility in children and its links with participation. Importantly, however, he highlights the tensions between the official position adopted by the state and what happens in practice, and between what happens in the public and private spheres. Unlike the Scandinavian countries, his analysis suggests that there is no shared view of what constitutes a 'good childhood' in Spain and that although the official position is one of a clear commitment to the promotion of children's rights under the UNCRC, social practices are at odds with this, reflecting clearly the influence of the Spanish cultural politics of childhood. This, he suggests, is partly because of the relatively recent development of a welfare state in Spain following its return to democracy in 1979, and the fear of many Spanish adults, in which they are by no means alone, that children's participation will undermine parental authority.

In this context, he goes on to explore the recent impact of information and communication technology on relationships between adults and children, partly as a consequence of the effect they have had in strengthening youth culture and increasing peer-group influence in the process of socialization. This in turn has had the effect of weakening their dependence on and thus the influence and authority of adults; however, it is also because it gives children access to authoritative sources of knowledge that are different from those traditionally controlled by adults, thereby challenging ideas about parental authority and inter-generational relationships. In such a context, Casas argues that determining what is in 'the best interests of the child' becomes more than usually problematic and represents a major challenge for adults in terms of how to realize the ambitions of the UNCRC in a context in which children and young people are showing themselves to be ever more active in creating their own cultures, from which adults are largely excluded.

In looking at recent changes in the social construction of childhood in Ireland, Dympna Devine also focuses on the challenge that children as active social agents represent to adult hegemony and the key role of power in the cultural politics of childhood. The historical similarities with Spain, described by Casas, in terms of the strong emphasis on the traditional authority of parenthood and an absence of welfare polices for children until very recently, are compelling. Equally compelling, however, is Devine's analysis of the evolving role of education in instilling Irish cultural values (cf. Norway), an understanding of Irish nationhood and the identification of what constitutes an Irish 'good childhood', with its focus on shaping (and reshaping) childhood and the very recent emergence of a recognition of the role of the state in fostering children's participation and children's rights, rather than national identity.

This new emphasis, however, has seen a growing tension between the advocates of children's rights and the traditional sources of adult power in Ireland and, as in Norway (cf. Kjørholt, chapter 2), it is children at the margins, such as Travellers and asylum-seekers, who put government commitments to children's rights and participation to the severest test. Thus, as with the analysis of developments in Spain (Casas, chapter 4), Devine points to the tensions and discrepancies between official polices and institutional practices, and to the challenge the construction of children as bearers of rights represents to the traditional power-knowledge relationship between adults and children. Mirroring the discussion of recent developments in the UK (James and James, chapter 6), her analysis also demonstrates a willingness on the part of government to use the rhetoric of children's participation but to deny them any effective involvement, which, she argues, 'raises key questions related to the political commitment to realize children's rights in practice'.

In chapter 6, James and James explore similar themes and issues, reflecting the ambiguities that currently permeate relationships between adults and children elsewhere in Europe. On the one hand, driven by the imperatives of the UNCRC, government policies employ the rhetoric of participation whilst, on the other, they reflect an apparent desire to re-establish a more traditional relationship between adults and children, a relationship based on the authority of adults and the protection and 'safeguarding' of children's futures as citizens and as the next generation of labour. Such changes are deeply rooted in the prevailing cultural politics of childhood in the UK, with its strong emphasis on children's futurity, although unlike developments elsewhere in the EU, their rationale is much more obviously rooted in the growing awareness of and sensitivity to the impact of the 'risk' society and related discourses of protection. Because such protective measures are so 'obviously' in the child's best interests, they provide a robust basis for legitimizing the extension of control over children and their childhoods, making the risk and protection paradigm central to government thinking and policy formulation.

As we argue, 'In a political environment such as this, the identification and allocation of "risk" becomes a mechanism to give authority to the state to intervene in the lives of groups who are deemed to be "dangerous", such as children.' The significant shift that is evident, however, is that the emerging strategy identifies not just some groups of children (e.g. offenders, school drop-outs, single mothers, etc.) as being in need of safeguarding, but *all* children. Moreover, under this strategy and under the direction of the state, *all* adults and professionals working with children, rather than just teachers, social workers and doctors, become responsible for safeguarding them. Thus relationships between adults and children are being fundamentally reconfigured as childhood itself is (re)constructed as being at risk.

Such developments are, however, not unrelated to broader issues of citizenship and national identity, particularly, although not exclusively, as far as children are concerned, since successive UK governments have struggled, to a greater extent than elsewhere in Europe, to identify what aspects of 'Britishness' comprise national identity. This has culminated in the announcement of plans for the radical overhaul of teaching in order to give pupils aged 11–16 a better understanding of 'Britishness' and to teach them about 'traditional British values', such as respect for other cultures and tolerance of religious and sexual differences. Endorsing these proposals, the Education Secretary, Alan Johnson, is quoted as saying: 'The values our children learn at school will shape the kind of country Britain becomes' (*The Independent*, 26 January 2007). In addition, it is becoming increasingly likely that proposals will be introduced compelling all young people to remain in full-time education until the age of 18. Such developments are also part of the government's response to 'risk' by safeguarding children's futures.

As Gulløv argues (chapter 7), with the development of modern European states, the rearing of children has become more and more professionalized and subject to state responsibility and authority, albeit that this process has not been uniform across the EU Member States. As a consequence, she argues, childhood and childcare institutions have become increasingly politicized, becoming objects of intense discussion concerning investment and societal outcomes, a process that has been particularly evident in Denmark where there has been state involvement in the construction of a 'good childhood'. Thus, current policies aimed at reinventing national culture have been pursued through heavy investment in public day-care institutions for pre-school children aged between six months and seven years, the age at which compulsory education begins (cf. Kjorholt and Nilsen on Norwegian developments). Indeed, she argues that 'day-care has become so much a part of the normal trajectory of the child that being at home is interpreted as potentially damaging for a sound development'.

As in Norway and Ireland, however (see Kjørholt and Devine, respectively), not all children in Denmark are embraced by the Danish version of 'the good childhood', including children from ethnic minorities who are unable to display the same competence in and mastery of the Danish language. This has become an indicator of capability to participate in democratic decision-making, its importance being exemplified by the introduction of legislation requiring the testing of Danish language fluency among pre-school minority children and singling out competence in Danish as an area for special educational intervention, for the sake of the individual child as well as the state. In addition, pre-school institutions aim to teach children the right way to behave, how to manage themselves and how to be co-operative and considerate towards others – in short, to be 'civilizing agents'.

In this way, a Danish version of 'risk' emerges, in which children not enrolled in day-care institutions are considered to be 'at risk' of not learning how to behave in socially sanctioned ways. Ironically, therefore, unlike in Spain (see Casas, chapter 4), it might be argued that in Denmark the authority of parents has been challenged by the state rather than by children. Gulløv also clearly demonstrates the cultural politics of childhood at work, however, and the fact that children are not only embedded in societies with specific historical and cultural ideas about childhood and the proper treatment of children, but also in fields of social relations (cf. Bourdieu), in which agents in different positions try to consolidate and extend their status and influence. As a result, as Gulløv argues, 'dominant conceptions of childhood reflect the distribution of power and dominance between the positions in the field'.

Chapter 8 explores similar themes and issues in terms of the role of education policy and practice in Cyprus as part of the process of cultural reproduction in a divided society, drawing on recent empirical data that illustrate how children respond to such processes. In exploring the role of the school as part of the apparatus of the state and how children are controlled by both the school and the family, Spyrou illustrates how children nonetheless become active participants in the process of creating a national identity. This they do at least partly through their interactions with their teachers, who act as mediators between policies and children. As Spyrou also shows, however, children's identities are never totally determined because of their ability to find ways to exercise their agency and to challenge or escape from some of the constraints imposed on them by external agencies.

Following Bourdieu, however, he concludes that the process of education in Cyprus has, until recently, as in so many other parts of the world, been one of exerting symbolic violence on them. In spite of official declarations about the liberating role of education and students' participation in the educational process, children are, more often than not, told what and how to think, what kind of children they should be and what kind of adults they should aim to be when they grow up. Latterly, however, following the accession of Cyprus to the European Union, a much more liberal influence has been exerted on education policy, in an attempt to move it away from its narrow ethnocentrism towards a system that will work to cultivate respect for diversity and pluralism. In spite of such changes, the impact of large-scale recent immigration has highlighted the difficulties faced by non-Greek-speaking children in Cypriot schools, giving further cause for reflection on the issues raised by Gulløv (chapter 7) concerning the emphasis placed by the Danish government on the language proficiency of the children of immigrant families.

Moving to the German context, Hengst explores how cultural pedagogy has developed outside the school as a result of the relative short hours of school attendance for German children, exploring its impact on notions of children's culture. Comparing this with the emergence of children's culture policy in Denmark in the 1970s, he observes that a key concern of such developments was, and continues to be, that children should be encouraged to play an active cultural role outside the family and the school, an emphasis that reflects a characteristic of such policies in the Nordic countries – that they are designed as policies of equality and pursued with the intention of enabling children to live their own lives independently of their parents' economic and cultural resources and as citizens with equal rights.

The increasing importance of developing an explicit cultural policy in Germany, not only in general terms but, in particular, for children and young people, is in marked contrast to the approach of other EU states, such as Britain and Ireland, to childhood. It reflects, Hengst argues, the search for re-integration in the face of the perceived breakdown of social institutions and is based on an understanding that children are, and have always been, autonomous participants in the cultural process. This approach assumes from the outset that children are independent beings and the policy questions that then arise centre on the areas in which children's independence should be suppressed, restricted, prevented or obstructed.

The German approach, which is largely extra-curricular and therefore not under the immediate control of the state, thus emphasizes the rights of children to their own culture, the advantages of the focus on cultural education processes being argued to lie in the fact that 'they are very powerful in helping individual sensitivities to express themselves, and in fostering in children and young people a conscious relationship to their own person, their own biography and future'. It can be argued that the development of the Third Way and the influence of communitarianism in British politics under New Labour reflect a similar concern with social re-integration. However, the British approach is predicated on a very different understanding of childhood and has produced a very different policy response in which the role of the state is of central importance (see James and James, chapter 6).

In a complementary chapter, offering another facet on childhood in post-unification Germany, Honig draws attention to the massive expansion in pre-school education, which he attributes primarily to changing economic and demographic factors. Not only is this important in terms of the development and welfare of children, Honig also argues that a reconstruction of childhood as an institution is taking place, which is making possible a re-contextualization of childhood and a realignment of the responsibilities of, and the relationships between, the state, the family, children and the market. In the process, he argues that 'child' has become 'an age-differentiated status where rights and responsibilities are subject to more detailed regulation than in any other phase of life', a description that also reflects the cultural politics of childhood in Germany today and that sounds very similar to the developments described by James and James in the UK (see chapter 6), particularly in terms of the shifting balance between risk, protection and control.

Importantly, however, his analysis focuses on the relationship between the detail of day-care arrangements for children and the macro-forces of socio-economic change and the demands of the labour market. Such issues go hand-in-hand with discourses relating to education, social and economic policies, which variously highlight the educational aspects of day-care arrangements, the role of day-care facilities in creating more equal opportunities in life and work, and the provision of childcare as it relates to the need to bring more women with children into the labour market. Empirical data demonstrate, however, the richness and complexity of the care arrangements made by many families, who expend significant resources to provide their children with a diverse and stimulating world of experience. Indeed, in many cases they go outside traditional childcare structures, thereby highlighting the duality of family and public education for the experience of children growing up in post-reunification Germany. More importantly, he argues that in the context of far-reaching economic and social changes, the structure of care arrangements and socio-cultural patterns of what comprises a 'good childhood' are linked and that by making explicit ideas about what a child *needs* or what additional support children *ought to be given* within certain social milieus, we can gain an insight into how the notion of what constitutes 'a good childhood' in Germany is changing.

In the final chapter, Qvortrup provocatively argues that children and childhood are not logically and necessarily a part of welfare state thinking, since children do not 'belong' to the state, let alone have any legitimate rights as claimants. This, he argues, is due to the fact that, in the main, children's status is that of dependants, and so they are subsumed under the household or, more specifically, the family – a view that explicitly echoes the position of children in Spain (Casas, chapter 4) and implicitly that in many other European countries. Consequently, any benefits they do receive do not accrue to them as a right but as an effect of targeting benefits at their parents. Indeed, Qvortrup goes further to ask whether children are really even the subject of the principle of need, or whether this too is delegated to someone else.

Importantly, however, he argues that even in advanced welfare states, such as the Nordic countries, the demands of the labour market on adults take precedence over child-rearing. Nonetheless, as he also points out, there are huge variations in the financial and service provisions made by different European countries, reflecting similarly large variations in the extent to which children's social citizenship is recognized as a legitimate claim. Since educational investments are for the common good, however, and thus of equal significance for all members and sections of society, Qvortrup argues that these investments must count as a contribution to maintaining and reproducing society as a whole, underlining the importance of schools and the education of children as the key mechanisms in cultural reproduction. As he points out, society has in effect colonized children's labour, leaving the costs to be paid by the family, with the consequence that 'those who are obliged to care for children do not benefit from it economically, while those who are profiting from children being brought up, do not contribute'. His analysis also suggests that children are, in fact, doing useful work in school and are therefore part of a new societal division of labour. Thus, by implication, children should be considered as members of society – as citizens – who deserve, as a right, a just proportion of societal resources.

Such observations not only mirror the major themes and issues raised in this volume, they also highlight the importance of the cultural politics of childhood in defining some of the major issues for social policy in relation to European childhoods and the relationship between children, their parents and the state. At the heart of this lies a question of fundamental importance to the analysis and understanding of childhood and more importantly to the lives of children, not only in Europe but throughout the world – what should be the balance between childhood as an end in itself, and childhood as a mean to an end?

Note

1   Norway, of course, is not a EU Member State.

References

James, A. and James, A. L. (2004) *Constructing Childhood: Theory, Policy and Social Practice.* Basingstoke: Palgrave Macmillan.
UNICEF (2007) *Child Poverty in Perspective: An Overview of Child Well-being in Rich Countries.* Innocent Report Card 7. Florence: Innocenti Research Centre.

2
Children as New Citizens: In the Best Interests of the Child?

Anne Trine Kjørholt

Nadia is two years old. She lives with her three siblings who are aged between five and twelve and her parents in an asylum seekers' reception centre in Norway. They are Sunni Muslims and their country of origin is Iraq, from where they were forced to flee for political reasons in 2005. When they first arrived as refugees in a country in southern Europe, they were met with violence and because they felt threatened, they continued on to Norway to apply for permanent leave to remain there. Nadia's father was detained and tortured in his home country and he is suffering from post-traumatic stress disorder. The family has been there for four months, waiting for a decision to be made about whether they will be interviewed by the Directorate of Immigration (UDI) and thereby get permission to apply legally to be asylum seekers in Norway.

Close to the reception centre is where Mari lives. She is the same age as Nadia and like the majority of pre-school Norwegian children, Mari attends kindergarten from 8 am to 4 pm while her parents are at work. Mari has two older siblings, aged eight and fourteen. Her mother was born in the same place as they live today and one of Mari's grandparents lives nearby. After school, Mari's sister and brother spend a lot of time participating in leisure activities, such as football and music. Oscar, who is fourteen, was recently invited to take place on the local youth municipal council, established to give children and young people the chance to take part in the political life of their communities. Though he was flattered, he turned down the offer and decided instead to give priority to his football team.

Introduction

This chapter discusses the dynamics between local notions of a (good) childhood, children's rights to participation and the principle of the 'best interests of the child' as stated in the UN Convention of the Rights of the Child (UNCRC), in the Norwegian context. According to the UNCRC, both Mari and Nadia and their siblings are rights-holders, but what are the implications of this for their day-to-day life and well-being? The Convention asserts that all children are independent individuals endowed with many of the rights that adults have, as well as enjoying a number of special rights linked to their status as children. Participation is one of these and one of the three 'P's on which the UNCRC is based (the other two being provision and protection; Cantwell 1993). Thus, Articles 12, 13, 14 and 15 provide children and young people with the right to participate actively in society and to take part in decision-making in the family, the school and the community.

The decision made by the Norwegian government to incorporate the UNCRC into its Human Rights Act in 2003 represented a legal strengthening of the UNCRC in Norway since it means that domestic law concerning children and family is now subordinate to the Human Rights Act and consequently these laws had to be changed in order to embrace the intentions of the UNCRC regarding children's rights. This chapter reflects on the implications of this for children and their well-being, focusing on the impact that the incorporation of the UNCRC into Norwegian domestic law might have on policy and practice, on notions of children as citizens and on changing what it means to be a child and an adult in contemporary Norway.

A core issue that this chapter addresses, taking Norway as its case-study, is how, and the extent to which, children's participation rights are interpreted and practised in different national and local contexts. For example, the degree to which children are regarded as subjects with participation rights is relative to their age and maturity, and depends in part on the emphasis put on other rights in the UNCRC, such as protection, since 'the best interests of the child', enshrined in Article 3, is an overarching principle. However, there is no universal yardstick by which children's best interests can be measured. Moreover, the degree to which children's rights, as stated in the Convention, will be guaranteed is dependent on how these are emphasized in different contexts and the extent to which they are consistent or come into conflict with other political interests and aims in any society.

Children's participation rights under the UNCRC have been used as a tool and frame of reference for policy-makers, NGOs and child researchers to assert that children are citizens or co-citizens. Governments around the world, on behalf of the states they represent, have taken on the responsibility of providing the conditions necessary for children and young people to exercise rights of participation, the expression of which increases as the child matures. However, it has been argued that rights to active social participation and citizenship are among the more fundamental rights and that they should embrace all age groups, including the very young. A central question to be addressed here then is what it means for children to be participating citizens in Norway and, furthermore, whether the recognition of children as citizens will contribute to their empowerment as social actors and to the improvement of their well-being and quality of life. The aim of this chapter is, therefore, to discuss the dynamic relationship between discourses on children and childhood, and the interpretation and practice of participation rights in the field of child policy in Norway in the context of the overarching principle of the 'best interests of the child'. The analytical point of departure is that before the UNCRC can become part of children's lives, it must be interpreted on the national level and rewritten as regulations that will determine local practices.

Until recently, the relationship between children and citizenship was largely un-theorized. However, over the last five years, researchers have contributed to the development of new theoretical approaches to children and citizenship, anchored in feminist and postcolonial thinking (Cockburn 1998; Jans 2004; Kjørholt 2004; Moosa-Mitha 2005). The construction of children as subjects with participation rights will be discussed with reference to these theoretical developments. In particular, I will argue that the construction of children as social participants in the context of rights discourses developed in a late modern Western context reflects moral values of what it means to be a child; that the relationship between participation rights and the principle of the 'best interests of the child' contains certain paradoxes and dilemmas that are often hidden due to the hegemonic character of the global rights discourses; and that the relative status and relationship between the different rights as formulated by the so-called three 'P's in the UNCRC are vague and ambiguous, resulting in confusion and inconsistency in the implementation of the UNCRC in different contexts.

In addition, there is a complex relationship between, on the one hand, participation rights and the child's best interests, which are claimed to be universal, and, on the other, the interpretation and practice of these rights in a local context. An important question to be addressed is what implications rights discourses have for children's well-being and quality of life, interpreted within the framework of the concept of 'the best interests of the child'. Related to this is the question of notions of childhood and the construction of the child-subject in rights discourses. Moreover, the construction of children as subjects with rights and as autonomous actors makes it imperative to consider the nature of the relationship between children and adults, and the extent to which the emphasis on children as new citizens also implies making children responsible for their own lives and choices. Provocatively, the following question can be formulated: 'Is the construction of children as citizens in "the best interest of the child"'?

This chapter explores the complex and dynamic interrelationship between global discourses on children's rights, which are claimed to be universal, and the politics of childhood at a national and local level, which is a complex and multi-directional process. Norwegian social policy on family issues and children's welfare has a long history and thus the new claims relating to children's rights meet this history in the context of established institutions, policy arrangements, norms and ideas. International regulations are therefore not simply enforced at the national level, but must be 'negotiated' into national and local arrangements (Rantalaiho 2004). This theoretical discussion of children as new citizens will therefore be related to two empirical contexts in Norway – children as citizens in the context of the kindergarten and child refugees in the context of asylum-seeking – using Mari, Nadia and their siblings to illustrate the discussion.

Children as new citizens?

The UNCRC has been described as revolutionary when compared to earlier declarations on children's rights, which did not recognize the child's autonomy and the importance of children's views (Freeman 1992; Verhellen 1997). The emphasis on participation rights in the UNCRC has been used by researchers, as well as by child rights advocates and politicians, as a frame of reference and a tool for treating children as fellow or co-citizens (de Winter 1997). However, it has also been argued that the rights to participation in the UNCRC are limited since they deny children political rights, such as the right to vote, and thus fail to recognize them as full citizens (Freeman 1992; Sgritta 1993; Opdal 1998).

In spite of this, much of the literature on children's participatory rights is characterized by universalizing and normative assumptions about the self-evident value of children's participation (see review in Kjørholt 2004), rather than providing a critical scrutiny of political discourses around the implementation of particular projects, or focusing on the actual experiences of child participants in these projects. International comparative studies are rare and consensus on common terminology and theory at the international level is lacking (Riepl and Wintersberger 1999), but those studies that have been done urge further empirical investigation of how national law and politics related to children's rights to participation affect children's lives and welfare, and how universal rights are implemented in different national and local cultural contexts.

In traditional citizenship theories (e.g. Marshall 1964) children are not seen as citizens in the formal political sense of the term since they are excluded from citizenship because they do not have political rights, such as the right to vote. What they do have are certain civic and social rights. Thus, a focus has been developed on the citizenship of children and young people in the social and legal sense (de Winter 1997) in which participation rights are seen as a fundamental part of children's citizenship (Hart 1992). Nonetheless, the use of concepts of rights to participation or citizenship that work in favour of giving children rights *as* citizens (see Kjørholt 2004) are issues that have only been touched on by the great majority of researchers and child rights advocates. Therefore, until recently, children have been largely excluded from theoretical discussions of citizenship and democracy (Kjørholt 2001, 2002). Giving children citizenship rights, however, raises fundamental questions associated with notions of citizenship, childhood and social and democratic participation. What does it mean to be a citizen? What is social and democratic participation? And what does it mean to be a child?

In recent years, some researchers have started to discuss these issues (Cockburn 1998; Jans 2004; Kjørholt 2004; Invernizzi and Milne 2005; Moosa-Mitha 2005), generating a body of literature that represents a valuable development in the theoretical and conceptual clarification of the meaning of citizenship and, as a consequence, prompting further discussion of children as subjects with rights of participation in society. In turn, this means that the social rights attached to citizenship are gradually receiving greater emphasis. This is important since giving children rights *as* citizens challenges traditional theories of citizenship based on liberal notions of democratic participation and the ideal of the rational autonomous individual.

As a consequence, new perspectives on children and citizenship are beginning to emerge. Thus, for example, Jans (2004) argues in favour of an alternative conceptualization of citizenship, a 'child-friendly citizenship', consisting of one or more of the following dimensions:

1. Citizenship as rights (I get to vote).
2. Citizenship as responsibilities (I have to be decent).
3. Citizenship as identity (I am Norwegian).
4. Citizenship as participation (I feel involved and can participate in community life) (Jans 2004).

Jans argues that a 'children-sized citizenship' is a dynamic and continuous learning process, demanding both participation and involvement. As part of this, citizenship as an identity, which places children in a position as contributing social actors in a community, represents a positive approach to the representation of children as citizens. Combined with an emphasis on citizenship as participation, it enables the identification of the variety of different ways in which children and young people participate in society.

Other researchers focus on the interdependency of children and adults, arguing for an alternative and relational model of citizenship (Cockburn 1998; Moosa-Mitha 2005). Such a relational approach, as conceptualized within difference-centred models, broadens the meaning of participation, challenging a dualistic split between the public and private spheres, placing citizens in many different subject positions in different contexts whilst at the same time coming together in solidarity (Moosa-Mitha 2005; Bjerke 2006).

Giving children rights as citizens is not unproblematic, however, and critics of children's social participation warn against the danger of placing a heavy burden on children by giving them too much responsibility and exposing them to inadequate care and protection (Nijnatten 1993, in de Winter 1997). They argue that adults have overall responsibility for creating an environment that ensures children have a good quality of life and for developing appropriate contexts for children's participation (Mollenhauer 1986, in de Winter 1997). Others have argued that citizenship is a tool that can be used to incorporate children in the social structure of society, to strengthen their influence and agency in society, and to educate them as future adult citizens (de Winter 1997).

It has also been argued that not only does children's participation in civil society benefit the child directly, it also has long-term significance for their community, their nation and the world because it encourages the development of knowledge, skills, values and attitudes that are fundamental in sustaining a democracy (Flekkøy and Kaufman 1997;

Kaufman and Rizzini 2002; Limber and Kaufman 2002; Smith et al. 2003). It has further been argued that encouraging children to express their opinions and feelings about their lives and events in their world and to participate actively in the world signals a respect for children as human beings (Weithorn 1998; Morrow 1999). Based on studies of asylum-seeking children's participation rights in Norway, Rusten also argues that there is a close connection between protection rights and participation rights in the sense that participation rights are essential for the realization of other rights and that, in order to meet children's protection rights, adults need to listen to children to understand their situation, their needs and what is in their 'best interests' (Rusten 2006). It is against this background that this chapter will discuss children's participation in Norway, beginning with an outline of the legal position relating to children's participation in Norwegian society.

The legal status of the UNCRC in Norway

Discourses that construct children as competent social actors with rights to participate in society and to have a voice in matters that affect their lives have been flourishing over the last 15–20 years among childhood researchers, non-governmental organizations (NGOs) and actors within the field of international and national child policy (McKechnie 2002; Halldén 2003; Kjørholt 2004). The position of children as social participants still depends, however, on the extent to which changed political and social practices eventually emerge from this incorporation. Thus, for example, the lack of incorporation of the UNCRC into the Human Rights Act when it was first adopted in Norway in 1999 illustrated ambivalence about the willingness to take children's right to participation seriously (Kjørholt 2004).

This lack of incorporation was met with criticism from both the UN's Expert Committee on children's rights (in their response to Norway's status report on activities connected to the implementation of the UNCRC in 2000) and from various political actors in Norway. A working group consisting of representatives from different ministries was therefore set up to discuss the issue further. As a result, in September 2003, the UNCRC was incorporated into the Human Rights Act by the Norwegian parliament. This was an expression of the political will to take children's rights in general, and their rights of participation in particular, more seriously. However, incorporation meant that national laws affecting children had to be redrafted in order to conform to the framework and the various articles of the UNCRC. Thus, for example, as a result of incorporation, the age limit in Norwegian law for children's rights to be heard in decisions concerning them was lowered from twelve to seven years. This has, however, created tension between the child's right to autonomy and participation on the one hand and, on the other, the extent to which the child is to be made responsible for difficult decisions (Sandberg 2004).

From a legal perspective, the impact of incorporation on the potential implementation of participation rights in different contexts is highly significant. Thus, for example, refugee and asylum-seeking children are protected with reference to two international conventions: the UNCRC and the Refugee Convention and its 1967 Protocol. Thus, in 1993, the UN High Commissioner for Refugees (UNHCR) adopted a Policy on Refugee Children that implemented the UNCRC as its 'normative frame of reference for UNHCR's action' (Rusten 2006). As noted above, the UNCRC endows children with three types of rights; provision, protection and participation. However, the relationships between, and relative weight given to, these different rights are discussed only briefly such that within policy and research literature, participation rights are often presented in terms of a dichotomous understanding of the child as either vulnerable or as a competent social actor (Kjørholt 2004). The former, which implies children's dependency and vulnerability, has been associated with the developmental paradigm and has been criticized for being adult-centric and as failing to recognize children as right-holders, which is implied by acknowledging them as competent social actors (Kjørholt 2004). The latter movement for empowering children that is anchored in universal discourses on children's rights, by contrast, seems to lack any concepts and approaches that can take account of children's *dependence* on the cultural and political context that they are part of. It is to a discussion of these opposing ideas, as they unfold in Norwegian society, that the chapter now turns.

Play and freedom of choice – in 'the best interest' of the child?

As stated in the introduction, Mari like the majority of pre-school Norwegian children attends kindergarten every day. The kindergarten, which is in a new building, is claimed to have a modern architectural style in line with 'new knowledge' about 'the modern child'. The new architecture is part of a policy aimed at improving the quality of the kindergarten by creating flexible places: more openness, more effective use of the locality and promoting active participation and freedom of choice for children as well as adults (Kjørholt and Tingstad 2007). This 'new knowledge' reflects prominent discourses in policy and research conceptualizing children's competence and autonomy from an early age, and rejecting earlier discourses on the developing and vulnerable child: the 'modern child' is asserted to be an individual with freedom of choice and the right to influence their everyday lives (Kjørholt and Tingstad 2007).

Mari attends a 'child meeting' in the kindergarten every morning after breakfast in order to exercise her rights, to take her own decisions and to influence everyday life in the kindergarten. This meeting is not obligatory, but it is a common practice in many Norwegian kindergartens. Forty children aged between 2½ and 6 years attend. As part of the agenda, children have to decide which room and what kind of activity they want to take part in during the next two hours. Once a child has made its choice, it is not allowed to change its mind, reflecting a moral value that it is important for children to learn responsibility and to accept the consequences of their decisions.

The implementation of participation rights for children in kindergarten is related to notions of what it means to be a child and notions of (a good) childhood in Norway. The construction of 'the tribal child' – as a group with a common, authentic culture – has been prevalent in child policy as well in research in Denmark and Norway since the 1990s (Kjørholt 2001, 2004; Kampmann 2001). The child's right to choose activities and with whom to play is emphasized in day-care institutions as well as in after-school activities in Norway and Denmark, and the emphasis on the opportunity for individual children to make their own choices and decisions in contemporary discourses is significant (Gulløv 2001).

Since the 1990s, the concept of 'children's own culture', referring to play and peer-cultural activities initiated by children themselves and representing a particular understanding of childhood, has had increasing discursive power among researchers and various professional groups in both Denmark and Norway. Former as well as contemporary notions of 'a good childhood' in Norway are connected to the right to move freely in the physical environment and to the potential for children to structure their time according to their own needs. Thus, autonomy, freedom and play with peers in the immediate neighbourhood and, in particular, in natural settings are promoted (Gullestad 1997; Nilsen 2000; Kjørholt 2001): childhood and nature are seen as closely intertwined. The cultural meaning of 'free play', practised among peers, is stressed especially when it takes place outdoors, preferably in a natural setting (see Nilsen, this volume). In this cultural context, children are constructed as a collective group with a common interest: the right to play together.

Commentators present the position as representing a shift from a focus on the *developing child* to the *competent child*, from *pedagogy* to *culture*, which are presented as dichotomous and opposite positions. Gulløv, for example, asserts that comparable discourses connected to day-care centres in Denmark are characterized by 'moral assumptions and understandings concerning individual autonomy, social coherence and conceptions of children and childhood' (Gulløv 2003: 24). These centres also emphasize the significance of individual children's capacity to make their own choices and ability to decide, and an analysis of changing practices in Danish day-care centres within the project 'Children as co-Citizens' reveals that the idea of citizenship is closely connected to practising participation rights. In this context, children's rights to participation are interpreted in terms of the exercise of individual autonomy and self-determination (Kjørholt 2005).

Since ratification of the UNCRC in early 1991, discourses on children's rights to participation have been powerful in Norwegian children's policy relating to school reform, political participation and local planning. However, it is only recently that these discourses have spread to the field of early childhood education and care. A government policy document ('Kindergartens in the Best Interests of Children and Parents') produced by the Ministry for Children and Family Affairs in December 1999, describes the political aims of kindergartens in Norway and illustrates how children's right to participation is interpreted:

> Children have to be children on their own terms, based on their own interests, and they must be protected against 'adult control'.
> (Government declaration to the Parliament,
> Stortings-melding – 27/2000:73)

As we can see, adults are thought of as a threat to children, the relationships between them being constructed only in the light of the concept of power.

In an article entitled 'Participation or Reactive Pedagogy', Pernille Hviid characterizes practices in Danish day-care institutions as a 'what do you want pedagogy', linking notions of 'the best interests of the child' to children's freedom of choice and 'free play' in daily life within the institutions. This pedagogy has the individual child's perspective as its starting point and relates to particular notions of 'freedom', 'desire', 'self-determination', 'diversity' and 'freedom of choice' (Hviid

1998). Self-determination is primarily understood as the individual's ability to 'decide for herself' and, she argues, to have as many opportunities for individual choice as possible. This is prevalent in different Danish institutions, from the early age of toddlers up to school age (Hviid 1998). Hviid is critical of this practice for a number of reasons, one of her arguments being that such practice makes children unduly accountable, since they are put in a position of taking responsibility for their own life and development, and also of being responsible for this choice (Hviid 1998: 213). She argues that the practice of encouraging individualism was introduced in the 1990s, and is different from pedagogical practices of the 1970s and 1980s. Writing at the end of the 1990s, she argues:

> the Danish day-care institution probably stands at the threshold of another kind of pedagogy, putting more emphasis on the social and learning aspects.
>
> (Hviid 1998: 208)

In the national curriculum for kindergartens, adopted in 2005, similar rights to participation are included. In the national law on kindergartens, rights to participation are emphasized in the following way:

> Children have the right to express their views on daily life in kindergarten. Children should regularly get the opportunity to active participation in planning and assessment of the activities. Children's views should be given due weight according to children's age and maturity.
>
> (Kindergarten Act 2005: 3)

Do these participation rights imply that Mari and other children in the kindergarten are constructed as citizens? According to recent theorizing about children and citizenship presented earlier in this chapter, we might argue that the recognition of children as competent actors with a right to have a say in everyday life in the kindergarten means including them as citizens. It can further be argued that the particular child-subject connected to play and child culture means including the 'different citizen' represented in difference-centred theories on citizenship (Misha-Mootha 2005).

There is an explicit reference to the UNCRC in the Framework for kindergartens, underlining Article 12 of the UNCRC. After an elaboration of the content of p. 3 in the National Framework, it is emphasized that children should have the opportunity to experience belonging and community, to exercise self-determination and to express their intentions. The National Framework does not fully link participation to self-determination and freedom of choice, however: individuality and the right to express an opinion are also connected to the ability to be empathetic and care for others. Furthermore, a relational approach is included, emphasizing the importance of adults listening to children and of their being responsible for all the children in the kindergarten.

It remains to be seen, therefore, how children's right to participation as outlined in the Kindergarten Act 2005 and the national Framework will be interpreted and practised in different kindergartens. Preliminary results from the Norwegian Centre for Child Research indicate that autonomy and individual choice are central issues in the practices that are developed (Seland 2006). The practice of participation rights furthermore presupposes a human subject who is able to make her own choices and to express her views verbally in a deliberate and rational manner. For Mari and the other children in the kindergarten this constitutes a particular challenge because their language skills are not fully developed at such a young age; desire and needs are often embodied, but are not always conscious, and are expressed more through body language than verbally. Thus, there is a danger that the new practices, representing the promotion of individual choice and self-determination consistent with the 'best interests of the child', will omit a discussion of related moral values.

There are, however, different and even competing discourses about childhood and the aims and content of the kindergarten and, as argued by Pernille Hviid regarding Danish day-care centres, there are similar trends in Norway that reveal a new emphasis on knowledge and learning. An illustration of this is that the name of one of the rooms in Mari's kindergarten has been changed from the 'building block room' to the 'maths room', underlining the point that using building blocks is not primarily a 'play activity' but is a 'maths learning' activity. Thus current Norwegian discourses are characterized by two different and competing positions; play, freedom of choice and an emphasis on 'children's culture' on the one hand, and learning, competence and knowledge on the other. This situation is reflected in the national administrative authority of the kindergarten. Until 2006 the Ministry for Children and Family Affairs was responsible for kindergartens; now they are administered by the Ministry of Knowledge. The new emphasis on learning, competence and knowledge, however, challenges 'traditional' discourses on (good) childhood in Norway. It remains to be seen how this will affect the content of everyday life in the kindergarten, as well as the normative assessment and moral values embedded in the practice of participation rights in everyday life in this setting.

Refugee children, citizenship and 'the best interests' of the child

In April 2006, approximately 2,000 children were living in Norwegian reception centres (Rusten 2006). Nadia is one of them. In contrast to Mari's day, Nadia spends most of her time with her parents at the transit asylum reception centre. If her parents want her to, she has can meet other pre-school children and their adult carers for a couple of hours a day. The children are of different nationalities and speak a variety of languages, however, which makes it difficult for them to communicate with each other. In relation to exercising participation rights, Nadia's situation contrasts markedly, therefore, with Mari's everyday life at the kindergarten.

There are potential problems in relation to the exercise of her legal rights. According to the Dublin Convention, which articulates the so-called 'first country practice', Nadia's family will probably not be allowed to tell their story in an interview and to apply for asylum: because they entered another country before fleeing to Norway, that country has the responsibility for handling their asylum applications. However, if an adverse decision is made, under the provisions of the Children's Act (adopted 8 April 1981, revised 7 April 2006), Nadia's two siblings will have a right to express their views in the proceedings: once they reach the age of seven their views should be given significant emphasis. As noted above, this lowering of age was made in 2003, with the Act also stating that children below seven years of age, who are able to express themselves, should be given the opportunity to do so.

In a case such as that of Nadia and her sisters, an important question arises about how the principle of 'the best interests of the child' should be determined when dealing with asylum applications. For example, do refugee and asylum-seeker children have their rights to express their concerns realized in immigration cases? In the Norwegian youth report to the UN on the Convention on the Rights of the Child in 2003, refugee children said:

> The interview is the only time we get to describe why we apply for permission to stay in Norway. At that time we're often anxious and

tired after a long journey. The interview should either take place later, or there should be more interviews.

(Sanner and Dønnestad 2003)

Evident here is the fact that fulfilling rights to participation requires time and communication; it involves the development of social relations characterized by mutual trust, something that is absent from the life of refugee children at reception centres in Norway. Indeed, this life has been characterized as a 'liminal phase', in which children and their families are placed in a situation of insecurity, often for a long period, having questions about their future 'answered' with silence (Knutsen 1998). This 'liminal phase' has further been characterized as a rite of passage for asylum seekers, who have the status of *non-citizens* (Archambault 2006).

Based on the argument that citizenship is a tool with which to include children in the social structure of society, strengthen their influence and agency in society, and educate them as future adult citizens (de Winter 1997), policies and practices which can improve the right of asylum-seeking and refugee children to express their views and to influence their daily life and society become extremely pertinent. Indeed, in their report to Norway in 2000 related to Article 12 of the UNCRC, the UN Committee stated that children's views in general were insufficiently heard and taken into consideration. It was therefore recommended that Norway should 'continue its effort to inform children and others, including parents and legal professionals, of children's rights to express their views and of mechanisms and other opportunities which exists for this purpose' (Supplementary Report 2004: 11). The conditions of children in families seeking asylum was made a particular issue in the report, and Norway was criticized for paying too little attention to asylum-seeking children's rights to participate in the proceedings or considering their views in the decision-making process (Report UN Committee 2000). Though the practices regarding children's participation rights had improved, the Forum for UNCRC (FFB) in their supplementary report to the Committee claimed that children were still rarely heard in immigration cases (Supplementary Report 2004).

A recent study (Rusten 2006) of children's right to participate in Norwegian asylum proceedings revealed that the authorities had addressed few of the problems and ethical dilemmas inherent in conducting interviews with children. Many respondents found it difficult to communicate and time-consuming, compared to conducting similar interviews with adults, while some respondents questioned the usefulness of talking to children when they believed the outcome would be that the parents had their application rejected.

In the Norwegian youth report to the UN, refugee children also claimed that they did not get the psychological support they needed to cope with difficult and traumatic experiences. They underlined the fact that they miss adults who care, with whom they can share their thoughts and feelings and with whom they can discuss their lives and aspirations for the future. One of the main wishes expressed by unaccompanied under-aged asylum seekers was to move in with a Norwegian family as soon as possible after arrival. Summarizing asylum-seekers' experiences in Norwegian reception centres, Sanner and Dønnestad (2003) conclude that: 'It is tough living with foreigners of the same age who speak different languages. There is little privacy and there are few adults in the reception centre. They [the children] say that the centre is an education in loneliness'.

It has been argued that 'children from minority groups constitute a double minority ... being considered as a minority group themselves, both as minors and as being members of any visible minority group' (Wintersberger, Bardy and Qvortrup 1993: 26). Wintersberger et al. also argue that 'children from minorities often display capabilities and competences that their parents do not have, which means that they are brought into a predicament as far as their relationships to authorities are concerned' (1993: 21). For example, their double minority status may place these children in a situation of conflicting social, cultural and generational relations, where authority relations between adults and children, as well as gender relations, become contested. Refugee and asylum-seeking children therefore often face additional challenges, having to reconcile traditional norms and values related to being a child in a particular ethnic minority with the new and different norms for childhood in Norwegian society.

Refugee children in Norway seem, therefore, to be a particularly marginalized group with regard to participation rights, since the process of applying for asylum often takes a long time, sometimes years. The wait means being involved in bureaucratic processes including interviewing and tracking of their journey (Archambault 2006). It leaves children in a situation of insecurity, with no control over their lives and, according to Forum for the UNCRC in Norway (FFB 2004), children are scarcely heard in immigration cases. Unaccompanied minors are especially vulnerable in Norwegian reception centres, where they are denied even the basic rights set out in the UNCRC (Save the Children, Norway 2004). In their recommendation to Norway in 2000, the UN Committee stated that the state party should 'review its procedures for considering applications for asylum from children, whether accompanied or unaccompanied, to ensure that children are provided with sufficient opportunities to participate in the proceedings and to express their concerns' (Supplementary Report 2004: 27).

These reports, and the experiences of refugee children cited above, clearly reveal that there are groups of children in Norwegian society who are denied the right to have a say in matters that affect their lives. They also expose the connections between different rights in the UNCRC: an asylum centre that is felt by children to be a place for 'an education in loneliness' is a place where children feel they are being excluded from society and deprived of relationships with others, socially, culturally and emotionally. Having an identity as a citizen in the present and in the future requires a sense of belonging, anchored in inclusive relationships with others. Being marginalized and excluded from social relationships and belonging means being deprived of the possibilities to practise citizenship. As difference-centred theoretical perspectives on citizenship underline (Misha-Mootha 2005), inclusion, regardless of age or group membership, is dependent on a sense of self being derived through active participation with, and belonging, to other human beings.

'The best interests of the child'

The comparison made between Mari's and Nadia's access to exercising their rights to citizenship and participation also highlights the difficulties that arise in relation to the idea of 'the best interests of the child': outlined in Article 3, it is an overarching principle of the UNCRC, but there is no universal standard defining what constitutes children's best interests. It is therefore a concept that is differentiated and dependent on normative and cultural evaluations made by different bodies and actors within the contexts in which the UNCRC is implemented. The welfare programme of the Norwegian Research Council clearly illustrates this point when it argues that:

> Many arrangements in the welfare society have children as users. Children's needs and interests often have to be interpreted and represented by parents and professionals. Everybody wants to realise the best interest of the child, but how do we know what this is?'
>
> (2004: 14)

So, for example, various studies focusing on court disputes over children's custody and visiting arrangements (Smart et al. 2003; Ottesen 2004; Skjørten 2004) argue from different viewpoints that the notion of the 'best interests of the child' is ambiguous, interpreted in different ways in different contexts, and that in many cases children are not heard. In Norway, children's role in divorce procceedings, for example, has been located firmly within the welfare discourse and is linked only to a 'caretaking' version of children's rights. So in mediation, which is primarily an adult-oriented process, the voice of the child is expressed almost entirely through its parents. The extent to which this accords with the provisions of Article 12 of the UNCRC is therefore questionable (Rantalaiho and Haugen 2004). In relation to immigration, Norway's third report to the Committee on the Rights of the Child in 2003 argues as follows:

> There is always emphasis on the best interests of the child in immigration cases that involve children. Many residence and work permits that are granted on 'strong humanitarian grounds' are justified on the basis of consideration for the children. Nevertheless, consideration for the child/children is not always decisive, nor is it always clear what the best interests of the child are.
>
> (para. 145, quoted in Rusten 2006)

Indeed, it has been argued that part of the state's obligation is to define the best interests of the child and that it is a matter of will, resources and procedures as to whether children's views, experts' views and parents' views are sufficiently heard and taken into account (Rusten 2006). In addition, it has been argued that rights discourses, constructing children as individual right-holders, and the assessment of 'the best interests of the child' might also contribute to children being used strategically as instruments to undermine principles in Norwegian immigration policies (Lidèn 2005).

Thus, the principle of the best interests of the child is not a neutral and global standard; rather, it is one that involves normative and ethical assessments, anchored in cultural contexts and notions of (good) childhood and quality of life. Although constructed as competent actors and individual rights claimants in Norwegian society, specific groups of children are nonetheless marginalized, which makes these children a target for different interest groups to use in the context of their own agendas. 'Best interests' is a standard with different meanings in different cultures, influenced by class, ethnicity, gender and other structural factors. Alston (1994) points out that, whereas a child's individuality and autonomy may be valued as being consistent with the principle of the 'best interests of the child' in Western societies, this may conflict with traditions and values in other cultures. The absence of standards defining the 'best interests of the child' therefore makes it possible to use this principle to legitimize a practice in one culture that in another would been seen as detrimental to children (Alston 1994). Notions of 'the best interests of the child' are therefore closely intertwined with cultural notions of a (good) childhood in a particular local context.

It is also important to clarify how the child's right to participation is to be linked with 'the best interests of the child'. Sandberg (2004) argues that in order to understand this, we must consider the degree of coincidence between the child's opinion and what is interpreted as the best interests of the child in different legal contexts. Alongside 'the best interests of the child', the concept of children's participation rights is also dependent on cultural interpretation, since there are no specific standards connected to the implementation of participation rights, a point which empirical studies clearly illustrate (Kjørholt 2004). Due to the universal character and hegemonic position of the discourses on children's rights, this is seldom discussed openly, since the dynamics between the global discourse on children's rights and national politics is a complex and multi-directional process. Thus, international regulations cannot simply be enforced at the national level, but must be negotiated into the form of national and local arrangements that can be reconciled with the perspectives, norms and practices of established institutions (Rantalaiho 2004: 3). This makes the universality of children's rights inherently problematic.

Human rights discourses have also been criticized for being rooted in the idea that human dignity and worth can only be realized by individual rights and by disregarding the alternative, that human worth may be rooted in care, interdependence and mutual needs (Diduck 1999). Rights discourses are anchored in the Anglo-American liberal tradition, which constructs human beings as legal subjects capable of speaking for themselves and acting in their own interests. The subject is constructed as a rational, autonomous individual, with the consciousness to formulate his or her own needs and wishes. It has been argued that there are some 'needs that are not easily expressed in rights claims – like the need to be loved, to receive emotional support and so on' (Mortier 2002: 83): care, dependencies, affection, affiliation, intimacy and love are therefore silenced by discourses on children's rights.

An important question that arises is what consequences this silence has for both children and children's citizenship. For example, studies of children's experiences of participatory projects reveal that they do not construct their *autonomy* as a counterpart to *dependency*: the construction of identities as competent social participants in their local communities derives from intertwined processes of autonomy and belonging to various kinds of communities, inter-generational as well as age-related (Kjørholt 2004).

Meanwhile, the studies of refugee children in Norway cited above reveal that children are only treated as autonomous, individual right-holders to a limited degree, indicating that their status as citizens may be questioned despite the change in Norwegian law. Indeed, Rusten concludes that children arriving in Norway as asylum-seekers are not fully treated as individuals in the administrative proceedings and that the principle of 'the best interests of the child' is not taken into consideration sufficiently. She asserts that:

> although the implementation of the UNCRC this far may not have had any major practical implications for the asylum administration; its status as Norwegian law has generally led to more focus on children's issues and shed light on the problems inherent in not treating children as individuals in the asylum process.
>
> (Rusten 2006: 72)

However, Rusten also argues that the asylum procedures with respect to child interviews are still not sufficient to satisfy the requirements of Article 12; that there is resistance among employees in UDI to listen to children's views and to give these sufficient weight in decisions that are made; and that the degree to which the principle of the 'best interests of the child' is taken into account when decisions are made by authorities is unclear (Rusten 2006).

Conclusion

The case studies considered in this chapter have explored the implementation of the UNCRC in the context of Norwegian kindergartens and they illustrate how the interpretation of participation rights is linked to notions of self-determination, play and individual choice, as well as to particular cultural notions of (good) childhood. The emphasis on freedom of choice and child autonomy in certain aspects of everyday life in the kindergarten, however, is riddled with ambiguity and paradoxes. Like the other children in the kindergarten Mari, aged 2½, is obviously dependent and vulnerable, and her ability to express her views verbally regarding daily life in the kindergarten and to make conscious decisions is limited. In order to be recognized as a competent social actor in the kindergarten, she needs to have her autonomy regarded in a relational perspective, taking into account the close interrelationship between autonomy on the one hand, and dependency and vulnerability on the other.

Fulfilment of participation rights in such a context is complex, requiring adult caretakers who do not construct autonomy and dependency as opposites but as mutually dependent, dynamic and fluctuating. In this sense, protection rights and participation rights are closely intertwined; a difference-centred approach to citizenship that broadens the concept of participation, relating the practice of participation rights to belonging and community, is therefore fruitful. It opens the way to recognizing children as citizens in manner that includes their vulnerability and dependency in the concept of citizenship.

As we have seen, however, Nadia and the other children at centres for asylum-seekers are not recognized as autonomous individual rights-holders, who have their participation rights fulfilled in decision-making processes. Their marginal position, the result of their belonging to different groups and communities, also indicates that their citizenship status may not be recognized and thus participation rights in decision-making, which are closely related to competence, inclusion and belonging in everyday life, may also be lacking.

As yet few empirical studies have been done since the incorporation of the UNCRC into the Human Rights Act in 2003 that explore how global discourses about children's participation rights are practised and interpreted in the context of Norwegian policy relating to refugee children. Thus if, as noted above, tensions and conflicts exist between practices relating to Articles 3 and 12, it is important to discover how children experience participation rights in their daily lives. Indeed, this has been underlined in a report about research on human rights in Norway, which recommends empirical investigation of children's experiences and perspectives related to policy and practice at both the local and national level (Lomell, All, Hvinden and Grøholt 1999). A central concern of such research must be to generate knowledge about *if* and, in the case refugee children, *how* children are constructed as subjects with rights to participate in society, and what consequences this construction (or lack of it) has for children, their relations to adults and other children, and for their inclusion in Norwegian society.

References

Alston, P. (1994) The Best Interest Principle: Towards a Reconciliation of Culture and Human Rights. In Alston, P. (ed.) *The Best Interest of the Child: Reconciling Culture and Human* Rights (pp. 1–25). Oxford: UNICEF and Clarendon Press.

Archambault, J. (2006) Refugee Children and Their Rights: Is Citizenship a Concern? Paper presented for the PhD course on Children's Rights. Trondheim: Norwegian Centre for Child Research, NTNU.

Bjerke, H. (2006) Conceptualizing Citizenship in Childhood. Working paper, unpublished. Trondheim: Norwegian Centre for Child Research, NTNU.

Cantwell, N (1993) Monitoring the Convention through the 3 'P's. In Heiliø, P. L. Lauronen, E. and Bardy, M. (eds), *Politics of Childhood and Children at Risk. Provision, Protection, Particiapation.* Eurosocial Report 45. Vienna: European Centre for Social Welfare Policy and Research, pp. 121–6.

Cockburn, T. (1998) Children and Citizenship in Britain. A Case for a Socially Interdependent Model of Citizenship, *Childhood* 5(1): 99–117.

de Winter, M. (1997) *Children as Fellow Citizens. Participation and Commitment.* Oxford and New York: Radcliffe Medical Press.

Diduck, A. (1999) Justice and Childhood: Reflections on Refashioned Boundaries. In King, M. (ed.), *Moral Agendas for Children's* Welfare (pp. 120–38). London and New York: Routledge.

Flekkøy, M. G. and Kaufman, N. H. (1997) *The Participation Rights of the Child: Rights and Responsibilities in Family and Society.* London: Jessica Kingsley.

Freeman, M. D. (1992) The Limits of Children's Rights. In Freeman, M. D. and Veerman, P. (eds.), *The Ideologies of Children's* Rights (pp. 29–46). International Studies in Human Rights. Dordrecht, London and Boston, MA: Martinus Nijhoff.

Gullestad, M (1997) A Passion for Boundaries: Reflections on Connections between the Everyday Lives of Children and Discourses on the Nation in Contemporary Norway. *Childhood* 1(4): 19–42.

Gulløv, E (2001) Placing Children. Paper presented at the research seminar, 'Children, Generation and Place: Cross-cultural Approaches to an Anthropology of Children', 19–21 May. University of Copenhagen, Network for Cross-Cultural Child Research.

Halldén, G. (2003) Barnperspektiv som ideologiskt eller metodologiskt begrepp. In *Barns perspektiv och barnperspektiv.* Pedagogisk forskning i Sverige 8(1–2), Institutionen för pedagogikk och didaktikk. Gøteborgs Universitet, Gøteborg, 12–23.

Harris, J. (1996) Liberating Children. In Leahy, M. and Cohn-Sherbok. D. (eds.), *The Liberation Debate*, London: Routledge.

Hart, R. (1992) Children's Participation. From Tokenism to Citizenship. United Nations Children's Fund. *Innocent Essays 4.*

Hviid, P. (1998) Deltakelse eller reaktiv pædagogik. In Brinkkjær, U. et al. (eds.), *Pedagogisk faglighed i dagistitusjoner* (pp. 207–26). Rapport 34. København: Danmarks pædagogiske universitet.

Invernizzi, A. and Milne, B. (guest eds.) (2005) Children's Citizenship: An Emergent Discourse on the Rights of the Child? *Journal of Social Sciences* Special Issue 9.

Jans, M. (2004) Children as Citizens. Towards a Contemporary Notion of Child Participation. *Childhood* 11(1): 27–44.

Kampmann, J. (2001) Hva er børnekultur? In Tufte, B. Kampmann, J. and Junker, B. (eds.), *Børnekultur. Hvilke børn og hvis kultur?* København: Akademisk Forlag A/S.

Kaufman, N. and Rizzini, I. (eds.) (2002) *Globalization and Children: Exploring Potentials for Enhancing Opportunities in the Lives of Children and Youth.* New York: Kluwer Academic/Plenum.

Kjørholt, A. T. (2001) 'The Participating Child' – A Vital Pillar in This Century? *Nordisk Pedagogikk/Nordic Educational Research* 21(2): 65–81.

Kjørholt, A. T. (2002) Small is Powerful. Discourses on 'Children and Participation' in Norway. *Childhood* 1(9): 63–83.

Kjørholt, A. T. (2004) Childhood as a Social and Symbolic Space. Discourses on Children as Social Participants in Society. PhD thesis. Trondheim, NTNU.

Kjørholt, A. T. (2005) The Competent Child and the 'Right to be Oneself': Reflections on Children as Fellow Citizens in a Day-care Centre. In Clark, A., Kjørholt, A. T. and Moss, P. (eds.), *Beyond Listening.* Bristol: Policy Press.

Kjørholt, A.T. and Tingstad, V. (2007) Flexible Places for Flexible Children? Discourses on the New Kindergarten Architecture. In Zeiher, H., Devine, D., Kjørholt, A. T. and Strandell, H. (eds.), *Flexible Childhood? Exploring Children's Welfare in Time and Space.* Cost Action A19: Children's Welfare, Vol. 2. Odense: Southern University Press.

Knudsen, John Chr. (1994) *'Hvis jeg hadde vært en fugl.' Asylsøker- og flyktningbarn i statlige mottak.* Rapport. Senter for samfunnsforskning (SEFOS), Universitetet i Bergen.

Lidèn, H (2005) *Barn og unge fra nasjonale minoriteter. En kunnskapsstatus.* Rapport 7. Oslo: ISF.

Limber, S. and Kaufman, N. H. (2002) Civic Participation by Children and Youth. In Kaufman, N. and Rizzini, I. (eds.), *Globalization and Children's Lives.* New York: Kluwer Academic/Plenum.

Lomell, H. M., Aall, J., Hvinden, B. and Grønholt, B. (1999) *Forskning om Menneske- rettigheter i Norge.* Oslo: NFR.

Marshall, T. H. (1964) *Class, Citizenship and Social Development.* New York: Anchor Books.

McKechnie, J. (2002) Children's Voices and Researching Childhood. In Goldson, B., Lavalette, M. and McKechnie, J. (eds.), *Children, Welfare and the State* (pp. 42–58). London: Sage.

Mollenhauer, K. (1986) *Vergeten Samenhang. Over cultuur en opvoeding.* Meppel: Boom.

Moosa-Mitha, M. (2005) A Difference-centred Alternative to Theorization of Children's Citizenship Rights. *Citizenship Studies* 9: 369–88.

Morrow, V. (1999) 'We are People too'; Children and Young People's Perspectives on Children's Rights and Decision-making in England. *The International Journal of Children's Rights* 10: 149–70.

Mortier, F. (2002) The Meaning of Individualization for Children's Citizenship. In Mouritsen, F. and Qvortrup, J. (eds.), *Childhood and Children's Culture* (pp. 79–102). Odense: University Press of Southern Denmark.

Nijnatten, C. H. C. (1993) *Kinderrechten in discussie.* Meppel: Boom.

Nilsen, R. Dyblie (2000) Livet i barnehagen. En etnografisk studie av sosialiseringsprosessen. PhD dissertation. Trondheim: NTNU, Fakultet for samfunnsvitenskap og teknologiledelse. Pedagogisk institutt.

Opdahl, P. (1998) Barnet – et menneske uten krav på fulle menneske-rettigheter? In *Barn* 3–4, Trondheim: Norsk senter for Barneforskning, 26–39.

Ottosen, M. H. (2004) *Samvær til barnets bedste?* København Socialforskningsinstituttet, 04.

Qvortrup, J. et al. (eds.) (1994) Childhood Matters: An Introduction. In *Childhood Matters: Social Theory, Practice and Politics* (pp. 1–23). Brookfield, VT: Avebury.

Rantalaiho, M. (2004) Childhood's Ambiguity – Politics and Practice on Children's Rights in Context of Family Change. Unpublished paper. Trondheim: Norwegian Centre for Child Research.

Rantalaiho, M. and Haugen, G. M. (2004) Family Change and Children's Rights to Participation in Comparative Perspective. Unpublished paper. Trondheim: Norwegian Centre for Child Research.

Riepl, B. and Wintersberger, H. (1999) Towards a Typology of Political Participation of Young People. In Riepl, B. and Wintersberger, H. (eds.), *Political Participation of Youth below Voting Age* (pp. 225–38). Eurosocial Report 66. Vienna: European Centre for Social Welfare Policy and Research.

Rusten, H. (2006) Making Children Visible to the Immigration Administration: A Study of the Right of the Child to Participate in Norwegian Asylum Proceedings. Submitted in partial fulfilment of the MA in the Theory and Practice of Human Rights, Norwegian Centre for Human Rights, University of Oslo, Department of Law.

Sandberg, K. (2004) Inkorporeringen av barnekonvensjonen i norsk rett, In *Kritisk juss*. 316–29.

Sanner, M. and Dønnestad, E. (2003) Life before 18. Dreams, Ideas, Life. Norwegian Youth. Report to the UN about the Convention on the Rights of the Child. Oslo: The project 'Life before 18'. Norwegian Department of Children and Family Affairs.

Seland, M. (2006) Kindergarten as a Bazaar. Paper presented at the third international seminar: The Modern Child and The Flexible Labour Market. Institutionalisation and Individualisation of Children's Lives in Modern Welfare Societies. Lofoten Island, 27–29 September, Norwegian Centre for Child Research.

Sgritta, G. (1993) Provision: Limits and Possibilities. In Heiliö, P. L., Lauronen, E. and Bardy, M. (eds.), *Politics of Childhood and Children at Risk. Provision – Protection – Participation*. Eurosocial Report 45. Vienna: European Centre for Social Welfare Policy and Research.

Skjørten, K. (2004) http://program.forskningsradet.no/vfo/nyhet.

Smart, C. et al. (2003) *Residence and Contact Disputes in Court*. Centre for Research on Family, Kinship and Childhood. University of Leeds. Research series no. 6/03.

Smith, A. B., Nairn, K., Sligo, J. Gaffney, M. and McCormack, J. (2003) *Case Studies of Young People's Participation in Public Life – Local Government, Boards of Trustees and the Youth Parliament*. Dunedin: Children's Issues Centre.

Verhellen, E. (1993) Children and Participation Rights. In Heiliö, P. L., Lauronen, E. and Bardy, M. (eds.), *Politics of Childhood and Children at Risk. Provision, Protection and Participation* (pp. 49–64). Eurosocial Report 45. Vienna: European Centre for Social Welfare Policy and Research.

Verhellen, E. (1997) *Convention on the Rights of the Child*. Leven and Apeldoorn: Verhellen and Garant.

Weithorn, L. A. (1998) Youth Participation in Family and Community Decision-making. *Family Futures* 2(1): 6–9.

Wintersberger, H., Bardy, M. and Qvortrup, J. (1993) *Children from Minorities*. Draft report prepared for the Government of Canada.

Forum for the Convention on the Rights of the Child (FFB)/Save the Children (2004) Supplementary Report 27.

The welfare programme of the Norwegian Research Council (2004).

Kindergarten Act, Norwegian Parliament, enacted 16 June 2005.

Children's Act, Norwegian Parliament, enacted 8 April 1981, revised 7 April 2006.

3
Children in Nature: Cultural Ideas and Social Practices in Norway

Randi Dyblie Nilsen

> *While spending the day outside as usual, one of the staff at the nature day-care centre initiates a game of snowballing with four boys. The boys run around and throw snowballs at the staff and at each other; one of the boys uses a sledge board [akebrett] as a shield. The member of staff laughs out loud when he scores a hit, and so do the children. When he throws a snowball at a colleague who has a girl sitting on his lap, the latter uses the girl as a shield. When she is hit by the snowball, she also laughs.*

Introduction

This chapter explores constructions of a 'good' or 'proper' childhood in Norway, focusing on traditional cultural values and social practices relating to nature and outdoor life and their interconnection with values of independence/autonomy (Gullestad 1997, 1992). In a Norwegian cultural context, outdoor environments in the fresh air, preferably 'in nature', where children engage in self-governed play, are central in traditional and contemporary constructions of 'a good childhood' (Telhaug 1992; Gullestad 1997). This chapter spells out the significance of such beliefs, with particular reference to day-care services and political issues, which also accord with the family context and beliefs among many parents (Nilsen 1999): as has been noted '[t]he majority of parents [in Norway] seem to hold the belief that happy children are children playing outside most of the day irrespective of season and weather' (Borge, Nordhagen and Lie 2003: 606).

Recently, support for such ideas has been manifested in the popularity and growth of nature day-care centres (*naturbarnehage*). The scene described above is drawn from a study of one such centre where two groups of twelve children and two adults set out from the base to walk and spend half the day (10 am–2 pm) in various locations in the nearby woodland area, regardless of the weather. These centres, which have proliferated in recent years, have chosen to stress 'nature and the outdoor life', which are already a traditional and important feature of Norwegian day-care centres (cf. OECD 1999); whatever the weather and in all four seasons, spending at least two hours a day out of doors is part of children's daily routine, in addition to occasional outings into the countryside. As will be illustrated, this provision and experience of a childhood spent outside in nature centres is backed by state policy and local initiatives.

Cultural analysis and discourse analysis (cf. Søndergaard 1999) direct our attention to the subtle, implicit and mundane – to what is taken for granted in specific contexts. Thus, the seemingly 'natural' is viewed as 'cultural' and thematized (Gullestad 1989). These are central approaches in this study, which takes as its starting point the social studies of childhood and the understanding that *childhood is socially constructed*, a perspective which requires that the view of children as 'natural' beings is abandoned. 'To describe childhood, or indeed any phenomenon, as socially constructed is to suspend a belief in or a willing reception of its taken-for granted meanings' (James, Jenks and Prout 1998: 27). In addition, various constructions of children and childhood are part of ongoing processes of cultural production and reproduction, acted out by agents at all ages, in different ways and in different contexts (cf. Jenks 1996).

Moving beyond the statement that childhood is socially constructed, James and James argue that the cultural politics of childhood requires that we be concerned 'with the precise ways in which this occurs in any society and the specificity of the cultural context to that construction' (2004: 12). It is therefore necessary to pay considerable attention to contextual issues and thus this chapter highlights the cultural values and practices of the Norwegian national context in which children are living and participating and which they help to (re)produce. Ideas of what is 'good' for children and the constructions of what constitutes a 'proper' childhood, which are the focus of this chapter, are thus shown to mirror core cultural values, both contemporary and historical (Gullestad 1992, 1997; Borge, Nordhagen and Lie 2003). These wider issues will be discussed later.

Before addressing the relationship between politics and the social practices of everyday life for children in the nature day-care centre that I studied, it is necessary to set the stage in terms of policies relating to

Norwegian day-care and outdoor life. In this respect, as I show, the everyday practices among children and staff that relate to 'nature' and outdoor life, and the ways children are constructed through these practices, illustrate continuous processes of cultural (re)production, which involve an understanding of children as active agents. In order to illustrate and highlight significant dimensions of 'children in nature', I will therefore present an empirical account of how what I term a 'robust' child subject is constructed in the nature centre.[1]

Although the particular subject explored in this chapter offers a local picture, it is also a part of a European context and of the much wider, multiple and complex mosaic that constitutes childhood in diverse contexts through the interweaving of different discourses, such as those related to 'the rights of the child' and other global processes. This chapter therefore discusses how a rational child subject is also being actualized through these practices and how this raises questions related to 'the child's best interest' in the Norwegian context.

The 'rights of the child' discourse

In recent years the UN Convention on the Rights of the Child (UNCRC) has contributed to the formation of a powerful and global discourse with a range of consequences for policy and social practices in European societies and beyond (James and James 2004; Kjørholt 2004; Moss, Clark and Kjørholt 2005). However, before the term became associated with the rhetoric of the UNCRC, 'the child's best interests' was a principle that was taken into account in the development of the Nordic welfare state, particularly during that latter half of the 1900s (Sandin and Halldén 2003). The Nordic countries are well known for their relatively long-standing and strong commitment to child-centredness, manifested for example in schooling, day-care and other aspects of the law and institutions, such as the establishment of a Children's Ombudsman (1981 in Norway). Both the family and the idea that a good or proper childhood should be secured by the state and local authorities have been to the fore in these developments. Childhood has therefore gradually become established as a distinct social category in the formal sense, with children becoming relatively separate from their parents in law and public regulations (Kjørholt 2004).

Since 2003, however, the UNCRC has been an explicit part of the domestic legal framework and the principle of 'the best interests of the child' is therefore widespread in law and policy. However, the notion of 'best interests' brings with it a range of problems. Being highly flexible and wrapped in consensus and universality has the consequence that the powerful normative and culturally-specific contents comprising a child's 'best interests' in different societies are easily overlooked (Sandin and Halldén 2003; Kjørholt 2004). In *Beyond Listening*, Kjørholt et al., for example, question the impact of a universal rights discourse that is

> based on Anglo-American liberal tradition, which constructs human beings as legal subjects capable of speaking for themselves and acting in their own interest. The subject is constructed as a rational autonomous individual, with the consciousness to formulate his or her own needs and wishes.
>
> (2005: 171)

In contrast with the idea of 'the natural and innocent child' (Jordanova 1989; Cunningham 1995), the children's rights discourse in Norway has undoubtedly had an impact on changing the qualities contemporary children are ascribed with (e.g. 'participatory', 'competent', 'rational', 'autonomous', 'independent'). This is also seen in the changes that have taken place in discourses about (young) children's needs and development that, to some extent, have been exchanged for, or extended to, a rights-based rhetoric (Kjørholt 2005). This can be witnessed in the newly revised[2] Day-care Institution Act of 1975, in which there is a paragraph about 'children's right to participation'. It is interesting to note, therefore, that the legal language and rights rhetoric is beginning to provide a new frame of reference for children's social position which, in Norway and the other Nordic countries, is traditionally derived from child-centred pedagogy (cf. Sandin and Halldén 2003).

Children and (nature) day-care centres in the cultural politics of Norway

In spite of the fact that increasing numbers of mothers with young children have joined the workforce in Norway since the late 1960s, the expansion of institutional day-care has been slow.[3] Although during this period social and educational policy supported traditional constructions of a good childhood as being situated in the family home, encompassing free play outdoors in the neighbourhood, preferably in a natural environment, a recurrent theme in political and public debates was the question of the best place for young children: family and home, or an institutional setting of day-care with professional adults?[4] (Telhaug 1992; Korsvold 1997).

Alongside such ambiguities, a present paramount concern in Norwegian state and local policy is how to expand the number of day-care centres in response to demands from parents and repeated political promises since late 1980s (Ellingsæter and Gulbrandsen 2003). Currently, many new day-care centres are being established by local authorities, which are given the responsibility (and some financial support) to translate national policies into action. There is substantial state funding of both privately and publicly run care centres, which is aimed at all children below the age of six rather than targeted groups. The vast majority of this provision is what policy documents refer to as 'ordinary' day-care centres (St.meld. nr. 27 (1999–2000): 64) and in order to increase the capacity rapidly, some centres have been set up at temporary locations, although now more nature centres/groups are being established.[5] This is similar to the situation in Denmark in the early 1980s where a lack of places meant that economic arguments were mixed with health, developmental and pedagogical issues (Eilers 2005). Thus, in Norway (Christiansen 2005: 82), recent arguments for establishing new centres/groups 'in alliance with nature' can be seen as a response to several current policy imperatives: the need to increase capacity faster, to obtain quality, variety and flexibility and to reduce costs compared to ordinary centres. It therefore appears as if traditional cultural ideas of a good childhood outdoors in nature are being neatly woven into current policy concerns.

Nature centres as well as variations[6] are subsumed under the same law and National Framework Plan,[7] which outlines the aims, content and pedagogical methods of ordinary centres. According to the newly revised Framework Plan (p. 13) all day-care institutions must aim at integrating care, upbringing, play, learning and social and linguistic competence, and provide an arena for transmitting culture and facilitating children's participation in creating their culture. In this way, children are defined as social actors, acknowledging present childhood and children's culture, as well as children as future citizens.

Children's rights are explicitly underscored in the revised plan and five subject fields are described in the Framework Plan. While balancing various child- and adult-initiated activities, learning is thought of as integrated into everyday life and activities. The following extract from the discussion of the subject 'Nature, environment and technique' illustrates the high value put on 'nature' and outdoor life for children in Norwegian day-care centres (cf. Korsvold 1997).

> The day care institution has to contribute to familiarizing children with plants and animals, landscape, seasons and weather. The

ecological perspective is paramount. An objective is to develop children's love of nature, an understanding of the interplay in nature and between man and nature.

Nature accommodates a multitude of experiences and activities in all seasons and in all weathers. Ample opportunities for play and learning are present in the outdoor areas and adjacent countryside.[8]
(Ministry of Children and Family Affairs 1996: 16)

The plan further states that outdoor life and contact with nature are important for pre-school children's 'overall development' and that nature and outdoor play are a part of everyday life in the institution.

Although the number of nature day-care centres is not specified in the national statistics, there are indications of a sharp increase in recent years (Borge et al. 2003; Lysklett 2005a[9]) and the main difference between ordinary centres and nature groups/centres[10] is the additional emphasis given to nature and outdoor life, which makes up both the dominant content and space at the latter. The first such centre in Norway opened in 1987; both Sweden and Denmark had established similar services earlier in the 1980s (Rantatalo 2000; Eilers 2005). Although the history of this type of day-care in Norway has not been systematically studied, it seems to have developed as a result of both idealism and local initiatives in urban and rural districts, with representatives from the pre-school teaching profession and colleges as central agents (Lysklett 2005b). Thus, if policy-making is regarded as an 'important *cultural*, rather than simply, [a] political process' (James and James 2004: 46), the public debates and policy concerning young children, day-care and nature reveal interesting ideas and ambiguities in beliefs about a 'proper' childhood in Norway (cf. Gulløv 2003 for Denmark).

Children as core agents in state policy

To gain a greater insight into national policy on children, youth and nature in general, and (nature) day-care centres in particular, a Ministry of the Environment White Paper on outdoor life (*friluftsliv*) (St.meld. no. 39 (2000–1)) and the related parliamentary debate is informative. Both environmental and health issues are high on the agenda. For example, it is stated that the government will work to 'enhance children and young people's opportunities to develop physically, mentally and socially through playing and walking about in, and experiencing, nature' (St.meld. no. 39 (2000–1) p. 11; author's translation). Although the focus on health has been stepped up in recent years, just as interesting is the focus on children and youth with respect to cultural (re)production processes. This is evident in the following quote from the document, in which children are positioned as core agents in the present and future:

> To maintain outdoor life [*friluftslivet*] as an important leisure activity in the future, subsequent generations must experience nature and have the opportunity to develop skills, in order that they will want and be capable of walking about in the woods and fields.
>
> (St.meld. no. 39 (2000–1) p. 11; author's translation)

Framed by a discourse of worry (see below), this illustrates the way in which children and young people are positioned as necessary agents in (re)producing traditional outdoor life in Norway where there is a law of common access (*loven om allemannsretten*), which gives everybody the right of access to the natural environment, whether this is privately or publicly owned. Those living in Norwegian towns (and many Scandinavian cities) are only a relatively short distance from the countryside and there is easy access to areas of woodland (Gundersen 2004). Along the coast, the seashore is easily accessed and there are vast mountain areas in which many people own or rent a simple cottage.

There are many opportunities for families and individuals to practise the Norwegian version of the 'love of nature': by locating themselves 'in nature' for a day, a weekend or a longer holiday, they can ski, walk, pick wild fruits or mushrooms, fish, swim or hunt if they wish, or simply enjoy being outdoors and building a camp fire to make coffee or grill sausages. Such practices illustrate what Norwegians think of as important aspects of outdoor life (Gullestad 1992, 1997; Repp 1996, St.meld. no. 39 (2000–1)). In this context, however, it is worth noting that 'nature' has multiple meanings that relate to different cultures and practices (Williams 1976a; Olwig 1989). Thus, in English, the terms 'country', 'countryside' and 'rural' seem to be used interchangeably (e.g. Jones 1999), but in Norway 'nature' has a wider – and wilder – meaning than that of the cultivated countryside, although in the Norwegian context, 'nature' can also encompass the rural and the countryside.

Thus, apart from the family, day-care and schools are highlighted in the White Paper as important arenas in which to acquire the skills necessary to experience nature and increasing attention has been given to such activities in these institutions. The government aims at stimulating this, and encouraging the growth of nature centres is viewed as one step on the way to achieving the ideal of 'offering all children in all day-care centres the opportunity for daily play in nature' (St.meld. no. 39 (2000–1) p. 84; author's translation). It is claimed that, by offering such experiences, these centres can also serve as a valuable resource to traditional day-care centres. In relation to this White Paper and other parliamentary debates, boosting nature centres (and nature schools) has been proposed, with one of the arguments being the belief that positive 'attitudes to nature and outdoor life must be established from an early age, ideally in the preschool years' (author's translation).[11]

When the White Paper was debated in parliament it received wide support: the focus on children and youth won approval, and (nature) day-care centres and their role in outdoor life activities were praised. The following extract from one of the speakers is interesting and illustrates several aspects of the debate, such as the importance of both outdoor life and children in the national context, as well as the assumed value of nature.

> The White Paper on outdoor life, which we are debating today, has the subtitle 'A way to a higher quality of life'. This is exactly what the outdoor life means to us in Norway.
>
> We are given the opportunity to enjoy fantastic nature for recreation and [other] experiences. But this also teaches us and gives is humility about the ecological cycle in the natural world. For our children this is an important part of growing up in this country, because nature is so close to us and because we have passed laws that make it possible. To a far greater degree than in many other countries closeness to nature is a shared value, which is an important part of being Norwegian and a natural part of our children's upbringing [*våre barns oppvekst*].
>
> (author's translation)[12]

Such images of 'the child' and 'childhood' are not natural, but cultural, just one of many possibilities. However, some understandings predominate and, in the above extract, the Member of Parliament draws on nature as a central cultural value, a key ingredient of Norwegian national identity (cf. Gullestad 1992, 1997). Thus, although not explicitly referring to it, one may speculate that the politician is expressing what is 'naturally' in 'the best interests' of Norwegian children.

A discourse of worry

Within a widespread discourse of worry, (post)modern childhoods are associated with many negative influences, the result of children's participation as consumers in a global (child) market (Tingstad 2003;

Buckingham and Bragg 2004). Thus, combined with the growth in sedentary indoor leisure pursuits ('screen' activities such as television, computer games, etc.), this is providing a negative contrast to the traditional image of an active, happy and healthy outdoor childhood (cf. Nilsen 1999). Not only is the natural environment seen as important for the development of good motor skills (Fjørtoft and Reiten 2003), and underscored as promoting health for both young and old (e.g. St.meld. no. 37 (1992–3); St.meld. no. 39 (2000–1)) but, as noted above, a key ingredient in Norwegian outdoor life and love of nature is *experiencing* nature for pleasure, as an end in itself. Thus, related to health, but going beyond that, one can observe a discourse of worry that the traditional outdoor life is in decline (e.g. St.meld. no. 39 (2000–1)). Anxiety has been expressed that family days out combined with picking wild fruits seem to be decreasing (Gundersen 2004) and that, snowboarding is gaining in popularity among young people at the cost of the traditional (and national) sport of cross-country skiing. Global processes, with spectacular activities like extreme sports, are also seen as encroaching on traditional outdoor activities in Norway.

Thus, in the White Paper (St.meld. no. 39 (2000–1)), nature and outdoor life are repeatedly defined as being of value for all, and children and young people in particular are positioned as promoters of outdoor life. Framed by this discourse of worry, children and educational institutions have been given the task of stimulating and motivating families that do not, or only seldom, take part in outdoor life. In other words, the cultural values and practices of nature and the outdoor life are assumed to fit into cultural constructions of the good life for children and other generations, now and in the future.

The study and further contextual indicators

As outlined above, the emphasis on nature and an outdoor childhood is a traditional and common aspect of all Norwegian day-care centres and indeed featured in the two ordinary centres where I did fieldwork in 1990–1 (Nilsen 2000). However, in order to study these issues in more depth, more recent fieldwork was carried out in a nature day-care centre with children aged 3–6 years. The methodological approach in the previous and present studies are the same, but fieldwork in the latter was carried out by an assistant (Line Hellem) between October 2003 and June 2004. Participant observation was the main approach to provide 'thick descriptions' (Geertz 1973). Field experiences were mainly documented in notes (sometimes using audio equipment) and some video-recordings were made.

Line focused on the practices of children and staff concerning 'nature' and outdoor life. Apart from making observations at the centre's premises, she concentrated on joining the groups on their regular visits to the nearby woodland, both on skis and on foot.[13] The boundaries of these areas, within which the children can run freely, are verbally defined by landmarks (trees, boulders, etc.). There are no buildings or other services (e.g. toilet facilities) here and everything children and staff need for the day they must carry in their rucksacks. They never bring any toys, but activity equipment and tools the children may use (e.g. a saw, sheath knives, magnifying glasses, binoculars, a bag for gathering things from 'nature' and fact books about flora and fauna). The mornings or afternoons and one day a week are spent at the centre's playground and house (with rooms and equipment like ordinary centres but to a lower building standard).

At this point it is necessary to provide a sketch of the kind of environment the children and adults are in. After a short walk, the terrain is mainly hilly woodland with some small streams, ponds, lakes, marshes and uncultivated grassland. Many narrow paths criss-cross the area, which, in addition to rocks, consists mainly of vegetation – heather, moss, grass, some flowering plants (and some wild berries). The mixed woodland is made up of many large evergreens (mainly spruce and some pines) and hardwoods (e.g. birch). This is an environment for birds and animals (e.g. hares, beavers, squirrels and moose). The woods are cultivated but only to a limited degree, and the area can be used by anyone for leisure, as well as by schools and other day-care centres (cf. the law of common access).

Constructing a robust child subject in 'nature'

It is worth noting that even within such specific locations as the nature day-care centre, diverse constructions of different child subjects are at play that are not necessarily in harmony with each other, as they can reflect different and sometimes contradictory aspects of the multiplicity and complexity of constructed childhoods. At the same time as children are perceived as acting subjects (or agents), other child subject positions are constructed and made available in both child and adult practices. From readings of the field notes made during the winter, what I term a *robust child subject* seems to be constructed between children and adults, as well as among children. The robust child signifies competence in this context and expresses adult expectations and challenges, which the children both encounter and participate in. These reflect practices and values at work in everyday life in nature, including physical and mental aspects, as well as knowledge, which are interwoven and coloured by endurance, resilience and vigour. In addition, a rational child subject, acting independently with agency, feeds into constructions of a robust child subject.

Bodily and mental aspects

The bodily aspect of 'the robust child subject' is explicitly illustrated in children's practices during the winter – viz. playing with and in the snow. I will therefore illustrate a few of a wide range of such possible practices in which, as illustrated in the introduction, adults are also actively involved.

> *One December day the branches of the [spruce] trees are covered with snow. A boy is standing under one of the trees and another boy asks him if he would like him to 'shower' him with snow. The offer is accepted and the first boy has a lot of snow dumped on his head. Later, a girl also takes part in this 'snow shower' activity.*
>
> *In another episode both adults and children are playing rough and tumble in the snow. One of the adults rubs snow on the face of a girl so that she is all white. She laughs. When Line [my assistant] wipes some of the snow off the girl's face, the adult comments with a smile that the children are expected to put up with that sort of thing. The girl throws snow at the adult and he in turn throws snow at the other kids.*

When children are playing with and in the snow we can clearly see their *agency* in constructing a robust child subject. Such vigorous activities inevitably lead to various degrees of (wet) snow on clothes and skin, but the children put up with it, and even enjoy it, in order to be able to initiate and participate in rough physical play.

Adequate material resources and 'expert' knowledge

These are needed in order to avoid freezing when daily life is spent outdoors in all kinds of weather, and they are particularly important during winter time. There is a saying in Norway: 'There is no such thing as bad weather, just bad clothing.' Knowledge and expertise about how to dress and what equipment to bring are prerequisites to feeling comfortable (both physically and mentally) and to avoiding illness. Thus, each child brings spare clothes (e.g. dry gloves) in their rucksack, and changes of warm woollen socks to wear next to the skin, while the adults make a fire and provide hot drinks. However, while parents and staff are responsible for providing the children with the necessary material resources, it is partly each child's responsibility to learn to *actively use their body* to keep warm. This is a 'side-effect' of the vigorous rough-and-tumble play in the snow, but it can also be the main objective, as will be illustrated later when we describe a situation in which one of the adults went for a walk with a few children and instructed an allegedly freezing boy (Edward) to take part in a catch and run game. The staff at the centre also encourage the children to go to the toilet soon after lunch, explaining that this will save energy necessary to warm up the body mass.

A rational child subject?

On the first day of fieldwork Line was told by one of the male staff that the adults in the centre teach the children not to whine, but rather to express their needs verbally: 'to whine is to make a victim of oneself', he stated, and the staff want to prevent victimization. The children, he said, will benefit from this in later life and he added that it is bad to have children in the group who whine, since it makes the staff's job more difficult and unpleasant; it might also make life for the other children less enjoyable.

In explaining the approach of staff in this way, in addition to dealing with the present situation, the teacher draws on a future orientation to argue for rejecting whining: constructions of the present (in)competent child and the future child (as an older child or as an adult) are combined. We might ask, therefore, whether in this case the construction of the ideal and competent child subject draws on ideas from within a child's right's discourse, in terms of a rational child who is or should be capable of stating her/his needs explicitly (cf. Kjørholt 2005). Here, a whining child is placed outside the ideal of a competent, robust and rational child subject. Thus, if children do whine, they are encouraged to adopt alternative strategies: to talk and take action.

To illustrate this I will refer to an incident on a day in November when the group, as usual, were going on foot to one of their places in the woods. Among others, this episode involves a three-year-old, Edward, who is in his first term at the centre. Each autumn the staff make special efforts to make the socialization expectations and rules of the centre clear and explicit to newcomers, something that is apparent in the following account:

> *It is about zero degrees [Celsius], wet and changing weather with snow and rain. The children and adults are eating their packed lunches and have hot*

drinks by a fire. Then Edward starts to cry and one of the adults tells him that he shouldn't cry, but talk and do something about his problem. The adult asks the boy repeatedly what is upsetting him and if his hands are cold, but he just cries. Another boy tries to help and he opens Edward's rucksack to get his mittens, but the adult stops him and says that Edward has to say what his problem is. The adult tells Edward that if his hands are cold, he must look for his mittens in his rucksack, but the boy keeps on crying. Another staff member approaches them, finds Edward's mittens and helps him put them on. After lunch the first adult takes Edward and a girl on a short walk because he thinks they are cold. When the three of them return Edward starts to cry again and the adult asks him what the matter is. Edward is still crying, and says he wants to go indoors. The adult replies that there is nowhere to go here. Edward cries more and more, and soon he is wailing loudly. The adult again asks the boy if he is cold, and Edward answers no, but continues to cry for a long time. The adults start to organize a run and catch game ('All My Chickens'). Edward does not want to join in but is told he must and after a while he stops crying, even smiles, and joins in the game. Afterwards they all return to the fire and an adult changes Edward's socks, to put the warm woollen ones next to the skin.

In this example, Edward is acting against the expectations of a robust child subject. We can observe how one of the adults in particular is trying to make him verbalize 'what his problem is', but he does not respond as a 'rational' subject. The adult wants Edward to act for himself and when another boy tries to help and care for Edward, he is prevented, the adult stating that Edward should find his mittens himself. Expectations of coping as an independent subject are put forward, although this is later overridden by another adult. Another aspect of the robust child subject therefore seems to be independence.

A robust, rational child subject acting independently with agency and 'expert' *knowledge*

Particular children may or may not act according to the ideal of a robust child subject. In the next example a robust child subject is constructed in the interaction between two girls.

Theresa is crying when they all are skiing back to the centre in a long line. Another girl, Rebecca, approaches her and asks Theresa several times in a caring voice if she is cold, if she is freezing, and Theresa says she is. Rebecca says that Simon [one of the boys] has borrowed the adult's mittens and that means Theresa cannot use them. Then Rebecca suggests that they should run to the centre and, supported by Line, they do so.

Children's agency is clearly illustrated here when one child helps another to act for herself, in accordance with the expectations of a robust child subject. The girls did not involve any of the staff in solving the problem and demonstrated their independent use of adequate skills, knowledge and reasoning during this episode. Alerted by the emotional expression of crying, Rebecca helps Theresa to *verbalize* her problem. Further, Rebecca obviously knows the importance of dry mittens and she refers to a caring adult practice: they may lend their mittens to children who need them. However, Rebecca reasons, this is not an option at the moment but the activity of running fast on skis is a way of helping Theresa to warm up.

In sum, Rebecca acts according to, and participates in, the construction of a robust, rational child subject, who acts independently with agency and 'expert' knowledge. However, when children fail to or only partly fulfil such expectations, they are also participating in the process by providing a contrast, which makes adult demands and expectations explicit to all the children – and to us. These children are *not* protected from the cold and wet weather, but rather are exposed to it as part of everyday life. The practices of playing with, and in, the snow manifest Norwegian cultural ideas where there are 'strong ideological associations among childhood, nature and rough, self-governed play' (Gullestad 1997: 29). That the adults kept so firmly to the theory that Edward (described in the earlier episode) was crying because he was cold, rather than for any other reason, highlights the construction of the robust child as a subject who should endure bad weather without whining, and be able to verbalize and *do* something about her/his needs: a rational and independent child is thus intertwined with a robust child.

Childhood and nature in time and space

As argued in the introduction, it is important that we consider the precise ways in which childhood is socially constructed in any society and the specificity of the cultural context of that construction (cf. James and James 2004: 12). The analysis of constructions of a robust child subject and the policy issues related to (nature) day-care centres will serve, therefore, as a sounding board in the following discussion, in which I will explore further how nature and outdoor life, and their interconnection with ideas of independence, are not only central in constructions of a 'proper' Norwegian childhood, but are consistent with cross-generational issues and historical events within the national context.

Nostalgia and romanticism?

In the context of a Nordic country, the above analysis suggests nuances of a legacy from (continental European) Romanticism, in which ideas of childhood and nature interconnect with constructions of an innocent, ignorant, vulnerable, dependent, authentic and sweet child subject (cf. Cunningham 1995). Such understandings seem to clash, however, with the competencies required of the child subject that I have conceptualized as 'robust'. Thus, although authenticity might be of relevance to a contemporary Norwegian context (Gullestad 1997), the understandings of children in nature in the above analysis involve the rational and independent subject that the global child's rights and participant discourses are currently forging.

However, there is widespread recognition that constructions of an ideal past childhood feed into contemporary ideas of a proper childhood (Hendrick 1994; Midjo 1994; Korsvold 1997). In this context it could be said that nature centres create a place that offers images related to memories of a happy, active and self-governed childhood in 'unspoiled nature' (e.g. Mjaavatn 2005), images on which constructions of a robust child subject might also very well be projected without inconsistency.

The current celebration of nature centres (e.g. St.meld no. 39 (2000–1); Lysklett 2005b) might also serve as a continuation and heightening of the idea, firmly rooted in Norway, that outdoor life and in particular 'nature' is an ideal setting for (young) children to act out their childhoods (Borge et al. 2003). Following on from this, one can speculate how nature centres might mediate some of the ambiguities noted above surrounding the placing of young children in institutions since, though the framing of family and home have changed, children can, nonetheless, spend everyday life outdoors 'in nature' and thus traditional cultural ideas of a good childhood are (re)produced in social practices, albeit within an institutional setting.[14]

The environments (actual and imagined) that children and childhoods move about in differ widely across Europe and beyond. I would certainly not suggest any material/environmental determinism, but such variations may well interact with different constructions of children and childhoods (cf. Jones 1999). The images embedded in ideas, as well as in the social practices that help to shape a Norwegian childhood 'in nature', are supposedly (but not solely) connected with 'unspoiled' nature of a more 'untamed' and different kind from national geographies with more widespread and systematic urbanization. Thus, for example, the physical natural environment for constructing a 'robust child subject' is different in the more cultivated and pastoral countryside of the UK (cf. Jones 1999).

'Love of nature' – the Norwegian version

The value of nature and spending time in the fresh air is not just connected to constructions of a proper childhood. As noted, it is generally accepted that special ideas about and a close relationship with nature are culturally dominant in Norway (and other Scandinavian countries) (Gullestad 1992; Repp 1996, 2001; St.meld no. 39 (2000–1)). The positive value of this is taken for granted but, nevertheless, selective processes are at play in order to identify

> that which within the terms of an effective dominant culture, is always passed on as 'the tradition' *the* significant past. But always the selectivity is the point; the way in which from a whole possible area of past and present, certain meanings and practices are chosen for emphasis, certain other meanings and practices are neglected and excluded.
>
> (Williams 1976b: 205)

Thus, spending time outdoors, preferably in (unspoiled) nature, as an unquestionably good thing, is based on culturally *selected* meanings and practices. Speaking from 'anthropology at home' and not particularly with children in mind, Marianne Gullestad describes the traditional version of experiencing nature in Norway:

> To be 'out in nature' is both a question of flora and fauna and a question of climate and seasons. Nature makes both body and soul hardier and fresh air gives new strength. Nature trains independence and the ability to cope in the wild. Nature offers harmony, peace of mind and distance from the hustle and bustle of society. Being out in the so-called fresh air offers solitude and freedom from society, as well as good friendship. This is how Norwegian men and women think, and to a greater or lesser degree this marks the upbringing of their children, their Sunday trips and holidays in primitive cottages.
>
> (Gullestad 1992: 204)

Nature and outdoor life are a part of the selective tradition in Norway which therefore replicates itself with astonishing force in different domains, including those of children and older generations.

Conclusion: constructing a national childhood?

The White Paper about outdoor life referred to in this chapter (St.meld. no. 39 (2000–1), and the related parliamentary debate, illustrate the fact that, with respect to the significance of nature and outdoor life, children are seen as important citizens and bearers of national culture (cf. Kjørholt 2002). Nature day-care centres (and schools) are viewed as important sites which (should) participate in such a cultural (re)production process. Supported by national and local policies, and in line with traditional constructions of a proper childhood, nature and outdoor life are selected from the national cultural 'curriculum' to be a part of children's everyday life in ordinary day-care centres and, as illustrated, are emphasized particularly in nature centres. As a part of the process of cultural (re)production, the present emphasis on an outdoor childhood 'in nature' points to cultural domination processes and one may speculate, therefore, if constructions of a national identity are at stake here. The robust child subject fits well within the national context: to become and be a subject who loves the Norwegian version of 'nature' encompasses an *independent* subject with the competence necessary to roam about in 'unspoiled' nature. The children in the nature centre *learned* through experiences how to handle the necessary tools for coping in such environments, whilst also learning about flora and fauna and environmental issues that reoccur in daily life.

Gullestad draws attention to the fact that '[i]ndependence has long been a key notion with much rhetorical force in the upbringing of children, as well as in many other contexts in Norway' (1997: 32). She further elaborates on national independence as a central feature of contemporary politics: for example, two referendums have rejected membership of the European Union and in 2005, public institutions (e.g. public broadcasting, the government, newspapers, etc.) were loudly celebrating Norway's 100 years of independence from the union with Sweden. Establising itself as independent nation has been a very significant part of Norwegian history since the 1700s and to this end (unspoiled) nature and the independent freeholder (*odelsbonde*) have become culturally selected key symbols (Christensen 2001).

What were selected as particularly Norwegian characteristics, however, such as celebrating the wilderness and practices of nature and outdoor life, are historically tied to trends in European science, art and philosophy and as such, one may view the development of nature centres as a renewed continuation of these trends, with a touch of modern ecology, philosophy and environmental concerns thrown in (Borge et al. 2003). Constructing a national identity related to nature has therefore been a long process, particularly during the nineteenth century. National romanticism in art and literature was a part of this (Sørensen 2001), as were the polar expeditions with national heroes like Fridjof Nansen, who is considered to be the founding father of (modern) outdoor life for all social classes (Repp 2001).

In the formation of nation states in previous centuries, constructions of a national identity and the question of what became selected as 'Norwegian' were on the agenda. Thus, the contemporary discourse of worry might point to a renewed debate and interest in issues of national identity which, being now located in the context of globalization, makes this a much more complex issue (cf. Kjørholt 2002). Constructing national identities is still part of ongoing cultural (re)production and, although more explicitly formulated in political documents and debates, it is also something that people as social agents *do* in everyday life, as well as on special occasions (e.g. celebrating national days), without necessarily reflecting on it as such (Frykman 1995).

Thus, past, present and future interconnect in complex ways. Sustaining (traditional) outdoor life in nature for 'future generations' with the help of 'the future generation' was a clearly stated aim of the White Paper (St.meld. no. 39 (2000–1)). Whether this is 'in the best interests of the child' is, however, an open question – it depends on the child, the contexts of their childhood and, not least, the values that frame this question. Children in (nature) day-care centres are experiencing the Norwegian version of 'love of nature' and are clearly envisaged as bearers of the national culture in political documents and debates. This involves constructions of a robust, rational and independent child subject, which ties in well to the global discourse of the Rights of the Child.

Notes

1   This chapter is based in the research project *Natural Childhoods in Norwegian Day-care Centres?* A sub-project within the larger project *The Modern Child and the Flexible Labour Market. Institutionalization and Individualization of Children in the Light of Changes to the Welfare State*. I thank the Norwegian Research Council Welfare Programme for funding this research.

The analysis of the 'robust' child subject is based on presentations and papers at: The Modern Child and the Flexible Labour Market, second international seminar, Norwegian Centre for Child Research, 3–5 June 2005; Internal Seminar at the Norwegian Centre for Child Research, 31 August 2005; The Seventh Conference of the European Sociological Association (ESA), Sociology of Childhood Stream, 9–12 September 2005. I thank the participants of these events for inspiring and helpful comments and discussions.

2   Barnehageloven av 17.juni 2005 nr.64, ß 3 Barns rett til medvirkning (cf. Kunnskapsdepartementet 2006). This revised Day-care Institution Act ('barnehageloven') came into force in January 2006.

3   The percentages of children aged 0–6 years in day-care are: 1968: 3%, 1978: 15%, 1988: 33% (Korsvold 1997: 419). In 1997 the age for starting school was reduced to six years, therefore the following data deal with children aged 1–5 years, 1998: 61% (St.meld. no. 27 (1999–2000)), 2003: 69% (Statistical Yearbook of Norway 2005).

4   During November 2005 the debate cropped up again. For the record: day-care in policy document is stated as a *supplement* to the family. The debates and promises made by both conservative and left-wing parties during the autumn 2005 election campaign revolved around: whether to provide a cash for care system for children aged 1–3, giving all children the opportunity to attend a day-care centre, funding questions and reducing the fee. The new left-wing/centre coalition government has reduced the fee, made a minimal decrease of cash for care, and are repeating the promises of increasing the capacity of day-care dramatically.

5   This is, for example, reported, in articles in the main paper for mid-Norway, *Adresseavisen*, 5 August 2005, p. 6 and 18 February 2006, p. 6.

6   One variation is family centres where a teacher or assistant and a maximum of five children make up a satellite group of an ordinary centre.

7   A Framework Plan was for put into action the first time in 1996. The day-care institution policy has recently been transferred from the Ministry of Children and Family Affairs to the Ministry of Education, which has since revised the plan (to be implemented from August 2006). Five subject fields are extended to seven and made compatible with school subjects (Communication, language and text; Body, movement and health; Art, culture and creativity; Nature, environment and technology; Ethics, religion and philosophy; Local environment and society; Number, space and form) (Kunnskapsdeparte mentet 2006, author's translation).

8   Extract from the presentation of the subject field 'nature, environment and technology', which is one of the seven subjects in the revised plan (cf. Kunnskapsdepartementet 2006). (The other five subject fields in the 1996 plan are: Society, religion and ethics, Aesthetic subjects, Language, text and communication, and Physical activity and health.

9   This author notes an increase from approximately 30 units in 1999 to over 250 in 2004.

10   Apart from the kind of nature day-care centre described in this chapter, there are ordinary day-care centres which have ambulant nature groups: two groups alternate in being located indoors or in a natural environment. Some

nature groups/centres are using a 'lavo' (a Saami tepee) to provide 'indoor' areas while spending time in the woods.

11 The proposals (in relation to the White Paper on Outdoor Life in 2002 and budget negotiations for 2006) were rejected by a narrow margin. The quotation is from the last event (Innst.S.no. 228 (2004–5). The proposals were put forward by the parties that in the late autumn 2005 formed a left-wing centre government.

12 Conservative MP Øyvind Halleraker. Parliamentary meeting, 11 April 2002. www.stortinget.no (at this time there was a Conservative/Centre coalition government).

13 No doubt this has been a great challenge doing fieldwork under different temperature and weather conditions and I am grateful to Line Hellem.

14 Such an argument parallels the earlier politics of making the family and home a model for Norwegian day-care services in policy and practices from the 1950s (Korsvold 1997; Nilsen 2000).

References

Borge, A. I. H., Nordhagen, R. and Lie, K. K. (2003) Children in the Environment: Forest Day-care Centres – Modern Day Care with Historical Antecedents. *History of the Family* 8: 605–18.

Buckingham, D. and Bragg, S. (2004) *Young Pople, Sex and the Media. The Facts of Life?* New York: Palgrave Macmillan.

Christensen, O. (2001) En nasjonal identitet tar form. Etniske og nasjonalkulturelle avgrensninger. In Sørensen, Ø. (ed.), *Jakten på det norske. Perspektiver på utviklingen av en norsk nasjonal identitet på 1800-tallet* (pp. 51–73). Oslo: Gyldendal Akamedisk.

Christiansen, T. (2005) Ett skritt på veien mot full barnehagedekning i en naturskjønn kommune. In Lysklett, O. B. (ed.), *Ute hele dagen!* (pp. 79–82). DMMHs publikasjonsserie no. 1. Trondheim: Dronning Mauds Minne. Høgskole for førskolelærerutdanning.

Cunningham, H. (1995) *Children and Childhood in Western Society since 1500.* London: Longman.

Eilers, C. (2005) Den Danske skovbørnehave – hva er det? In Lysklett, O. B. (ed.), *Ute hele dagen!* (pp. 41–3). DMMHs publikasjonsserie nr.1. Trondheim: Dronning Mauds Minne. Høgskole for førskolelærerutdanning.

Ellingsæter, A. L. and Gulbrandsen, L. (2003) *Barnehagen – fra selektivt til universelt velferdsgode.* NOVA Rapport no. 24. Oslo: Norsk institutt for forskning om oppvekst, velferd og aldring.

Fjørtoft, I. and Reiten, T. (2003) *Barn og unges relasjoner til natur og friluftsliv. En kunnskapsoversikt.* HiT skrift nr. 10/2003. Porsgrunn: Høgskolen i Telemark and Friluftslivets fellesorganisasjon.

Frykman, J. (1995) Nationell och annan kulturell identitet, *Tradisjon* 25(1): 17–30.

Geertz, C. (1973) *The Interpretation of Cultures.* New York: Basic Books.

Gullestad, M. (1989) *Kultur og hverdagsliv. På sporet av det moderne Norge.* Oslo: Universitetsforlaget.

58   *Randi Dyblie Nilsen*

Gullestad, M. (1992) *The Art of Social Relations. Essays on Culture, Social Action and Everyday Life in Modern Norway*. Oslo: Scandinavian University Press.

Gullestad, M. (1997) A Passion for Boundaries. Reflections on Connections between the Everyday Lives of Children and Discourses on the Nation in Contemporary Norway. *Childhood* 4(1): 19–42.

Gulløv, E. (2003) Creating a Natural Place for Children. An Ethnographic Study of Danish Kindergartens. In Fog Olwig, K. and Gulløv, E. (eds.), *Children's Places. Cross-cultural Perspectives* (pp. 23–38). New York: Routledge.

Gundersen, V. S. (2004) Urbant skogbruk. Forvaltning av skog i by- og tettstedkommuner. *Aktuelt fra skogforskning*. Rapport 3/4: 1–33.

Hendrick, H. (1994) *Child Welfare. England 1872–1989*. London: Routledge.

Innst.S. no. 228 (2004–5).

James, A. and James, A. L. (2004) *Constructing Childhood. Theory, Policy and Social Practice*. London: Palgrave Macmillan.

James, A., Jenks, C. and Prout, A. (1998) *Theorizing Childhood*. London: Polity Press.

Jenks, C. (1996) *Childhood*. London: Routledge.

Jones, O. (1999) Tomboy Tales: The Rural, Nature and the Gender of Childhood. *Gender, Place and Culture*, 6(2): 117–36.

Jordanova, L. (1989) *Children in History. Concepts of Nature and Society*. New York: Cambridge University Press.

Kjørholt, A.T. (2002) Small is Powerful. Discourses on 'Children and Participation' in Norway. *Childhood*, 9(1): 63–82.

Kjørholt, A. T. (2004) Childhood as a Social and Symbolic Space: Discourses on Children as Social Participants in Society. PhD dissertation. Trondheim: Norwegian University of Science and Technology, Faculty of Social Sciences and Technology Management.

Kjørholt, A.T. (2005) The Competent Child and the Right 'to be Oneself': Reflections on Children as Fellow Citizens in an Early Childhood Centre. In Clark, A., Kjørholt, A. T. and Moss, P. (eds.), *Beyond Listening. Children's Perspectives on Early Childhood Services* (pp. 149–70). Bristol: Policy Press.

Kjørholt, A. T., Moss, P. and Clark, A. (2005) Beyond Listening: Future Prospects. In Clark, A., Kjørholt, A. T. and Moss, P. (eds.), *Beyond Listening. Children's Perspectives on Early Childhood Services* (pp. 171–83). Bristol: Policy Press.

Korsvold, T. (1997) Profesjonalisert barndom. Statlige intensjoner og kvinnelig praksis på barnehagens arena 1945–1990. PhD dissertation. Trondheim: Norwegian University of Science and Technology, Faculty of Arts.

Kunnskapsdepartementet (2006) Forskrift om rammeplan for barnehagens innhold og oppgaver [Revised Framework Plan for Day-care Institutions in Norway by the Ministry of Education].

Lysklett, O.B. (2005a) Uteleik året i rundt i kjente omgivelser. In Lysklett, O. B. (ed.) *Ute hele dagen!* pp. 15–22. DMMHs publikasjonsserie nr.1. Trondheim: Dronning Mauds Minne. Høgskole for førskolelærerutdanning.

Lysklett, O. B. (ed.) (2005b) Ute hele dagen! DMMHs publikasjonsserie no.1. Trondheim: Dronning Mauds Minne. Høgskole for førskolelærerutdanning.

Midjo, T. (1994) Den nye barndommen. Individuering og subjektstatus. In Aasen, P. and Haugaløkken, O. K. (eds.), *Bærekraftig pedagogikk. Identitet og kompetanse i det moderne samfunnet* (pp. 88–114). Oslo: Ad Notam Gyldendal.

Ministry of Children and Family Affairs (1996) Framework Plan for Day-care Institutions. A Brief Presentation.

Mjaavatn, P.E. (2005) Natur- og friluftsbarnehager – et gode for barn? In Lysklett, O. B. (ed.), *Ute hele dagen!* (pp. 51–6). DMMHs publikasjonsserie nr.1. Trondheim: Dronning Mauds Minne. Høgskole for førskolelærerutdanning.

Moss, P., Clark, A. and Kjørholt, A. T. (2005) Introduction. In Clark, A., Kjørholt, A. T. and Moss, P. (eds.), *Beyond Listening. Children's Perspectives on Early Childhood Services* (pp. 1–16). Bristol: Policy Press.

Nilsen, R. Dyblie (1999) Fysisk aktivitet, helse og oppvekst. Report no. 53. Trondheim: Norwegian Centre for Child Research.

Nilsen, R. Dyblie (2000) Livet i barnehagen. En etnografisk studie av sosialiseringsprosessen. PhD dissertation.Trondheim: Norwegian University of Science and Technology, Faculty of Social Sciences and Technology Management.

OECD (1999) *OECD Country Note. Early Childhood Education and Care Policy in Norway.*

Olwig, K. R. (1989) Nature Interpretation: A Threat to the Countryside? In Uzzell, D. L. (ed.), *The Nature and Built Environment* (pp. 132–41). London: Belhaven Press.

Parliament Meeting 11 April 2002, 10 am, www.stortinget.no.

Rantatalo, P. (2000) Skogmulleskolan. In Sandell, K. and Sörlin, S. (eds.), *Friluftshistoria. Från 'härdande friluftslif' till ekoturism och miljöpedagogik.* Stockholm: Carlsson Bokförlag.

Repp, G. (1996) Norwegian Relationships to Nature through Outdoor Life. In Neuman, J., Mytting, I. and Brtnik, J. (eds.), *Outdoor Activities.* Proceedings of International Seminar, Prague 1994, Charles University. Lüneburg: Verlag edition erlebnispädagogik.

Repp, G. (2001) Verdier og ideal for dagens friluftsliv. Nansen som føredøme? PhD dissertation. Oslo: The Norwegian University of Sports and Physical Education.

Sandin, B. and Halldén, G. (2003) Välfärdsstatens omvandling och en ny barndom. In Sandin, B. and Halldén, G. (eds.), *Barnets bästa – en antologi om barndomens innebörder och välfärdens organisering.* Stockholm/Stehag: Brutus Östlings Bokförlag Symposion.

Statistical Yearbook of Norway 2005.

St.meld. no. 37 (1992–3) *Utfordringer i helsefremmende og forebyggende arbeid.* Oslo: Sosial- og helsedepartementet [White Paper on Health Policy].

St.meld. no. 27 (1999–2000) *Barnehage til beste for barn og foreldre.* Oslo: Barne-og familiedepartementet [White Paper on Day-care Policy].

St.meld. no. 39 (2000–1) *Friluftsliv. Ein veg til høgare livskvalitet.* Oslo: Miljøverndepartementet [White Paper on Environment Policy].

Søndergaard, D.M. (1999) *Destabilising Discourse Analysis – Approaches to Poststructuralist Empirical Research.* Working paper no. 7, Insitut for Statskundskab. University of Copenhagen.

Sørensen, Ø. (2001) Hegemonikamp om det norske. Elitenes nasjonsbyggingsprosjekter 1770–1945. In Sørensen, Ø. (ed.) *Jakten på det norske. Perspektiver på utviklingen av en norsk nasjonal identitet på 1800-tallet* (pp. 17–48). Oslo: Gyldendal Akamedisk.

Telhaug, A. Oftedal (1992) Den moderne barndommen som utvidet institusjonalisering. In Aasen, P.and Oftedal Telhaug, A. (eds.), *Takten, takten. Pass på takten. Studier i den offentlige oppdragelsens historie.* Oslo: Ad Notam Gyldendal.

Tingstad, V. (2003) Children's Chat on the Net. A Study of Social Encounters in Two Norwegian Chatrooms. Doctoral dissertation. Trondheim: Norwegian

University of Science and Technology, Faculty of Social Sciences and Technology Management.

Williams, R. (1976a) *Keywords. A Vocabulary of Culture and Society*. Glasgow: Fontana.

Williams, R. (1976b) Base and Superstructure in Marxist Cultural Theory. In Dale, R., Esland, G. and MacDonald, M. (eds.), *Schooling and Capitalism*. London: Routledge & Kegan Paul.

4

Children's Cultures and New Technologies: A Gap between Generations? Some Reflections from the Spanish Context

Ferran Casas

If we analyse the answers from the adult samples of the Eurobarometer 34 and 39 surveys for Spain (Commission of the European Communities/ Commission des Communautés Européennes 1990; 1993), we find that, as in other European countries, the most important value the Spanish place on the education of their children is *responsibility*. In fact, in 1993 Spain had the highest preference for responsibility of all European countries.

Debates on how to teach responsibility to children have often concluded with practical recommendations, such as how to create spaces where responsibility can be exercised, an idea that allows a link to be made with the 'participation' principle contained in the UN Convention on the Rights of the Child. Promoting responsible participation programmes has even become a goal for some local authorities in Spain, for example, by the means of the Child Friendly Cities programme.

There is a marked difference, however, between local initiatives and mainstream welfare policies in Spain. The latter are restricted to social protection policies that target the most marginalized groups (e.g. abused and neglected children) or social problems highlighted by public opinion (e.g. violence against women). In general, however, policies relating to public services and programmes for children focus principally on children as *students and users of paediatric services*.

At present, neither the national government nor most of the regional governments recognize children as active social participants, a view that, as will be explored in this chapter, reflects the attitude of many Spanish parents. As this chapter will show, most parents think of themselves as having primary responsibility for children's socialization into future adults, even when their children reach adolescence, a view that is challenged by children's use of ICTs (information and communication technologies). This reveals the existence of a new and strong peer culture in Spanish society that may represent a challenge to the authority relations characteristic of relationships between parents, teachers and children, and which have traditionally been regarded as representing the 'optimum model' from the adults' point of view.

Family and child policy in Spain

According to OECD reports (2004), Spain spends the least on families and has the lowest family services rates among the Member States. Public expenditure on the family, as a percentage of GDP in 2001, was 0.5 per cent, while the OECD (30 countries) mean was 1.8 per cent and the EU (19 countries) mean was 2.1 per cent. Allowances for families with newborn infants are also among the lowest in the industrialized West, which is probably not unrelated to the fact that the fertility rate in Spain is one of the lowest in the world.

Spain also has no national Children's Ombudsman; only one of the 17 *Comunidades Autonomas* into which the country is divided for administrative purposes has an independent Ombudsman for children and one other has a Deputy Ombudsman for children with powers derived from the General Ombudsman.

Over the past 20 years, policies in Spain have given priority to developing a competitive economy as the principal way to raise the country's standard of living. In this context children have had no priority in terms of public policy; furthermore, in the social arena more generally, few voices have been raised in support of improving their position in society. Children's NGOs are few and in general are neither large nor well funded. Thus people engaged in children's welfare and rights are a small, although very active, minority. Consequently, it is NGOs, together with some municipalities and a few provincial authorities, that have taken most of the initiatives in promoting children's rights and social participation programmes.

In contrast to public policy in Spain, children have become increasingly important in the private life of families. Most couples have just one or two children (in 2000 the fecundity rate was 1.23, the lowest in the EU) and the trend is for them to have them increasingly later in life.

So when a Spanish couple have a child, it is usually a carefully planned event, couples being acutely aware of the economic and time costs of childrearing. Because measures to help couples balance their work and family responsibilities are still very scarce (in 2002 only 11 per cent children under the age of three in Spain was offered a place in public childcare, with all over three year olds having a place), parents also need to organize the extended family (particularly grandmothers) to help with childcare, and they tend to buy many material goods for their children as a way of compensating for the lack of time spent with them.

The low priority given to children in public policy is in marked contrast to the increasing interest that advertisers have shown in recent years. Companies have become aware of the desire of Spanish parents to spend on their children and since children receive pocket money from an early age, they have become consumers in their own right and a very important target group for advertisers.

In such a context, the question of what is good or proper for children must be analysed along two different axes: the official version versus what happens in practice; and the private versus the public version. In the official version, Spanish authorities are working for children's rights and quality of life, and reports to the Committee on the Rights of the Child (CRC) underline the substantial volume of legislation intended to guarantee such rights. In practice, however, public investment is aimed at ensuring (a) a well-educated workforce, and (b) healthy children, thanks to the public health service. In private life, enormous efforts are made by parents to get 'the best' for their child – for example, if they can afford it, many families prefer the services of a private paediatrician, because they believe private health care offers better quality, and they use public services only for emergencies or very expensive treatments. They also spend substantial sums on extra-curricular activities. In terms of the public sphere, however, nobody feels responsible for children – they are mostly 'other people's' children for whom there is no collective sense of responsibility.

Furthermore, although experts (developmental psychologists, educationalists, paediatricians and other professionals) tend to focus on what is good for child development and what is in 'the best interests of the child', there is no consensus about what this means and the standards that should be applied. It is popularly believed that experts often change their mind. In addition, parents may disagree with them and, in a society with a large immigrant population from different cultures, it is also becoming apparent that there are no viable cross-cultural criteria against which such issues can be determined. Consequently, there is increasing awareness that there are important (cultural) differences (or diversities) in determining what is good for children in the Spanish context (Casas 1997).

Quality of life and children's best interests

Improving 'quality of life' has emerged as the new social aspiration offered by all kinds of advertising and all political parties in Spain. However, the concept is understood very differently by the various social groups and all too often is hardly more than rhetoric and bears little relationship to research findings on the subject.

In Western societies during the first half of the twentieth century, the standard of living was widely regarded as the best indicator of well-being and of progress in terms of welfare and the quality of life. However, from the 1960s onwards, social scientists increasingly argued that what is important is how people *experience* their lives and that material conditions may therefore reveal little about people's worries and needs (Campbell, Converse and Rodgers 1976). As a result, different conceptualizations of and scientific models for the quality of life (QOL) started to be developed, which sought to articulate both material ('objective') and non-material ('subjective') aspects of the human and socio-cultural environment. However, it was very easy to demonstrate that in many situations these two components of QOL do not correlate and that, for example, experts' 'objective' measures and the 'subjective' satisfaction of service users may not correlate at all, triggering debates about who is right. Thus, it took some years to become aware that what is scientifically relevant is not *Who is right?*, but *Why do they disagree?'*

During the 1980s and 1990s, a clear consensus began to emerge that how people experience their lives is a crucial psychosocial component of QOL. Such non-material and 'subjective' phenomena as perceptions, evaluations and aspirations have therefore become of key scientific value and are now taken into account in most serious QOL studies (Campbell et al. 1976; Casas 1996).

There are several lessons to be learned from these debates about how to define and evaluate QOL and how to understand the meaning of quality in terms of children's lives. When different social agents (e.g. children and parents) do not agree about what is good or best for children, we must now consider whether *Who is right?* is the question we should be asking.

When we review the research exploring children's quality of life, however, we find very few publications in which the question has been put to children themselves. Typical research in this field is about the attribution of needs, or the perceptions of quality that *adults* (experts or parents) have about children. This is, however, a misuse of the concept 'quality of life' as it is now understood, since it undermines its very foundations – the centrality of people's *own* perceptions, evaluations and aspirations. So, in practice, what is referred to as research on children's QOL is often not about their perceptions of the quality of their lived experiences but about adults' perceptions of, or opinions about, children's lives.

Traditionally, what is considered good or best for Spanish children, as elsewhere in Europe, has been decided by their parents or experts. Experts 'know' about children's needs because of their expertise; thus, it has also been assumed that experts take into account the perspective of the child, because this may be different from that of an adult. But even though this change of perspective is very important, it has still been taken for granted that children themselves should not be asked, because they do not know (or are not yet capable of knowing or competent to know or understand) what is good for them: who is right and who is wrong. In short, who knows and who is not capable of knowing has been decided in advance.

When we *do* ask children, however, we find that sometimes they agree and sometimes they disagree with adults, which in turn raises a question about the reasons for any disagreements from which we might learn. Such disagreements – between children's perspectives on their own lives and adult's perspectives on children's lives – are an important dimension of social life. For example, adolescents and young people in general are well known for being greater risk-takers than adults; having new and challenging experiences and discovering their limits are very important to them. For adults, however, 'security' has a much higher priority. But for young people, the protective measures imposed on them by adults in their 'best interests' may be perceived and experienced as adults seeking to control their lives or limit their freedom – something not considered by adults to be of sufficient importance to take into account.

We must not forget, however, that the psychosocial context in which such perspectives emerge is based on both adults and young people defining each other as belonging to different social groups or categories, something that social psychologists call *processes of inter-group categorical differentiation* (Casas 1995). A major challenge that arises from this is the struggle to understand why, as adults, 'we' are so 'interested' in keeping children and teenagers as a completely differentiated social category, instead of trying to build a social consensus with the younger generations. The answer is also likely to help us to understand why many adults often feel uncomfortable when we speak about the need to increase children's social participation (Casas 1994).

Children's rights as traditionally understood (e.g. the right to the provision of key services such as health and education, and to protection) are an attempt to increase children's QOL. In this regard the universal and growing consensus about the importance of children's rights must be seen as a positive step. However, we must not forget that it is adults who have formulated these rights. When we ask children, they usually agree (although there are some problems, for example, with the right not to work), but often children will express 'rights' in different terms. When we explore the question of children's civil rights (freedoms) or their right to participation, however, many adults waver (as became clear in Spain from Aguinaga and Comas's survey results (1991)) and the difference between adults' and children's perceptions can be surprising.

Traditional conceptions of children and childhood in Spain and the audio-visual media contradiction

In Spain, traditional conceptions of children and childhood are deeply rooted in the fabric and principles of Roman law: children were historically regarded as the property of their parents (originally, the property of who had the *patria potestas*) and did not figure in public policy considerations until recently, when the concept of social protection was adopted. In fact, social policies in general did not seriously appear in Spain until a democratic constitution was again adopted in 1979. However, childhood and family policies, as noted, have not been a priority in recent history and consequently the Spanish welfare state is still far from achieving the level reached in Northern Europe, which is often taken as a standard for comparison.

As a result, although general attitudes towards children in Spain have undergone rapid change at the level of interpersonal relationships – from authoritarian to more democratic and tolerant – the fundamental perception of and belief in adults' authority over children is still evident as a kind of miasma, present everywhere in the context of intergenerational relationships. Thus in recent televised debates (e.g. TV3, 24 January 2006), the risk of losing parental authority clearly emerged as the main reason for many adults' opposition to children's participation, in both family life and society more generally.

In the last two decades, however, a new phenomenon – audio-visual media – has started to destabilize adult–child relationships, initially in subtle ways but more recently in very obvious ways. First, in the 1980s, videos and video games appeared in homes and often the person programming the video was the child. This could be for practical reasons – children's familiarity with the technology meant that they could do this faster and without using the instruction manual – but this was considered unimportant by adults. Second, children showed impressive mastery of the video games, although these too were dismissed by adults as 'childish' and most parents did not want to play or even to talk about video games with their children. For example, in a sample of Spanish parents, 53.9 per cent reported never talking about video games with their children and 60.2 per cent admitted never playing video games with them (Casas 2000, 2001). Those who did were often unable to outperform their children, which for proud adults was an unsettling experience. Computers started to penetrate Spanish households in the mid-1990s, and the Internet at the end of the 1990s; since then the mobile phone has appeared (Casas et al. 2005). As in most European countries, the presence of a child in the family was likely to facilitate the early introduction of computers and the Internet (Suess et al. 1998; Livingstone and Bovill 2001).

However, the ways in which new information and communication technologies (ICTs) have dramatically increased in Spanish households in such a short period is not the aspect of these changes we want to analyse here; crucially, it includes human interaction and the creation of non-material products. We therefore need to understand much better what roles new technologies are playing in human relationships, in the socialization of children, in parent–children interactions and in intergenerational relationships if we want to improve them.

It soon became evident, for example, that the attitudes of children to ICTs were different from those of adults and that ICTs play a key role in children's, adolescents' and youngsters' cultures. Recent research exploring the use of and attitudes towards ICTs amongst children aged 12–16 years and their parents revealed the following (Casas et al. 2001):

- children's use of audio-visual media shows them to be competent social actors;
- access to information through ICTs makes children less dependent on adults as sources of knowledge;
- the knowledge and skills related to the use of ICTs are more often acquired from peer groups than from adults; and
- children's conversations about audio-visual media-related activities with adults tend to be unsatisfactory but very satisfactory with young

people, particularly with peers. Dissatisfaction with intergenerational communication seems to be related (amongst other things) to a generation gap in the evaluation of activities related to ICTs.

The importance of peers in children's lives is not new. However, ICTs are making this more evident and everyday life seems to lend increasing support to the hypothesis that socialization is more peer group-dependent than we have traditionally accepted (Harris 1995). Such evidence threatens adults' traditional and deep-rooted beliefs about how children are dependent on them and, of course, adults are reluctant to abandon such beliefs.

In highlighting these issues, however, it is the ICTs that become the 'problem', although as in other European countries Spanish adults' opinions on this point are divided, a phenomenon that has been labelled binary determinism: optimistic vs. pessimistic (Sefton-Green 1998). Optimists believe that computers *themselves* (and other ICTs) will improve people's lives and facilitate global communication; they therefore view them as having enormous potential for children, the challenge being to maximize their positive use. Pessimists, by contrast, think that the growth in ICTs will result in more control over our lives and greater dehumanization and, as a consequence, they see them as a risk for children and argue that they should be strictly controlled or even banned.

In addition, many parents and teachers feel they are losing control, not only because they feel unskilled in relation to ICTs and are reluctant to change traditional methods of knowledge transmission, but also because ICTs give children access to alternative authoritative sources of knowledge, which differ from those that adults have traditionally controlled. Thus, not only are ideas of parental authority changing but, as elsewhere in Europe, there is growing concern in Spain that schooling is being deposed from the top of the tree of knowledge (Sefton-Green 1998). Indeed, although school has traditionally been considered as the prime means of securing entry into democratic society, far-reaching questions are now being asked about how this will happen in the future. The next section presents empirical data that flesh out these issues.

The 'problem' of the new technologies as new socializers: a generational misunderstanding

Data from adolescents' use of different audio-visual media and about their relationships related to media were collected in Spain in successive biennial surveys (1999, N = 1,634; 2001, N = 3,424; 2003, N = 1,936) from samples of 12–16-year-olds. As described below, the results make interesting reading (Casas et al. 2005) in revealing considerable differences between parents' and children's views about ICT ownership, use and value.

Adolescents were asked, from a list of four items of audio-visual equipment (television, computer, console and mobile) and some of their facilities (educative CD-ROMs, the Internet and games) if they had access to them *at home* and if any of them were their *own*. Television emerged as by far the most common piece of equipment that adolescents have access to. However, during the period 1999–2003, there was an impressive increase in the availability of all the items, with the fastest increase being access to the Internet, with the percentage more than doubling in 1999–2001, from 23.15 per cent to 49.5 per cent. It is also worth mentioning that mobile phones were not included in the 1999 questionnaire because at the time they were scarcely used by Spanish teenagers. However, the landscape changed so fundamentally in such a short time that when they were asked about mobile phone ownership in 2001, they were found to be used by more than three-quarters of the adolescents in the sample.

Differences are evident between boys and girls in relation to consoles and console games, with the percentage of availability much higher for boys than for girls in the three samples. In contrast, more girls than boys have educational CD-ROMs and access to a mobile phone. Ownership percentages are always higher for boys than girls with the exception of mobile phones, and girls' and boys' responses differ in relation to the equipment they report using the most when visiting friends: the highest percentage for girls is TV and for boys games. In short, if we consider children's access to ICTs, not only at home but in friends' homes, at school and elsewhere, their potential for facilitating increased social interaction is impressive and has increased dramatically – much faster than for the large majority of adults.

In the 2003 survey, adolescents were asked to what extent they were interested in different audio-visual equipment and in their facilities at present. They were also asked whether they were concerned about being well-informed about each of these pieces of equipment or facilities. The same questions were asked of their parents, who were also asked to report on the degree of interest in and information they believed their own child had.

Both in terms of present degree of interest and of considering themselves well-informed about what they could watch or do with the different audio-visual media, the highest mean rate for adolescents was in relation to TV, whereas CD-ROMs scored very low. By gender, the highest mean rates for boys were for computer and Internet use, followed by

TV, while the highest for girls were the mobile phone, followed by the Internet. The lowest mean scores for boys were for educational CD-ROMs, whereas for girls they were for games. Overall, however, and despite these differences, young people reported a high degree of interest in and knowledge about ICTs.

Parents' reported own interest in all audio-visual media was lower than that reported by their own child, except in relation to girls' interest in video consoles. In fact, most parents reported having more interest in and information about games than their daughters did. Additionally, parents reported having more information about television then their own child, while they reported less information than the child about other audio-visual media.

When parents were asked about the interest they thought their child had in each medium, they tended to slightly overestimate the interest their child reported about games and, more specifically, their daughter reported about computers, and they tended to underestimate their child's interest in all other media. When they were asked about the information available to their child about each medium, they tended to overestimate the child's responses for all media, except the Internet.

Different usage of computers and the Internet was also explored. Parents reported doing any of the possible activities with the computer less frequently than their child, except writing, in the case of parents of boys. When we asked about the frequency of activities on the Internet, parents only reported searching for information more frequently than their child; all other possible activities were less frequent, with the exception of sending emails, in the case of parents of boys.

Another topic explored were parents' and children's estimates of different audio-visual media use. We found that parents frequently regarded their children as gaining greater entertainment from using computers or video games than did the child, while they attributed them with higher levels of boredom in relation to television viewing and Internet use than their children reported.

In terms of learning, therefore, TV seems to be regarded by adolescents as much more learning-related than by parents, while parents tend to overestimate learning from computers in comparison with their children's answers: watching TV was generally considered by parents as less useful than it was by their children, while exactly the opposite applied in relation to computer use. Adolescents also reported feeling more actively involved in front of the TV than their parents perceive them to be, while the opposite was reported in relation to the computer and the Internet. Similarly, children felt that using a computer was a more lonely activity than their parents thought it was for them, while they reported feeling more in company in front of the TV and using the Internet than their parents believed.

However, in the case of TV, differences are very important. TV continues to be the medium showing clearer or even more extreme discrepancies between parents and children when any evaluation about it is made. As in previous research (Casas and Figuer 1999), therefore, important and significant discrepancies appear when parents and children are asked separately about their attitudes towards and evaluations of the use of different audio-visual media, but in the case of TV clear discrepancies are observed in more then 45 per cent of the families, while extreme differences are observed about the 'utility' of TV in more than 20 per cent of the households. Differences in the evaluations of ITCs, particularly in relation to TV, are often very important, suggesting a generational gap in attitudes (see Table 4.1).

Adolescents were also asked how much they liked to talk about things they watch or do with audio-visual media. In a 5-point Likert scale (from *I don't like it* to *I like it very much*), it is beyond doubt that their level of satisfaction is much higher in talking to peers or friends about their use of audio-visual media than in talking to parents or teachers.

Table 4.1 Concordances and discrepancies between children and parents when evaluating different audiovisual media (%)

	Coincidences				Discrepancies		
	Negative	Neutral	Positive	Sub-total	Clear	Extreme	Sub-total
Computer							
Learning	1.4	4.2	50.3	**55.9**	34.8	9.2	**44**
Wasting time	2.8	7.2	43.6	**53.6**	36.2	10	**46.2**
Utility	0.9	2.8	73.7	**77.4**	17.4	4.4	**21.8**
Console							
Learning	61.9	5.1	0.4	**67.4**	25.8	6.7	**32.5**
Wasting time	51.8	4.8	1.4	**58**	26	16.1	**42.1**
Utility	45.6	4.7	1.3	**51.6**	23.8	17.3	**41.1**
Television							
Learning	8.4	21.8	10.2	**40.4**	47.3	12.3	**59.6**
Wasting time	19.3	19.8	3.3	**42.4**	46.9	10.6	**57.5**
Utility	6.3	15.6	10.9	**32.8**	45.7	21.4	**67.1**

- Concordance = the child and the parent score the same, only ±1 point difference in a 5-point Likert scale is observed.
- Clear discrepancy = ±2 or ±3 points difference in the scores.
- Extreme discrepancy = ±4 points difference in the scores.

Spanish sample N = 1,634.

Source: Casas and Figuer (1999).

In the 2003 sample, talking about what they have watched on TV with their *father* was the conversational activity they liked the most, a similar result to the 1999 sample; console and computer games and educational CD-ROMs are among the topics children liked least to talk about with their father. In 2001 and 2003, boys' mean satisfaction of reporting how much they liked to talk with their fathers about any equipment was higher than girls', with the exception of talking about the computer. Responses to the question about how much they liked talking to their *mothers* showed similar patterns to talking with the father in all samples, with TV scoring the highest and video games the lowest. In general, girls were more likely to report that they prefer talking with their mothers about any audio-visual activity than boys, with the exception of console and computer games, where girls scored even lower than boys.

Questions about how much children liked talking with *teachers* produced the lowest mean scores in all samples; computer and Internet use scored best, and CD-ROMs, console and computer games the worst. Boys' and girls' responses were very similar across the samples.

When considering the mean scores obtained in relation to how much they liked talking with peers, we found the highest satisfaction rates in talking with anyone regarding any of the equipment and facilities, although TV was the medium that obtained the highest percentages and CD-ROM the lowest. Some gender differences were found in that boys generally preferred to talk with peers about console games and girls about TV.

Overall, parents tended to overestimate their child's satisfaction with talking to their father or mother about such activities, with the exception of TV, although an exception to this is boys' satisfaction with talking to their fathers about computer use, which was clearly underestimated by parents. In addition, parents greatly overestimated their child's levels of satisfaction with talking about these activities with their teacher. Last but not least, parents tended to underestimate their sons' levels of satisfaction with talking with their peers about any media-related activity, while they seem to overestimate girls' satisfaction from talking with peers, except in the case of TV.

ICTs, interpersonal relationships and children's cultures

Although it seems likely that communication between parents and children about audio-visual media cannot be separated from their communication about other topics, and that some parents talk to their children about many things whilst others talk to their children very little, the high levels of enthusiasm that can be observed among children in relation to audio-visual media suggests that these media may be a good starting point for trying to understand parent–child communication in a volatile environment, in which adults are not always and necessarily 'competent'. To make sense of this, we must take what children say – the perspective of the child – more seriously.

As the data show, parents' perceptions and evaluations often reflect gender stereotypes, as well as stereotypes about the value of different forms of ICTs: parents tend to believe that children are very interested in educational CD-ROMs, whereas children do not express any great enthusiasm for them, particularly if we compare them with other media. Both boys and girls like computer games, even violent ones (Casas 2000), but parents tend to deny this in relation to their own child.

Probably the most surprising aspect of our results concerns the question of to whom children like to talk about what they watch or do with ICT media. From the point of view of many of the children in the three samples, the least popular choice of an adult with whom to talk about audio-visual media is their teacher. This offers an important reflection about how schools connect with the 'real world'. Mothers and fathers are also not a popular choice – young people clearly prefer their peers, followed by siblings and older friends. One implication of this is that adults in general do not seem to be taking advantage of the opportunities created by these media to establish relationships with children in new ways.

These results reinforce the belief that Spanish children are constructing their own culture – one that is separate and distinct from adults' culture, or at least has little dialogue with adults. The range and volume of information and discourses in the media that contain contrasting values constitute another point for critical reflection. It would appear that many children in contemporary Spanish society are being socialized through the mediatory influences of ICTs without much (or any) adult input, relying solely on the interpretations of their peer group, in the context of their own culture. What has happened to the many adults who, from their children's perspectives, no longer have a credible voice or views in terms of discussions about audio-visual media and related values? This question requires further research but, from the evidence outlined above, many children are dissatisfied with the competence of adults to discuss their activities with ICT media.

Clearly we cannot think about children only as the 'future'; they are also a vital and relevant part of the 'present', as active members of society. We must therefore 'understand' how children themselves think about new media and technologies, how they are using them and how they are relating them to their own futures, through present expectations, wishes and value-related aspirations. What Llull (1980) said about the six different types of social use of TV by parents may be a useful starting point for analysing children and young people's current use of other media. Llull argued that audio-visual media:

- may act as an environmental resource;
- can be used for regulating daily activities;
- may facilitate communication by offering common topics for talk;
- can be used for seeking or avoiding contact with other people;
- may be means for social learning; and
- may be used for demonstrating competence or dominance.

The potential of new technologies for children as competent social actors and participating citizens

Adults traditionally attribute children with less competence than themselves. This implies that they have less capacity for knowledge and lower levels of information and understanding of the world 'as it is' (Postman 1982). Adults have also traditionally taken the view that it is self-evident that some information should not be given to children and that other information can only be given if adapted to their more limited understanding.

These assumptions about children were, however, challenged by the United Nations Convention on the Rights of the Child (UNCRC), which included the child's right to information amongst its provisions:

Art. 13. The child shall have the right to freedom of expression; this right shall include freedom to seek, receive and impart information and ideas of all kinds ...

...

Art 17. States Parties recognize the important function performed by the mass media and shall ensure that the child has access to information and material from a diversity of national and international resources, especially those aimed at the promotion of his or her social, spiritual and moral well-being and physical and mental health. To this end, States parties shall:
(a) Encourage the mass media to disseminate information and material of social and cultural benefit to the child ...

Lack of information on the part of children does not now seem to be the problem, however. The real 'problem', thanks to TV, seems to be just the opposite: children have a huge amount of information, sometimes more than adults, about all topics, because they tend to spend more time watching TV than adults (Von Feilitzen 1991). This information includes a range of topics traditionally considered inappropriate for children, including those where there is a broad consensus that they are prejudicial to children's well-being (e.g. violence, unlimited consumerism, and so on). If different amounts of information (or knowledge) were an important element for the differential categorization of children therefore, as proposed by Postman (1982), the old categories must now be in crisis!

In the light of the Spanish data discussed above, it would seem that it is adults who must adapt, who must accept and understand children's enhanced capacities and competences as a consequence of the emergence of new ICTs. By doing so, we will be able to explore ways of promoting and using ICTs in different contexts: improving children's situation in the world is not only about protecting them, but also enhancing their quality of life. However, in our postmodern, iconic societies, we also have the challenge of developing new images of children and childhood, and the new media certainly have the potential to change the traditional social representations of children in ways that are – but also may not be – in the best interests of the child.

In the international macro-context in which child research takes place, the UNCRC has posed challenges for the international research community and gives strong support to changes in the focus of child research. Indeed, as many authors have pointed out, the UNCRC opened a new historical period for children across the world (see Verhellen 1992) as, in both a sociological and a psychosocial sense, the Convention has started to frame a 'new childhood', a new image of what children are as a social group or social category (Qvortrup 1990; Casas 1991, 1998). However, the consequences for the international research community remain uncertain, a situation that parallels the ever-quickening pace of social change in relation to ICTs and childhood in Spain. It is becoming increasingly clear, therefore, that both new technologies and new social and cultural phenomena are taking us towards a very different society but, as yet, we do not know what it will be like.

These rapid changes not only demand that people understand one another across countries and across generations but also that the increasing cultural diversity of European nations requires more young people to understand and work with people who have different perspectives. It is clear that children's democratic socialization is extremely important if we are to develop a citizenry that is flexible, cooperative, responsible and caring. What is not clear is how we should socialize our children so that they can live responsibly in a world where many of its parameters are still unknown.

Authors debating modern socialization processes in Europe have been arguing for many years that children's socialization is dependent on three major social agents: the family, school and television. But, as revealed by our Spanish data, we must also consider the effect of the 'new screens' – videos, computers, the Internet and mobile phones (Barthelmes 1991; Casas 1993, 1998) – and the influence these are having on the impact of the peer group. Indeed, other recent European research has shown that the importance of peer influence in this area may have been underestimated. Suess et al. (1998) suggest, for example, that TV and other new technologies seem to play an important and influential role through peer relationships among children aged 6–16 years in many European countries. In addition, in the broader international arena, new theories are emerging that seek to explain why it is that, as in Spain, parents' influence on their children's socialization is lower than expected (Harris 1995).

The influence of media interacting with the influence of peer groups suggests, therefore, that we may be seeing the emergence not only of new children's cultures, but also of children's and young people's cultures that are very often very different, and increasingly autonomous, from adults and adults' cultures. Although adolescents have always wanted to have their own identity, one that is clearly differentiated from adults', this psychosocial process seems to be starting ever earlier in children's lives in much of Europe. Thus young people are moving into and occupying spaces in our cities and our social life, when adults are absent. In the summer, in the squares and bars of many Spanish towns, for example, we find hundreds of young people concentrated in places where adults prefer not to go at night. Even if they do not feel able to occupy such spaces physically, young people often do so symbolically – for example, with graffiti.

This indicates that in Spain, as elsewhere, children and young people are becoming evermore active social agents. A classic example, reported in the scientific literature, is that some years ago, when Son-Goku cartoons first appeared on a Spanish TV channel, a merchandising mistake meant that children could not find products related to the cartoon characters in Barcelona's shops. As a consequence, many parents of under

12-year-olds were urged by their children to go to one of the Sunday morning markets (*Mercat de Sant Antoni*). Here children had organized themselves to swap photocopies of their own designs of the cartoon characters (Munné and Codina 1992). Demonstrating that they could be active and organizing their own spaces and interests proved to be so motivating for children that it can still be observed in the market. It also served to demonstrate the power of children as highly competent social actors, with the potential to build new relational networks for the future, rather than remaining passive, responding only to changes led by adults' interests.

Conclusion

> Children have the chance to reinvent communications, culture and community, to address the problems of the new world in new ways.
>   (Katz 1996, in Sefton-Green 1998: 1)

In much of European society there is a growing concern and awareness that the child population as a whole is demanding more attention from us in the immediate future at all social levels. We can therefore perceive a great challenge ahead: new 'methods' are required so that children will be able to face and take responsible decisions about new issues in new situations (Council of Europe 1996).

Change already requires a debate about the new rights and responsibilities of children, since the UNCRC (especially in Articles 12–16) establishes civil rights for children. Taken as a whole, the recognition of such rights creates new forms for children's presence in society, new means for children to assume social responsibilities, new ways for adults to be with children and to listen to them as competent people and as subjects with rights.

The implementation of such rights is arguably one of the most profound challenges which the UNCRC poses to European society and probably to all industrialized countries. Those who have direct responsibility for children, or for childhood policies, understand its importance whilst also appreciating the profound doubts and uncertainties that it creates, which reflect, above all, the lack of any tradition of giving a leading social role to our child population.

As this chapter has argued, using data from Spain, we now have powerful tools with which to address such challenges: new media and communication technologies have opened up opportunities for children to create their own cultures, independent of adults' cultures and even from youngsters' cultures. Spanish data show that by their use of ICTs, children are developing such cultures. In this context, children's own motivation and enthusiasm for using these technologies and for developing skills and competences are enabling them to create novel forms of interpersonal relationships and to modify existing ones. New communication technologies are also giving some adults innovative ideas about how to improve children's social participation and 'suggesting' to us how important it is that children are listened to and taken into account in all areas of social life. Children's cultures are offering us new kinds of potential for participation and for improving human relationships, which are, in fact, the major contributors to our quality of life (Casas 1996, 1998).

Most important of all, however, is that children are now presented with opportunities to exercise real responsibilities in practical situations. They are demonstrating their ability to be very active as social agents – for example, by creating new communication codes and new 'languages' using the mobile phone or SMS messages in the Internet. We should therefore try to develop new participative experiences *with* children, to put into practice other desirable values, both trans-nationally and trans-culturally – co-operation, solidarity, democracy, and so on – and thereby try to contribute, with children, to improving the quality of life of many other children in the world.

According to Bressand and Distler (1995), most of the old, well-known social utopias were reactions against something. Now that we have 'R-tech' (relational technologies), we have an historic opportunity to develop utopias without an enemy (Breton 1992), because new technologies can be harnessed to the task of developing social aspirations and making them real. We must remain clear, however, that such technologies are not ends in themselves; rather, they offer the means to an end. Aims and goals must be defined and appropriate tools for each goal must be chosen.

In some European fora (e.g. the Council of Europe 1996) it has been suggested that we cannot continue to analyse and try to understand new social phenomena with old theories and perspectives; that the continued understanding of children as a social category who are 'not yets', 'becomings' and not 'beings', can no longer be defended and that there is a need to adopt new ways of relating to children as citizens.

The research results reported here have, for example, clearly shown that there are important gender-based differences in relation to the degree and style of use of ICTs. Since 2003 girls, for example, have shown a spectacular increase in their interest in mobile phones and in Internet chatrooms and emailing: over a short period, they have overtaken boys in terms of enthusiasm for the 'media world'. Boys' and girls' different interests in and sensibilities towards ICTs might therefore be a fruitful departure point for any intervention or programme. In addition, carefully planned intervention will be needed to reduce the potential for the emergence of inequality of access to ICTs among different groups (e.g. children of immigrant families, in rural areas, or those from families in the lower socio-economic groups).

These issues need to be situated in a context in which new and different kinds of research perspectives are being developed, which place children at the centre and that ask children about their lives, experiences and standard of living. Such developments, which are promising initial steps at the start of a new stage of exploring children's 'real' quality of life, are helping us to understand a different interpersonal and social world and to engage with the idea of 'children's cultures'. We can only make sense of this, however, when we understand how children themselves form their opinions, experiences, evaluations and aspirations, and that these are no longer necessarily constructed in interaction with adults. Such a changed understanding is demanded by the findings of research on the use of audio-visual media and on the interpersonal relationships related to or mediated by these technologies.

References

Aguinaga, J. and Comas, D. (1991) *Infancia y Adolescencia: La Mirada de los Adultos*, Madrid: Centro de Publicaciones. Ministerio Asuntos Sociales.

Barthelmes, J. (1991) Infancia y Cultura, *Infancia y Sociedad* 7: 13–32.

Bressand, A. and Distler, C. (1995) *La Planète relationnelle*, Paris: Flammarion.

Breton, P. (1992) *L'Utopie de la communication*, Paris: La Découverte.

Campbell, A., Converse, P. E. and Rodgers, W. L. (1976) *The Quality of American Life: Perceptions, Evaluations and Satisfactions*, New York: Russell Sage Foundation.

Casas, F. (1991) El Concepto de Calidad de Vida en la Intervención Social en el Ámbito de la Infancia, *III Jornadas de Psicología de la Intervención Social*, 2: 649–72, Madrid, November 1991: M.A.S., 1992.

Casas, F. (1993) Medios de comunicación e imagen social de la infancia, *Intervención Psicosocial* 6(II): 55–65.

Casas, F. (1994) Children's Participation in European Society, *Proceedings of the Conference on Evolution of the Role of Children in Family Life: Participation and Negotiation*, Madrid, 1–3 December, Strasbourg: Council of Europe.

Casas, F. (1995) Social Representations of Childhood. *European Intensive Course in Children's Rights*, ERASMUS Programme, Salerno.

Casas, F. (1996) *Bienestar Social. Una Introducción Psicosociológica*, Barcelona: PPU.

Casas, F. (1997) Quality of Life and the Life Experience of Children, in Verhellen, E. (ed.), *Understanding Children's Rights. Second International Interdisciplinary Course on Children's Rights*, Ghent: University of Ghent.

Casas, F. (1998) *Infancia: Perspectivas psicosociales*. Barcelona: Paidós.

Casas, F. (2000) Perceptions of Video Games among Spanish Children and Parents. In von Feilitzen, C. and Carlsson, U. (eds.), *Children in the New Media Scopes*, Göteborg: The UNESCO International Clearinghouse on children and violence on the screen.

Casas, F. (2001) Video Games: Between Parents and Children. In Hutchby, I. and Moran-Ellis, J. (eds.), *Children, Technology and Culture. The Impacts of Technologies in Children's Everyday Lives*, London: Routledge/Falmer.

Casas, F., Alsinet, C., Pérez, J. M., Figuer, C., Leiva, E., González, M. and Pascual, S. (2001) Information Technologies and Communication between Parents and Children, *Psychology in Spain* 5: 33–46; http://www.psychologyinspain.com.

Casas, F. and Figuer, C. (1999) Usos del ordenador e interacción padres/hijos en la adolescencia. *III Congreso de Investigadores Audiovisuales. Los Medios del Tercer Milenio*, Madrid: Facultad de Ciencias de la Información. Universidad Complutense de Madrid, July.

Casas, F., González, M., Figuer, C., Malo, S., Alsinet, C. and Subarroca, S. (2005) The Penetration of Audio-Visual Media in Adolescents' Cultures in Spain between 1999 and 2004: Its Use at Home, School and at Friends'. *Childhoods 2005*. Oslo.

Commission of the European Communities (1990) Public Opinion in the European Community, *Eurobarometer* 34, August, Brussels.

Commission des Communautés Européennes (1993) Les européens et la famille, *Eurobaromètre* 39. December. Brussels.

Council of Europe (1996) *Documents for the Closing Conference of the Childhood Policies Project*, Leipzig, 28 May–1 June, Strasbourg: CDPS – Council of Europe Publications.

Harris, J. R. (1995) Where is the Child's Environment? A Group Socialization Theory of Development, *Psychological Review* 102(3): 458–89.

Livingstone, S. and Bovill, M (eds.) (2001) *Children and Their Changing Media Environment. A European Comparative Study*, London: Lawrence Erlbaum Associates.

Llull, J. (1980) The Social Uses of Television, *Human Communication Research* 6(3): 197–209.

Munné, F. and Codina, N. (1992) Algunos Aspectos del Impacto Tecnológico en el Consumo Infantil del Ocio, *Anuario de Psicología* 53: 113–25.

OECD (2004) *Social Expenditure Database (SOCX), 1980–2001*; http://www.oecd.org.

Postman, N. (1982) *The Disappearance of Childhood*, New York: Dell.

Qvortrup, J. (1990) Childhood as Social Phenomenon. An Introduction to a Series of National Reports, *Eurosocial* 36.

Sefton-Green, J. (1998) *Digital Diversions: Youth Culture in the Age of Multimedia*, London: UCL Press.

Suess, D., Suoninen, A., Garitaonandia, C., Juaristi, P., Koikkalainen, R. and Oleaga, J. A. (1998) Media Use and the Relationship of Children and Teenagers with their Peer Groups. *European Journal of Communication* 13(4): 521–38.

Verhellen, E. (1992) Los Derechos de los Niños y las Niñas en Europa. *Infancia y Sociedad* 15: 37–60.

Von Feilitzen, C. (1991) Influencia de los Medios de Comunicación en los Niños y Jóvenes. *I Congreso Internacional sobre Infancia, Juventud y Comunicación Audiovisual* (pp. 217–34). Valencia: Generalitat V.-M.A.S.

5
Children at the Margins? Changing Constructions of Childhood in Contemporary Ireland

Dympna Devine

Irish society has undergone significant change in the past 30 years, characterized by membership of the European Union, rapid economic and social development and changing patterns of immigration. Social change inevitably brings with it changes in both the lived experience of childhood and in the construction of childhood itself within society. In Ireland, investment in education has been pivotal to social and economic change, with the schooling of children in line with particular goals central to the project of modernization. When such change is explored through the lens of broader legislative and educational policy contexts, key shifts in adult thinking about the role and position of children in contemporary Ireland are evident. In this chapter it will be shown that the concept of children's participation has varied meanings, mediated by the role of powerful 'adult' stakeholders who often have competing interpretations of what it means to act in the 'best interests of the child'.

The chapter begins by providing a brief overview of central theoretical concepts used in the analysis, in particular how concepts of children's participation in the social order are mediated by dominant discourses related to their rights and status within society. This is followed by a consideration of the evolving constructs of children and childhood in Irish society and how such constructs are both produced and reproduced through key legislative and policy texts. Particular reference is made to the educational context, given its predominance in the process of social (re)production in society (Bernstein 1975; Bourdieu and

Passeron 1977; Bourdieu 1993). Finally, consideration is given to the current context with reference to the shifting terrain in the cultural construction of childhood. Conclusions are drawn by highlighting the implications of recent trends in government policy for the empowerment of all children in Irish society.

Discourse, power and practice – conceptualizing children as participants

The proliferation of research into children's lives in recent years, coupled with the growing awareness of children's rights and status as a social group, is deeply implicated in what has been referred to as the 'cultural politics of childhood' (James and James 2004). Politics is itself intertwined with the exercise of power and Michel Foucault's emphasis on the impact of disciplinary power in modern societies provides a useful framework within which to explore the exercise of power between adults and children (Devine 2003). Foucault's (1979) analysis draws our attention to the significant role of discourse in mediating disciplinary practices, framing our very understandings of what is normal and 'other' and, in so doing, contributing to the process of identity formation and subjectification (1979: 194). Discourses themselves form part of the backdrop to the structural condition of society, framing the norms and expectations, rules and regulations that govern social behaviour and practice.

Applied to child–adult relations, particular constructions of childhood become embedded in the way in which adults think about and relate to children, and importantly, in the way in which children think about and position themselves. Such constructions are integral to a cultural politics of childhood and are reflected in the laws that regulate social behaviour (both children and adults) as well as the practices that permeate institutions in which children spend much of their time. Here the question of power becomes paramount: in the capacity of adults to exercise control over both the definition and experience of childhood, and in children's own capacity, as reflective agents, to resist, accommodate to or subvert such control. The remainder of this chapter structures the discussion of the cultural politics of childhood in Ireland in terms not only of changes in the discourse surrounding children and childhood, but also the key role of power in this process and the differential access to resources by various stakeholders in shaping the nature of change in both the experience and structuring of childhood, and debates that give rise to it.

'Cherishing children of the nation equally'?
Constructing childhood in contemporary Ireland

The construction of childhood in contemporary Ireland cannot be separated from the political and economic context of Irish society over the past century. This has been a period of significant change for a country located on the fringes of Western Europe, with the establishment of a republic for three-quarters of the island in 1922, membership of the European Economic Community in 1972 and the shift from a rural-based economy to one now commonly referred to as the 'Celtic Tiger' – a post-industrial liberal market economy of the 1990s. Broadly speaking, however, three distinct phases in the cultural construction of childhood from the earlier years of the foundation of the state, to the present can be identified: 1920–1960, 1960–1990 and 1990 onward. Key social policy and legislative frameworks are evident in these phases that signal a gradual shift in the discourse surrounding children and childhood coinciding with economic and political developments in the broader sphere.

1920–1960

The first phase marked the transition from a colonial to a postcolonial society and attempts to consolidate the position of the new republic in a relatively unstable and war-torn Europe (Garvin 2004). As a nation with a strong Roman Catholic tradition, the mix of nationalism and Catholicism had significant implications for the construction of childhood in particular terms. Initial aspirations within the declaration of the Irish Republic in 1916, that the state would 'cherish all the children of the nation equally', gave way to the subsidiary role of the state in family – hence the way in which children were addressed in the Irish constitution of 1937, strongly reflecting Catholic social teaching and the powerful role of the Catholic hierarchy in the fledgling republic (Duncan 1996; Inglis 1998; Kennedy 2001). Thus Article 42.1 asserts that the state will:

> Respect the inalienable right and duty of parents to provide, according to their means, for the religious and moral, intellectual and social education of their children.

Prioritizing the responsibility of parents/the family in the upbringing of their children resulted in a *laissez-faire* approach by the state to the development of any systematic child policy, reflected in the absence of any significant legislation concerning the welfare of children between the Children's Act 1908 until the Childcare Act 1991 (Devine et al. 2004).

The absence of any distinct provisions for the rights of children within the constitution reflected a wider discourse that viewed children as subordinates, the property of their parents, there to serve adult needs and demands. Ethnographic research into childhood in rural Ireland up to the 1960s (Curtin and Varley 1984) reveals a general discourse on children that defined them in terms of their capacity to fulfil three major functions: generational continuity; a source of cheap labour on farms and in urban centres; and security in old age. While this functional definition of childhood did not preclude emotional involvement with children, especially with mothers (Arensberg and Kimball 1968; Curtin and Varley 1984), it did result in a highly instrumental orientation to children, with an emphasis on reinforcing status differentials between themselves and adults. Children were expected to be relatively silent and passive in adult company, and were frequently assigned the terms 'boy' and 'girl' to denote their lower status. The capability of adults, especially fathers, to exercise such power over their children was underpinned by patterns of property inheritance and social norms which instilled in children a respect for authority and an unquestioning acceptance of the roles assigned to them by their parents.

Such norms in turn were legitimated by religious/Catholic ideology, which constructed childhood as a period of 'uncontrollable passions and instincts' (Inglis 1998: 151), which could only be civilized through a process of strict adherence to the rules and regulations laid down by those in authority (i.e. parents and local priests). State policy towards children was very much predicated on this process of civilization and normalization in line with Catholic and nationalistic ideals. Within the school system this was particularly evident, where a radical change in education policy took place, reflecting the nationalistic fervour of political leaders of the time (Farren 1995). Curricular experience in the new republic became redefined in terms of adherence to Catholic teaching and the re-establishment of Gaelic civilization (Coolahan 1983; Hyland and Milne 1992). Inspired by the ideology of cultural nationalism and a heightened patriotic fervour, a central role was accorded to the Irish language with an Irish emphasis on courses in literature, history, geography, mythology, games, music and dancing. Through schooling, a cultural revolution was envisaged that would provide a solid grounding in nationhood, conceptualized in terms of

Gaelic rituals and ideals. As Akenson states:

> In defining the goals of the schools, the successive governments paid
> little attention to actual children. As long as the collective political
> purpose was being served by the school curriculum, the development
> of the individual bore scant notice.
>
> (1975: 60)

This absence of a distinct child focus had negative implications not
only for the status of children and childhood within Irish society generally, but also for any attempt by the state to address differences in status
between groups of children themselves. In this sense children were
viewed predominantly as a homogeneous group, with little or no attention given to the needs of those at the margins of society, including
Traveller children and those with a range of (dis)abilities. While efforts
were made to develop a child health service through school medical
inspections and school meals, the provision of such services was on an
ad hoc basis, reflecting a level of indifference by the state to frame social
policy in general and, more specifically, in relation to children (Breen
et al. 1990; Richardson 2005).

Structural definitions of children up to the 1960s clearly constructed
them as 'other', in need of normalization in line with nationalistic and
religious ideals. The principle of subsidiarity endorsed in the constitution precluded the state from any serious attempt to address inequalities
between children and adults, or among groups of children at a national
policy level. This had disastrous consequences in subsequent years for
the life chances of those who did not conform to the dominant norm
and/or for those whose parents did not have the economic, cultural
and/or social resources to safeguard their interests.

As a group, children had little power. They were constructed as passive recipients of adult mores and norms, their agency exercised
through adaptation and accommodation to such norms, with severe
consequences for those who resisted or questioned adult authority
(McCourt 1996). Cultural constructions of the 'good' child centred on
obedience and subservience at home and in school, with children,
through their labour, fostering the production of a Gaelic and
Catholic Ireland. Institutionalized practice within schools, for example, reflected this policy in the structuring of the school experience
around a highly subject-centred and traditional curriculum, as well as
patterns of teacher–pupil relations, which were hierarchical and
authoritarian in tone.

1960–1990

A change in discourse in relation to children and childhood in Irish society is evident from the 1960s onwards. The period 1960–1990 was marked by rapid change, expressed in a move towards an industrialized economy, membership of the European Community and a greater openness to international influences (Garvin 2004). The implications of such change for children were twofold. First, the breakdown in traditional neighbourhood and kinship structures characteristic of the move towards industrialization and urbanization led to a reappraisal of the role and function of children in the family (Hannon and Katsiouni 1977). Life chances were no longer determined solely by property inheritance, but increasingly by the acquisition of educational credentials – the primary basis on which allocation to position was made in the rapidly changing social structure.

The resultant decline in average family size (Devine et al. 2004), given the long-term commitment of time and money by parents for their children's education, paved the way for a less authoritarian and more emotionally supportive family environment. While there was still minimal intervention by the state in family life, the implementation of both the Adoption Act 1952 and the Guardianship Act 1964, in spite of resistance from the Catholic Church, signalled the first sign of recognition by the state of the need to safeguard the interests of children, independently of their biological parents (Richardson 2005).

More substantively, however, state intervention in children's lives was directly reflected in a radical shift in education policy (O'Sullivan 2005). Industrialization led to calls for a more technically proficient and literate population, reflected in a greater willingness to invest in education generally and a greater onus on those responsible for education to bring about change. The highly instrumental view of education articulated by influential economists of the time portrayed a view of children as vital to serve the future needs of the industrializing economy. This instrumental orientation mirrored the views of parents, who saw education as a means of improving the life chances of their children. The interrelation of these trends is evident in the rhetoric surrounding the move towards a child-centred curriculum in primary schools, where explicit recognition is made of childhood as a distinct period of human development and of children having distinct and individual needs:

> All children are complex human beings with physical, emotional, intellectual and spiritual needs and potentialities ... because each child is an individual he deserves to be valued for himself and to be

provided with the kind and variety of opportunities toward stimulation which will enable him to develop his natural powers at his own
rate to his fullest capacity.

(Department of Education 1971: 13)

The emphasis on sensitivity to children's needs and a less authoritarian approach to their education highlighted an openness to international discourses on children that called for a more supportive and
sensitive approach to their education. Equally, the highly individualistic
emphasis inherent in progressive education, and the essentialist and
meritocratic orientation that informed the writing of the Irish primary
school curriculum, ensured that it gained approval from those who
pointed to the importance of maximizing the development of individual talent for the betterment of the economy. The curriculum itself was
broadened, with a greater emphasis on active learning and, while priority was still accorded to learning the Irish language, oral skill rather than
literacy was increasingly stressed. Changes in pedagogical and disciplinary practices were recommended (although corporal punishment was
not outlawed in schools until 1982) with sensitivity to children's needs
and capacities emphasized.

Despite this changing orientation, however, educational discourse of
the period continued to be influenced by Catholic ideology:

Each human being is created in God's image. He has a life to lead and
a soul to be saved. Education is therefore concerned not only with
life, but with the purpose of life

(Department of Education 1971: 3)

The moralization of the young through religious instruction was now to
be implemented in a child-centred and integrated manner, and Catholic
feast days and rituals remained central to the structuring of the school
experience. While the curriculum continued to be grounded in Gaelic
traditions and customs (e.g. in dance, music, literature) patriotic fervour
and cultural nationalism evident in the earlier period of the state were
curtailed in favour of a less directive and more open approach to children's learning.

This incorporation of a child-centred ideology into discourse on primary
education, at a time of rapid social change, resulted in a broader approach
to framing the activities of children within what remained a predominantly instrumental framework (O'Sullivan 2005). While changes were
envisaged in the nature of teacher–pupil relations, in practice this resulted

in a move towards a less authoritarian approach to interaction, while keeping traditional structures of domination (Giddens 1984) between teachers and pupils intact. In terms of the construction of childhood, structural patterns of adult–child relations continued to focus on the normalization of children in line with goals for economic growth and development, although these were now expressed in terms of the fulfilment of children's 'needs'. Thus, the discourse of the period failed to challenge the 'other' status of children in any serious way. What did change was the manner in which their 'otherness' was expressed.

The investment in children through their education was limited however, with the state reluctant to invest substantially in safeguarding the interests of those outside the dominant norm (e.g. children with special needs), underpinning the predominance of a welfarist rather than a rights-based approach to the construction of childhood in Irish society of the time. While discourse in relation to child protection became more widespread, following the publication of the Kennedy Report (1970) into children in care in industrial and reformatory schools, it was predominantly the voluntary sector rather than statutory services that filled the gap in provision for children in need of community care (Richardson 2005). The period can also be noted as one characterized by the absence of any specific legal provisions for children, including a lack of coherence over the exact legal definition of a child (Nic Ghiolla Phadraig 1990; Richardson 2005).

1990 onwards

A marked change is evident after 1990 in the discourse *about*, if not necessarily practice *with*, children. National and international developments have spearheaded such change. At the national level, publicity concerning child abuse scandals in state industrial schools over a period of 40 years (Kilkenny Incest Report 1993) signalled a growing recognition of the rights of children to bodily integrity and privacy, although the discourse surrounding such abuse rarely focused on the position and status of children *per se* within society at large. The past 15 years have heralded a number of government-sponsored reports and the publication of national guidelines in this area, although government policy has fallen short of the introduction of mandatory reporting.

This shift towards a more proactive stance on child welfare issues was indicated through the publication of the Child Care Act 1991. Described as a watershed in childcare policy in Ireland (Richardson 2005), this Act consolidated the responsibility of the state, through the health service, to safeguard the welfare of children through child protection, care for children who cannot remain in the home and the provision of family support. In so doing the Act signalled the intention of the state to become more proactive in the lives of children, a direction which in itself was underpinned by commitments made through the ratification of the United Nations Convention on the Rights of the Child by the Irish state in 1992.

Criticisms over the fragmented implementation of the Convention indicate, however, the serious shift that had yet to be taken at government level in relation to the implementation of the Convention as a whole. The Report of the UN Committee (CRA 1998) highlighted the predominance of a welfarist and paternalistic discourse in state policy on children, with legislation (e.g. the Child Care Act 1991/1997 and the Children's Bill 1997) defining the rights of children negatively in terms of protection from abuse and inadequate care, rather than in terms of the empowerment of children within society as a whole.

In this sense, dominant constructions of childhood as a period of vulnerability and innocence eschewed consideration of the construction of children as citizens, with the right and capacity to make a more active contribution to shaping their everyday lives. This absence of a fully articulated rights discourse in relation to children was noted by the UN in their criticism of the lack of a national policy on children's rights, underpinning criticisms made two years earlier related to the position of children in the constitution (Duncan 1996). Criticisms were also expressed in relation to the rights and welfare of specific groups of children including those in poverty, children with disabilities and Traveller children.

Shifting terrain in the cultural construction of childhood – The National Children's Strategy

Such criticism provided the impetus for a significant shift in the cultural construction of childhood in Ireland, evident in the publication of the National Children's Strategy in 2000. Developed as a response to the UN Committee's Report (1998), the Strategy outlines a coherent and integrated policy in relation to children's rights and welfare in the new millennium, placing at the core of its focus three major goals that signal changing constructs in relation to a 'good' and 'proper' Irish childhood. They are:

1. Children will have a voice.
2. Children's lives will be better understood.
3. Children will receive quality supports and services.

As a policy document the Strategy is significant in the emphasis that is placed on children's voice and participation, challenging traditional constructs of children solely in terms of their vulnerability and dependence. Discourse related to the 'whole child' permeates the strategy, such discourse being clearly grounded in national and international studies of childhood, as well as the UNCRC itself:

> The strategy has adopted a 'whole child' perspective, which provides a more complete understanding of children's lives. It draws on the most recent research and knowledge about children's development and the relationship between children and family, community and the wider society ... this perspective anchors the Strategy to a coherent and inclusive view of childhood ... The perspective is endorsed as good practice underpinning legislation and policy and service developments internationally. It is also compatible with the spirit of the UN Convention on the Rights of the Child.
>
> (Government of Ireland 2000: 24)

The complexity of children's lives is illustrated through consideration of nine core dimensions related to their well-being: physical, mental, emotional, behavioural, intellectual, moral and spiritual, identity, self-care, family relationships, social and peer relationships and social presentation. Policy commitments are specified in relation to children's health and well-being, learning and education, play, leisure and cultural opportunities, children in crisis, poverty and homelessness, children with disabilities, discrimination in children's lives and concern for the environment. A 'good' childhood as presented in the Strategy is one in which children's rights as citizens are acknowledged and supported in an integrated manner through experiences which are child-centred, family-oriented, equitable and inclusive (Government of Ireland 2000: 10). Diversity in culture, lifestyle and need among different groups of children is recognized, the best interests of the child now being defined in social, affective and developmental terms, rather than solely in terms of the fulfilment of economic or national goals for development. The very development of the Strategy is justified on the grounds that 'Children matter ... Children deserve to be highly valued for the unique contribution they make through being just children' (Government of Ireland 2000: 6).

Such discourse signals a radical shift from unitary constructs of children, defined as cultural products to be moulded in line with nationalistic/Gaelic ideals (pre-1960s), to key forms of human capital serving the needs of a developing economy (1960s onwards). Absent from the Strategy is any specific indicator of national identity to which children are encouraged to subscribe. Rather, the Strategy embraces constructs that acknowledge the diversity within childhood while holding central key values related to the importance of family and local community in children's lives. Such constructs are embedded in the rapidly changed context of the modern 'Celtic Tiger' Ireland and an acknowledgement not only of the diversity such change brings, but also of children's right to benefit from the fruits of economic development:

> Especially at a time of major social and economic change every effort should be made to enhance children's status and improve their quality of life.
>
> (Government of Ireland 2000: 6)

At the level of discourse the Strategy represents an important step forward in the promotion of children's rights and, as a policy document, reflects a construction of childhood that is far removed from what prevailed in the past. While there is still a strong welfarist thrust in the document, this is counterbalanced by a clear acknowledgement of children's voice and a willingness (not yet realized) to consider the legal position of children as a group in the Irish constitution. Children themselves actively participated in the development of the Strategy through a series of public consultations, and their comments are interspersed throughout the document. In so doing, the document challenges the 'other' status of children in Irish society and, for the first time, lays down a coherent framework for placing children's welfare, in the broadest sense, at the heart of government policy. Furthermore, the appointment of the Ombudsman for Children in 2004 provides an important mechanism within which the rights and welfare of children can be advanced, not only for individual children but also for children as a group.

Empowering children – empowering childhood(s)?

At policy level it is clear that a change has taken place in the manner in which childhood is being constructed in modern Ireland. Valuations of the 'good childhood' (Kjorholt 2004) are increasingly made with reference to international norms. The development of a national set of child well-being indicators (NCO 2005a) is a prime example, coupled with the framing of legislation relevant to children, in line with commitments under the UNCRC (1989) to act in the 'best interests' of the child, broadly defined.

Analysis indicates the emergence of tensions and contradictions in the implementation of the strategy in practice, however, as the new children's rights agenda competes with traditionally more powerful (adult) interests in Irish society and continual battles ensue between child advocates and government agencies over how children's best interests are being safeguarded. This is especially the case where the rights of children at the margins of Irish society (e.g. migrant children, children of the Traveller community, children with special needs and children who are economically and socially disadvantaged) are concerned.

Thus, in spite of government commitments to act in 'the best interests of the child', legislation governing aspects of children's lives (e.g. Education Act 1998; Education for Persons with Special Educational Needs Act 2004) is not rights-based. Commitments made are continuously framed in aspirational terms (e.g. 'as resources permit'), in spite of the unprecedented economic growth in the economy in recent years. It is also reflected in the protracted debates that took place over the implementation of ASBOs (Anti-Social Behaviour Orders) in contravention to provisions in the Children's Act 2001 for more community-based approaches to juvenile crime, as well as debates about the removal of the automatic right to citizenship of all children born in Ireland, irrespective of the citizenship status of their parents.

While the discourse regarding childhood may be changing, the extent to which such discourse permeates practice in institutions of direct relevance to children's everyday lives is also open to question. Here the question of power becomes paramount and, with it, the access to resources that power implies. In this context Giddens's (1984) distinction between allocative and authoritative is useful, providing a framework within which to consider differences in the access to resources, and hence to power, between adults and children in Irish society. In terms of authoritative resources (i.e. the capacity to control the social environment through organization of life chances, time, space and the body), for example, while the adult voice clearly predominates in Irish society, a number of important initiatives have been taken to strengthen the voice of children in policy-making and to prioritize areas of specific interest to children themselves. The establishment of the National Children's Office (now Office of the Minister for Children) to oversee the implementation of the National Children's Strategy provides a significant resource in moving the agenda for children's rights and welfare forward. This is reflected in its overseeing role regarding the launch of a national play policy (2004) and the establishment of a national longitudinal study for children.

Furthermore, a number of initiatives to improve the political participation of children have been instigated through the establishment of
Dáil Na nOg (the Children's Parliament) and, at local level, Comhairle
áitiul na nOg (local youth committees), although both initiatives are
very much in the early stages and not yet accessible to the majority of
children in Irish society. The Children's Office has also published guidelines to facilitate the active involvement of children in decision-making
across a host of organizations (NCO 2005b). Such initiatives, while very
much in their infancy, signal the strengthening position of children as a
social group with the right to involvement in decisions affecting their
everyday lives. They suggest a move towards a concept of the social citizenship of children, with the accompanying rights of participation this
implies (Marshall 1950, 1981; Roche 1999).

While respect for and recognition of the distinctiveness of children
and childhood as part of the life-course underpins this more broad-
based approach to children's welfare, issues of distribution (access to
allocative resources) are equally core to the advancement of children's
rights. This applies to the rights of children as a group distinct from others (e.g. adults), as well as to different groups of children in relation to
one another. As in most countries, it is difficult to gain an accurate
measure of the resources that are allocated to children in Ireland, or
indeed children's own active contribution to the economy, given the
adult-centred focus of much survey research (Qvortrup 1995; Fitzgerald
2004). Recent data confirm, however, that while there are fewer children
living in poverty in Ireland than hitherto, the risk of poverty is still
greater for a child than an adult, especially among more marginalized
groups (Nolan 2001; Devine et al. 2004; Combat Poverty Agency 2005).

This is all the more serious when one considers that, in spite of the
level of sustained growth and economic stability in Ireland in recent
years, child poverty rates are the third highest among developed countries (UN Human Development Report 2005). Crises over childcare and
the absence of a coherent child-centred policy in this area, coupled with
increasing urban expansion, often without appropriate infrastructural
support for children and their families (e.g. schools, youth facilities,
etc.), are indicative of the ad hoc approach of the state to investment in
areas that directly affect children (Brooke 2004; CDI 2005/2004;
Ombudsman for Children 2005).

While the establishment of the office of Ombudsman for Children
demonstrates a positive commitment to the promotion of children's
rights and welfare, delays in the appointment as well as the allocation of
sufficient funding to the office suggest a lack of urgency in moving the

agenda for children's rights forward. With increasing immigration, concerns have been expressed at the absence of a coherent immigration policy that would provide stability and greater rights for immigrants and their children (Immigration Council of Ireland 2004), while the position of Traveller children remains one of considerable marginalization and exclusion (Kenny 2001; McDonagh 2004; Pavee Point 2006).

While substantial investment is being made in children through education (to the long-term benefit of the society), the concentration of such investment in that part of the system which yields a more immediate labour market return – the higher education sector (Clancy 2005) – has given rise to a primary school system that struggles under larger than European average class sizes (OECD 2005) and poorly equipped buildings, which have been the subject of recent negative media attention. Furthermore, progress on the development of a fully integrated service for children with special needs remains slow and the expansion of the fledgling school psychological service inadequate (Shevlin and Rose 2003).

The capacity of government to make a qualitative difference to the lives of all children rests on the state's willingness to invest substantively in the implementation of the National Children's Strategy (2000), rather than in a piecemeal fashion as currently prevails. Tensions and contradictions between policy regarding children's rights and welfare and institutionalized practices are fundamentally linked to issues of power and control and the willingness by adult stakeholders to take the issue of children's rights and welfare seriously.

For example, given the amount of time spent by children in schools, many of the structural dynamics between adults and children are crystallized in the practices that permeate schools as institutions. In this sense schools are central to the cultural politics of childhood – producing, reproducing and resisting dominant constructions of childhood that exist within the broader sphere. Thus conceptualizations of a good Irish childhood as one where all children are guaranteed an experience of inclusion and equality in the education system are enshrined in the provisions of the Education Act 1998. However, research consistently highlights the reproduction of inequalities related to social class, gender, disability and ethnicity at all levels of the school system (Clancy and Wall 2000; Lynch and Lodge 2002; Deegan et al. 2004; DES 2005; Devine and Kelly 2006; MacRuairc 2006), which suggests that a 'good' childhood is not available to all.

While the reproduction of inequalities in and through education is a multifaceted and complex phenomenon (Bourdieu 1993; McLaren

1993; Apple 2001; Baker et al. 2004), the marginalization of certain social groups through insufficient access to both economic and cultural capital cannot be divorced from the ad hoc nature of government policy in relation to children and the absence of co-ordinated and sustained investment in the area. Not surprisingly, in the first annual report of the Ombudsman for Children (2005) over half of the complaints related to education issues, one fifth of these concerning access to resources for children with special needs.

Fundamentally, conceptualizations of children in terms of their rights challenges the traditional power–knowledge relationship between adults and children, and the former's authority and positioning that enables them always to act in and define the 'best interests' of the child. Nowhere is this more clearly seen than in the school system. In terms of the authoritative resources of children and their capacity to exercise some influence over the experience of schooling, concepts of children's active participation in decision-making are also reflected in the Education Act 1998. However, provisions that accord children consultative rights in relation to their schooling experience are positioned alongside others that clearly define adults (teachers, parents, the school inspectorate, etc.) as the primary stakeholders in education, with the capacity to exercise greater control over what happens in the classroom.

Thus, for example, protracted discussions were required with the teachers' unions over the wording of the Act, limiting the rights of consultation of children in schools (Devine 2003). Furthermore, student councils are only required to be established at second level and are subject to board of management (all adult representatives) approval, while grievance procedures can only be taken by a child who is 18 years of age – a relatively meaningless provision given that this is typically the age of the final year of schooling.

Such conditionalities suggest that children's rights remain constrained within boundaries set by adults, encouraging them to assert themselves in relation to bullying (among peers) and child abuse, but failing to allow them to make a meaningful and relevant contribution to the organization of school life. The revised primary curriculum (1999), developed after extensive consultation with education 'partners', makes welcome reference to the construct of the child as an 'active agent' – incorporating changing constructs of childhood that emphasize notions of participation and agency – yet the process of consultation leading to its formulation did not include children at any stage.

While the development of critically reflective skills is emphasized throughout the curriculum, nowhere in the lengthy document is the education of children with respect to their own rights mentioned. While citizenship is included in the new curriculum area of Social, Personal and Health Education (SPHE), it is framed in terms of the preparation of children for active and responsible citizenship (i.e. as future adults) and has undertones of the more moral and social control aspects of citizenship studies noted in similar programmes in the UK (Bailey 2000; Osler and Starkey 2005; see also James and James, this volume). More recent policy documents directed at improving practice in schools and furthering accountability and transparency in education (e.g. School Development Planning and Whole School Evaluation) eschew reference to the potential of children's active contribution to these processes.

The education system which judges, monitors and evaluates children on a daily basis is not open to scrutiny and evaluation by children, suggesting that in spite of provisions in the Education Act, they are not yet taken seriously as partners in education. That representatives of the children's parliament (Dáil Na bPaisti) recently met the Minister for Education (www.nco.ie) signals the potential of future approaches to dialogue with children about their experience of school at a more formal level. While the Department of Education and Science has produced guidelines for second-level schools on the effective running of student councils (DES 2002), research at both primary and second level suggests that issues of power, status and democracy in teacher–pupil relations are key concerns children retain about their experience of school (Lynch and Lodge 2002; Zappone 2002; Devine 2003). More recent research into the operation of student councils in second-level schools indicates concerns over the extent to which the councils are taken seriously by teaching staff and of the absence of real influence of students at school or board of management level (Children's Research Centre 2005).

Such findings suggest, therefore, that in spite of legislative provision and an awareness by policy-makers of the discourse about children's rights, the gatekeepers of key institutions in children's lives (in this instance teachers) can draw on their more authoritative position to minimize the effects of policy changes in practice. As Devine et al. (2004) note, the silence and invisibility of some groups cannot be divorced from the power and dominance of others. Notwithstanding the rights of children as articulated in the UN Convention 1989 and the Education Act 1998, teachers, concerned for their own professional standing in a time of rapid social change, can draw on a discourse of discipline breakdown (DES 2006), fear of student rule and a weakening of their authoritative position in schools, to minimize the impact of measures which accord students greater rights of consultation in schools. In the absence of a concerted effort by the state to encourage a cultural shift in schools (through greater publicity regarding children's rights and appropriate support and in-service training to teachers on the potential merits and benefits of student consultation), the involvement of children in the organization of school life in practice remains a matter of choice for teachers rather than a matter of the right of children to have their voices heard and their views taken into account.

Conclusions

It appears that the cultural politics of childhood in Ireland is at a point of transition, the child being positioned discursively somewhere between 'other' and citizen, with children's capacity for transformative action limited in both potential and practice. The idea that children may be considered as competent actors and have rights which need to be safeguarded is gaining momentum, although the manner in which this is given constitutional recognition remains to be seen (CRA 2007). Nonetheless, structural recognition is being given to children's rights as the discourse of familialization, which traditionally framed child protection issues, is increasingly being replaced in both policy and legislation by a broader understanding of children's needs and welfare, including their rights (Richardson 2005). Children's greater access to authoritative resources through the office of the Ombudsman for Children and the work of the office of the Minister for Children, for example, points the way to a significant potential for change in their subordinate positioning within Irish society. However, initiatives to include the voices of children in policy-making remain ad hoc and dispersed, and children do not yet constitute a sufficiently formidable constituency that politicians and policy-makers are unable to ignore them.

Tensions and contradictions at the broader level are reflected in institutionalized practice on the ground. Within education, for example, provisions related to the greater participation of young people in second-level schools are being implemented, some with greater success than others (Children's Research Centre 2005). That the issue of participation by primary school children is entirely ignored is indicative of a discourse that continues to determine competency and rights of participation in terms of age criteria alone. While considerable curriculum development has taken place at all levels of the education system, reflecting the intention to make the system more relevant and meaningful to young people's lives, children on the whole lack any real and meaningful input into the organization of their schooling.

Furthermore, substantial differences remain between groups of children in their capacity to access and participate in the education system – inequalities which are all the more serious given the strength of the economy over a sustained period. New inequalities are being compounded upon old, as migrant children are distinguished from others in their right to Irish citizenship and their access to educational supports is on a limited and predominantly narrow basis (Devine 2005; Devine and Kelly 2006). Substantively, in spite of the rhetoric of commitment to children's welfare as children, the absence of a rights-based focus in safeguarding the best interests of each child raises key questions related to the political commitment to realize children's rights in practice.

For their part children exercise their agency according to the material, cultural and social resources to which they have access, as well as by their positioning as children within the interdependent context of their lives with adults. While there are some examples of children actively bringing about change through their own initiatives and self-mobilization (e.g. the establishment by students of a union for secondary students to articulate their interests in the wake of a protracted industrial strike by teachers), their position as a group is at best ambiguous in relation to the adult group as a whole. Thus, while the discourse of citizenship is increasingly incorporated into policy on children, the actualization of children's rights through their participation in policy-making in all aspects of their lives remains fragmented and as yet relatively tokenistic.

At the level of practice there are some notable examples of real consultation with children who, through exercising their agency, challenge misconceptions adults may have about their competency. Richardson (2005), for example, notes the surprise expressed by senior civil servants over the process of including children in the selection panel for the position of Ombudsman for Children, while research by McLoughlin (2004) on the operation of a student council in a primary school confirms the positive nature of the experience for teaching staff and children alike, in spite of reservations of teachers that such a council could work.

In spite of such examples, a discourse of children's rights is not widespread and has not filtered into common-sense understandings of what it is to be a child and the experience of childhood in Ireland. Debates over children's rights in the public sphere become crystallized in the main over issues of protection and safety, with popular media frequently referring to the 'loss' of childhood in modern Ireland, reinforcing constructions of childhood rooted in notions of the vulnerability and innocence of the child. Such debates are rarely framed at an ideological level to include issues related to the rights and status of children, relative to adults, in society at large.

It is clear, however, that some changes are occurring in the cultural construction of childhood in Irish society. Globalized discourses have merged with local circumstance as the issue of children's rights and participation has become increasingly prevalent in public policy-making. However, relations of power between adults and children, which are themselves complex and differentiated, mediate the instantiation of these constructions in practice. Thus, although traditional structures of domination between adults and children are being challenged and gradually replaced by more democratic forms of interaction (Whyte 1995), instances appear to be predicated on individual and local initiatives, rather than through prescribed, system-wide recognition of the rights of children to be consulted in all matters which affect them. Nowhere is this more clearly seen than in the education system, a key mechanism for the cultural (re)construction of childhood, but one in which often opposing interests (religious groups, parents, teachers, the state) have traditionally sought to speak 'on behalf of' the child.

More broadly, the availability of a national data-set on all aspects of children's lives is required to highlight the diversity of childhood in Ireland and to move government policy beyond reaction to pro-action in tackling the considerable inequalities that exist. In the midst of rapid cultural and social change, underpinned by a neoliberal market economy, serious questions need to be asked about the experience of identity, belonging and participation of all children. Although important progress has been made in recent years, bringing children in from the margins in public policy and practice is a challenge that has yet to be met.

References

Akenson, D. H. (1975) *A Mirror to Kathleen's Face: Education in Independent Ireland 1922–1960*. Montreal and London: McGill-Queen's University Press.

Apple, M. (2001) *Educating the 'Right' Way – Markets, Standards, God and Inequality*. New York: Routledge/Falmer.

Arensberg, C. and Kimball, S. (1968) *Family and Community in Ireland*. Cambridge, MA: Harvard University Press.

Bailey, R. (2000) *Teaching Values and Citizenship across the Curriculum*. London: Kogan Page.

Baker, J., Lynch, K., Cantillon, S. and Walsh, J. (2004) *Equality from Theory to Action*. New York: Palgrave Macmillan.

Bernstein, B (1975) *Class Codes and Control*, Vol. 3, London: Routledge & Kegan Paul.

Bourdieu, P. (1993) *Sociology in Question*. London: Sage.

Bourdieu, P. and Passeron, J. C (1977) *Reproduction in Education, Society and Cutlure*. Beverly Hills, CA: Sage.

Breen, R., Hannan, D., Rottman, D. and Whelan, C. (1990) *Understanding Contemporary Ireland*. Dublin: Gill and Macmillan.

Brooke, S. (2004) *Children and Housing Problems*. Dublin: Children's Research Centre.

Childhood Development Initiative (CDI) (2004) *How are our Kids? Children and Families in Tallaght West, Co Dublin*. Childhood Development Initiative and Dartington Social Research Unit, Devon.

Childhood Development Initiative (CDI) (2005) *Experiencing Childhood Citizenship – Consultations with Children in Tallaght West*, Childhood Development Initiative. Jobstown, Dublin.

Children's Research Centre (2005) *Second Level Student Councils in Ireland: A Study of Enablers, Barriers and Supports*. Dublin: Trinity College Dublin.

Clancy, P. (2005) Education Policy in Ireland. In Quin, S. P., Kennedy, A., O'Donnell, A. and Kiely, G. (eds.), *Contemporary Irish Social Policy*. Dublin: UCD Press.

Clancy, P. and Wall, J. (2000) *Social Background of Higher Education Entrants*. Dublin: Higher Education Authority.

Clarke, M. (2000) Creating Listening Schools. In Pearce, N. and Hallgarten, J. (eds.), *Tomorrow's Citizens: Critical Debates in Citizenship and Education*. London: Institute for Public Policy Research.

Combat Poverty Agency (2005) *Ending Child Poverty*, Dublin, Combat Poverty Agency.

Coolahan, J. (1983) *Irish Education: History and Structure*. Dublin: Institute of Public Administration.

CRA (Children's Rights Alliance) (1998) *Children's Rights – Our Responsibilities – Concluding Observations of the UN Committee on the Rights of the Child*. Dublin: Gentian Press.

CRA (Children's Rights Alliance) (2007) The Constitution and Children – A Position Paper on the Proposed Referendum, www.childrensrights.ie; accessed 8 February 2007.

Curtin, C. and Varley, A. (1984) Children and Childhood in Rural Ireland: A Consideration of Ethnographic Literature. In Curtin, C. et al. (eds.), *Culture and Ideology in Ireland*. Galway: University Press.

Deegan, J., Devine, D. and Lodge, A. (2004) *Primary Voices – Equality, Diversity and Childhood in Irish Primary Schools*. Dublin: IPA.

Department of Education (1971) *Curaculum Na Bunscoile*. Dublin: Stationery Office.

Department of Education and Science (DES) (2002) *Student Councils: A Voice for Students*. Dublin: DES.

Department of Education and Science (2005) *Literacy and Numeracy in Disadvantaged Schools: Challenges for Teachers and Learners*. Dublin: Government Publications.

Department of Education and Science (2006) *School Matters – Report of the Task Force on Student Behaviour*. Dublin: DES.

Devine, D. (2002) Children's Citizenship and the Structuring of Adult–Child Relations in the Primary School. *Childhood* 9(3): 303–21.

Devine, D. (2003) *Children, Power and Schooling – How Childhood is Structured in the Primary School*, Stoke-on-Trent: Trentham.

Devine, D. (2005) Welcome to the Celtic Tiger? Teacher Responses to Increasing Ethnic Diversity in Irish Schools. *International Studies in Sociology of Education* 15(1): 49–71.

Devine, D. and Kelly, M. (2006) 'I just don't want to get picked on by anyone' – Dynamics of Inclusion and Exclusion in a Newly Multi-ethnic Irish Primary School. *Children and Society* 20(2): 128–39.

Devine, D., Lodge, A. and Deegan, J. (2004) Activating Voices through Practice – Democracy, Care and Consultation in the Primary School. In Deegan, J., Devine, D. and Lodge, A. (eds.), *Primary Voices – Equality, Diversity and Childhood in Irish Primary Schools*. Dublin: IPA.

Devine, D., Nic Ghiolla Phadraig, M. and Deegan, J. (2004) Time for Children – Time for Change? – Children's Rights and Welfare in Ireland during a Period of Economic Growth. In Jensen, A., Ben-Arieh, C., Conti, D., Kutsar, M., Nic Ghiolla Phadraigh, M. and Warming Nielsen, J. (eds.), *Children's Welfare in Ageing Europe*. Trondheim: Norwegian Centre for Child Research.

Duncan, W. (1996) The Constitutional Protection of Parental Rights in Government of Ireland. *Report of the Constitution Review Group*, Dublin: Government Publications Office.

Farren, S. (1995) *The Politics of Irish Education 1920–1965*. Belfast: Institute of Irish Studies.

Fitzgerald, E. (2004) *Counting our Children – An Analysis of Official Data Sources on Children and Childhood in Ireland*. Dublin: Children's Research Centre, Trinity College.

Foucault, M.(1979) *Discipline and Punish: The Birth of the Prison*. New York: Random House.

Garvin, T. (2004) *Preventing the Future – Why was Ireland Poor for so Long?* Dublin: Gill and Macmillan.

Giddens, A. (1979) *Central Problems in Social Theory, Action, Structure and Contradiction in Social Analysis*. London: Macmillan.

Giddens, A. (1984) *The Constitution of Society – Outline of the Theory of Structuration*. Los Angeles, CA: University of California Press.

Government of Ireland (2000) *National Children's Strategy*. Dublin: Stationery Office.

Hannon, D. and Katsiouni, L. (1977) *Traditional Families? From Culturally Prescribed to Negotiated Roles in Farm Families*. Dublin: Economic and Social Research Institute.

Hyland, A. and Milne, K. (1992) *Irish Educational Documents*, Vol. 2. Dublin: Church of Ireland College of Education.

Immigration Council of Ireland (2004) *Voices of Immigrants: The Challenges of Inclusion*. Dublin: Immigration Council of Ireland.

Inglis, T. (1998) *Moral Monopoly*. Dublin: Gill and Macmillan.

James, A. and James, A. (2004) *Constructing Childhood: Theory, Policy and Social Practice*. London: Palgrave Macmillan.

Kennedy, F. (2001) *Cottage to Creche: Family Change in Ireland*. Dublin: Institute of Public Administration.

Kenny, M. (2001) Traveller Childhood in Ireland. In Cleary, A., Nic Ghiolla Phadraig, M. and Quin, S. (eds.), *Understanding Children*. Vol. 2: *Changing Experiences and Family Forms*. Dublin: Oak Tree Press.

Kjorholt, A. (2004) Childhood as a Social and Symbolic Space: Discourses on Children as Social Participants in Society. PhD thesis. NTNU, Trondheim: Norwegian Centre for Child Research.

Lynch, K. and Lodge, A. (2002) *Equality and Power in Schools*. London: Routledge/Falmer.

Marshall, T. H. (1950) *Citizenship and Social Class*. Cambridge: Cambridge University Press.

Marshall, T. H. (1981) *The Right to Welfare and Other Essays*. London: Heinemann.

MacRuairc, G. (2006) Schools and Teachers and all them Poshies' Language, Culture and Class: A Comparative Examination of Cultural and Linguistic Experiences in School Space and Non-School Space. PhD thesis, UCD. Dublin: School of Education and Life Long Learning.

McCourt, F. (1996) *Angela's Ashes – Memoirs of an Irish Childhood*. London: HarperCollins.

McDonagh, W. (2004) Travellers and Education: A Personal Perspective. In Deegan, J., Devine, D. and Lodge, A. (eds.), *Primary Voices – Equality, Diversity and Childhood in Irish Primary Schools*. Dublin: IPA.

McLaren, P. (1993) *Schooling as Ritual Performance: Towards a Political Economy of Education*. London: Routledge.

McLoughlin, O. (2004) Citizen Child – The Experience of a Student Council in a Primary School. In Deegan, J., Devine, D. and Lodge, A. (eds.), *Primary Voices – Equality, Diversity and Childhood in Irish Primary Schools*. Dublin: IPA.

National Children's Office (2005a) *The Development of a National Set of Child Well-Being Indicators*. Dublin: National Children's Office.

National Children's Office (2005b) *Dail Na nOg Delegate Report*, http://www.nco.ie/upload_documents/DNN_2005-final.pdf.

National Children's Office (2005c) *Young Voices – Guidelines on How to Involve Children and Young People in Your Work*. Dublin: National Children's Office.

Nic Ghiolla Phadraig, M. (1990) *Childhood as a Social Phenomenon. National Report, Ireland*. Vienna: European Centre for Social Welfare Policy and Research.

Nolan, B. (2001) Children and Poverty. In Cleary, A., Nic Ghiolla Phadraig, M. and Quin, S. (eds.), *Understanding Children*. Vol. 1: *State, Education and Economy*. Dublin: Oak Tree Press.

OECD (2005) Education at a Glance – OECD Indicators, www.oecd.org.

Ombudsman for Children (2005) *Annual Report*, Dublin: Millenium House; www.oco.ie.

Osler, A. and Starkey, H. (2005) *Changing Citizenship: Democracy and Inclusion in Education*. Maidenhead: Open University Press.

O'Sullivan, D. (2005) *Cultural Politics and Irish Education*. Dublin: IPA.

Pavee Point (2006) *Assimilation Policies and Outcomes – Travellers' Experience*. Dublin: Pavee Point Traveller Centre.

Phillips, A. (1999) *Which Equalities Matter*. Cambridge: Polity Press.

Qvortrup, J. (1995) From Useful to Useful: The Historical Continuity in Children's Constructive Participation. In Amber, A. M. (ed.), *Theory and Linkages Between Theory and Research on Children/Childhood*. Special volume of *Sociological Studies of Children*. Greenwich, CT: JAI Press.

Richardson, V. (2001) Legal and Constitutional Rights of Children in Ireland. In Cleary, A., Nic Ghiolla Phadraig, M. and Quin, S. (eds.), *Understanding Children*. Vol. 1: *State, Education and Economy*. Dublin: Oak Tree Press.

Richardson, V. (2005) Children and Social Policy. In Quin, S., Kennedy, P., O'Donnell, A. and Kiely, G. (eds.), *Contemporary Irish Social Policy*. Dublin: UCD Press.

Roche, J. (1999) Children: Rights, Participation and Citizenship. *Childhood* 6(4): 474–93.

Shevlin, M. and Rose, R. (eds.) (2003) *Encouraging Voices*. Dublin: National Disability Authority.

Tovey, H. and Share, P. (2003) *A Sociology of Ireland*. Dublin: Gill and Macmillan.

UN Development Report (2005) *UN Human Development – International Co-Operation at a Crossroads*. UN Development Programme, New York: Hoeschstetter Press.

Whyte, J. (1995) *Changing Times: A Comparative Study of Children – Belfast, London, Dublin*. Aldershot: Avebury.

Young, I. (1991) *Justice and the Politics of Difference*. Princeton, NJ: Princeton University Press.

Zappone, K. (2002) *Achieving Equality in Children's Education in Primary Education: Ending Disadvantage – Proceedings and Action Plan of National Forum*. Dublin: St Patrick's College.

6
Changing Childhood in the UK: Reconstructing Discourses of 'Risk' and 'Protection'

Adrian James and Allison James

Introduction

The study of childhood, it would seem, has finally come of age. No longer confined to the traditional disciplinary straitjackets of sociology or developmental psychology, social science is engaging with childhood in a variety of new and interesting ways. Multidisciplinary and, although perhaps less frequently, interdisciplinary inputs from sociology, anthropology, social policy, social geography, history, law and social work are now making their mark on our understanding of childhood and children's everyday lives. Since the paradigm shift of the 1980s–1990s (James and Prout 1990), it is no longer remarkable to speak of children as social actors or, more properly as Mayall (2002) puts it, as social agents – that is, people who make things happen; nor does it seem novel to describe children as competent informants about issues that matter to them.

Recent policy developments that seem to reflect a desire to re-establish a more traditional relationship between adults and children therefore merit close attention. In seeking to understand such developments, it is to the 'cultural politics of childhood' that we turn (see James and James 2004), since these are central to any account of childhood change. In sum, what this theoretical construct facilitates is an exploration of the relationship that exists between ideas about childhood, as embodied and reflected in various politico-cultural discourses, the experiences of children as a social category and the impact that both of these have on the everyday life of any individual child. To engage with the cultural politics through which the social space of contemporary

British childhood is currently being mapped requires us to explore the discursive politico-cultural parameters of this process, which therefore involves not only untangling the ways in which ideas about childhood come to shape the everyday lives of children and children's responses to and experience of those ideas, but also a consideration of the mechanisms and processes through which this dance of ongoing social construction takes place.

For us, law and policy are key elements in this process. As we have argued (James and James 2004), the framework and operation of law as a socio-legal institution in large part shapes the interactions that take place between, on the one hand, the political, economic and social structures and institutions that constrain children's lives and, on the other, the different kinds of agency that children as individuals choose, or are allowed, to adopt. As Ewick and Silbey (1998) argue in their perceptive analysis of 'the commonplace of law', law does not just exist 'outside' of social life as an external agent to shape what we can or cannot do; rather 'it operates through social life as persons deliberately interpret and invoke law's language, authority and procedures to organise their lives and manage their relationships' (1998: 20).

This conceptualization of the cultural politics of childhood, in our view, provides a theoretical space in which we can locate and consider the production and reproduction of childhood and, in doing so, allows us to account for changes in the forms and ways in which childhood unfolds in any society. Thus, as we shall discuss, changes in law and policies relating to childhood reflect the dynamic process through which children's everyday lives are experienced and conceptualized. As we shall show, recent years have seen an increasing determination on behalf of the government to reverse the evolutionary changes that have taken place in the cultural politics of British childhood, which have become increasingly liberal with the greater recognition of children's social agency.

This development, which has met with little effective opposition from adults in general or from those who work on the behalf of children (since children are seldom if ever able themselves to mount effective opposition against adult hegemony), has seen the government encouraging the stricter enforcement of existing laws, alongside the creation of new ones, in order to maintain the status quo for children and young people and to resist changes that children might seek in fashioning their own childhoods. It is through this process of redefining and reordering the everyday practices of children that the cultural politics of childhood operates, as concepts of 'childhood' and 'the child' begin to change and these changes feed back into the everyday lives and experiences of children. (For a more detailed discussion of this theoretical proposition, see James and James 2004: chapter 3.)

In order to further this theoretical approach and to reveal its explanatory potential in practice, this chapter examines the interplay between three different, but complementary discourses that are shaping the contemporary cultural politics of childhood in the UK. The first is communitarianism; the second the notion of risk and, closely related to this, the idea of protection; and the third moral panic (Cohen 1973).

The communitarian agenda revisited (and revived!)

As we have argued elsewhere (James and James 2001) the policies of the New Labour government, which came to power in 1997, have sought to revitalize social democracy in the UK. Based on an approach elaborated by Giddens as the 'Third Way', which embraces many of Etzioni's ideas on communitarianism, the principles that emerge from this political philosophy, and New Labour's political practices, are still very much in evidence in a range of social policy developments aimed at revitalizing civic society and developing social capital.

As we also suggested, however, many of these policies can be seen as attempts to increase social control over children since their effect has been to restrict children's agency and rights. Thus, in spite of an apparent increase in measures to enable children's participation (see Children and Young People's Unit 2001a and b; Wade et al. 2001; Wyness 2001; Combe 2002; Kirby et al. 2003), children have continued to be marginalized. As we argued:

> the control of children's behaviour is increasingly a focus for policy initiatives under New Labour for it is through shaping the form that 'childhood' takes that the socialisation of children can be most effectively regulated. And it is through the regulation and control of children in the present that a particular kind of future, adult community can be produced.
>
> (James and James 2001: 215)

Such developments, although evident across the social policy board, are particularly significant in relation to what is seen as the anti-social behaviour of children and young people. This is perhaps inevitable since, as we suggested (James and James 2001), childhood constitutes a prime site for managing the tensions between conformity and autonomy.

These are tensions that a communitarian agenda has to manage, and the way in which this is usually done is through censure of different kinds. As Etzioni points out, censure represents

> a major way that communities uphold members' commitments to shared values and service to the common good – community order. And indeed, community censure reduces the reliance on the state as a source of order.
>
> (1996: 5)

In the context of children and childhood, such censure is particularly important since it is children who are envisaged as the community's and the nation's future. It has, however, reached unprecedented levels: as the Council of Europe's Commissioner for Human Rights comments in a recent report, the UK has witnessed

> the introduction of a series of civil orders aimed at reducing urban nuisance, but whose primary effect has been to bring a whole range of persons, predominantly the young, within the scope of the criminal justice system and, often enough, behind bars without necessarily having committed a recognisable criminal offence.
>
> (Gil Robles, 2004: para. 83)

In relation to children, childhood and the communitarian agenda, there is much more of interest and relevance in this report, which has the particular merit of presenting an external perspective that offers a mirror in which we can see reflected a rather different view of developments in the UK from that presented by the government. In a tacit acknowledgement of the communitarian agenda, the report argues:

> What is so striking, however, about the multiplication of civil orders in the United Kingdom, is the fact that the orders are intended to protect not just specific individuals, but entire communities. This inevitably results in a very broad, and occasionally, excessive range of behaviour falling within their scope as the determination of what constitutes anti-social behaviour becomes conditional on the subjective views of any given collective ... At first sight, indeed, such orders look rather like personalised penal codes, where non-criminal behaviour becomes criminal for individuals who have incurred the wrath of the community.
>
> One cannot but wonder, indeed, whether their purpose is not more to reassure the public that something is being done – and, better still,

by local residents themselves – than the actual prevention of the anti-social behaviour itself.

(paras. 110–11)

As a recent front-page article in a national newspaper pointed out:

Children are the subject of more anti-social behaviour orders than adults, leading some commentators to warn that the Government is in danger of making it a 'crime to become [*sic*] a child.

(*The Independent*, 20 June 2005)

Such an analysis of contemporary developments justifies our concern (James and James 2001) that the communitarian principles underpinning the broad-based political agenda of New Labour would result in a significant extension of control over children. What is new, however, and what is central to our specific focus here, is the contemporary framing of such measures through discourses of risk and protection. At least part of the significance of this discursive framing lies in the fact that it makes more problematic any critique of such policies, since what right-minded adult can be critical if new measures are taken in order to protect children?

Risk, protection and moral panic

A signal feature of the changing cultural politics of childhood in the UK is that the languages of welfare and of risk are being transmuted, not to say hijacked, as part of an apparently growing 'moral panic' about childhood. However, this is part of a process that has been evident since the late 1960s, when the separation between welfare and justice, treatment and punishment, was at its clearest. Thus, for example, during this period and in the context of the Children and Young Persons Act 1969, children in trouble were regarded as deprived rather than depraved. They were therefore considered deserving of adult understanding and treatment through a range of compensatory mechanisms. Such a concern for children's welfare was based on recognition of the structural disadvantages faced by many of those children whose behaviour was defined as criminal or anti-social. Far less emphasis was placed at that time on the notion that children might choose to behave in such ways and that they were therefore in need of punishment.

Over the next three decades, however, successive governments sought increasingly to deny, or at least to obscure, the links between structural disadvantage and anti-social or delinquent behaviour, preferring instead to emphasize choice, thereby justifying the use of increasingly punitive measures against children and young offenders. This shift towards individualism in respect of responsibility and punishment could be regarded as an ironic feature of postmodernity since it appears to have gone hand-in-hand with the increasing recognition of children as 'social agents', normally regarded as a positive indicator of empowerment.

There has also been an increasing politicization of crime, through its figuration as an increasingly prominent election issue since the early 1990s as politicians sought to gain party political advantage out of the public's fear of crime and disorder. This process was clearly evident in the 2005 general election and was reflected in the recent widespread media attention given to the banning of young people wearing 'hoodies' from an Essex shopping mall. This move received very public support from the newly elected Labour government, even though recent evidence from the Greater Manchester Police, one of the largest police forces in the country, showed that only 1.2 per cent of robberies in the previous 12 months involved someone wearing a hooded top (Barrett 2005).

If, as Stanley Cohen argued in his seminal book *Folk Devils and Moral Panics*, a moral panic can be said to exist when

> [a] condition, episode, person or group or persons emerges to become defined as a threat to societal values and interests; its nature is presented in a stylized and stereotypical fashion by the mass media; [and] the moral barricades are manned by editors, bishops, politicians and other right-thinking people
>
> (1973: 9)

then contemporary UK perspectives on childhood might reasonably be argued to constitute just such a moral panic.

One of the key ways in which this moral panic is currently being inflamed is through the deployment of the language of 'protection' in relation to childhood across an increasingly wide range of perceived risks as a feature of the changing cultural politics of childhood in the UK. In sum, discourses of risk and protection are becoming increasingly important in providing a populist political justification for what is a growing raft of measures that work to control and discipline children. The communitarian agenda, underpinned by the tougher enforcement of existing laws and the introduction of new laws, draws on the discourse of risk to amplify a growing moral panic amongst adults about children.

What is of particular interest and concern, however, is that in the context of this moral panic, it is not just a particular group of children or young people, such as the Mods and Rockers Cohen wrote about, who are the focus of this moral crusade. It is, we suggest, childhood itself and therefore, by implication, all children. Such a perspective has gradually crystallized through the tendency, in recent years, to present childhood as a time of risk, in which children are defined as being in need of protection, in their best interests, in order to fulfil their potential as adults. From stranger-danger through to the banning of games of conkers in school playgrounds, childhood is presented by adults, and to adults and children, as a time of risk (see Freeman 1992; Scott et al. 1998; Scott, 2000).

What is particularly noteworthy about this development, however, is the bowdlerizing of the language of child protection. By promoting strategies as being in children's best interests through offering them protection against various risks, a semblance of welfare is recreated. As Parton (2005) argues, however, whilst such a reformulation of the concept of protection is entirely consistent with the emphasis placed by the Children Act 1989 on safeguarding and promoting children's welfare, it has a whole variety of intended and unintended consequences. Therefore, as we argue in our discussion of the strategy that has emerged around the recent Green Paper, *Every Child Matters* (Chief Secretary to the Treasury 2003), this reformulation must also be understood in the context of a developing cultural politics of childhood that is fostering polices that are actually less about the welfare of children and more about the protection of adult communities, in both the present and the future. Before looking in detail at this, however, the issues of risk and protection merit some further consideration.

What *exactly* is 'at risk'? Discourses of risk *as* protection

The significance of the concept of 'the best interests of the child' in the context of the cultural politics of contemporary childhood lies in the fact it constitutes a central rhetorical plank in many of the decisions made in determining children's welfare. Indeed, as we have shown (James, James and McNamee 2004a), it is the site of, and therefore reflects, some of the main struggles over the social construction of childhood: in the process of defining what is in the best interests of any individual child, the best interests of children as a category are also defined and thus the dominant (and changing) views of adults towards children also become apparent.

'The best interests of the child' is, however, premised on the notion of children as 'becoming' rather than 'being', as part and parcel of a welfare commitment to a predominantly developmental and psychological understanding of children (James, James and McNamee 2004a). Such a perspective plays down any diversity between children, as well as masking their individuality: the 'best interests of the child', a phrase that implies a high degree of individuality, is in fact used in relation to *all* children and, as a recent study of family court welfare practice showed (James, James and McNamee 2004a, 2004b), the developmental paradigm and its prescriptions for what children need can easily overshadow any divergent wishes and feelings expressed by an individual child.

Interestingly, then, within these discourses of 'protection' and 'best interests', children are most often regarded collectively and most often valued as proto-adults. Just so with risk. The discourse of children at risk is, like that of protection, similarly oriented to the future and, like that of protection, is linked to a set of unknowns in adulthood: the being of the child in the present has to be safeguarded against risk in order to protect the future adult s/he will become.

This overlap between risk and protection is therefore interesting and important and, lest our argument be seen simply as a critical commentary by two cynical academics, we need to unravel the ways in which risk and protection are being deliberately entwined: we need to ask why references to risk in government policies continually accompany those to protection, best interests and welfare; why, on occasion, concern with risk, rather than protection, gains the upper hand; and we need to understand what advantage this might offer to government, and what disadvantages this might bring to children.

We turn first to Ulrich Beck's classic account of the linkages between processes of individualization and reflexive modernization in the risk society, a thesis usefully summarized by Taylor-Gooby and Zin as follows:

> the key cultural shift among the citizens of risk society is towards 'reflexivity': individuals are conscious of their social context and their own roles as actors within it. Managing the risks of civilization becomes both a pressing issue and one that is brought home to individuals. At the same time, however, confidence in experts and in accredited authorities tends to decline as people are more aware of the shortcomings of official decision-makers and of the range of alternative approaches to problems available elsewhere on the planet. The breakdown of an established traditional order in the life-course

provided by work, marriage, family and community leads to greater individualization and increased uncertainty and anxiety. In this context, the individualized citizens of world risk society are increasingly conscious of the responsibility to manage the risks they perceive in the context of their own lives, and, in this sense, self-create their own biographies.

(2005: 6)

However, in relation to changing perspectives on childhood, such an apparently emancipatory outcome for children simply does not apply. Instead, as we shall see, by virtue of their supposed need for 'protection' *against* risk, children are not permitted (or are less and less so) to make choices and take risks. The institutional structures that 'protect' them also prevent them from making their own choices and constructing their own biographies as good, postmodern individuals and citizens. They are instead 'freed' from risk-taking, under the guise of protecting them and their future status as adults, whilst running the risk of coercive control and punishment if they continue to take risks. In consequence, in that children's 'becoming' – their childhood – is being entrusted to adults rather than to children themselves, this risk-free cultural environment turns out to be one that is highly governed and controlled: it is certainly not an environment that nurtures reflexive individuality!

One reason for this is the government's failure to engage effectively with many of the structural underpinnings of the problems that continue to face a significant number of children and young people today and their preference instead to curtail or deny them their agency through the restoration of adult control. With the important exception of agentic individuals who offend, and who are therefore punished as fully competent individuals, children and young people are, in the contemporary cultural politics of childhood, being rendered less rather than more able to manage the risks (and opportunities) they face.

Beck's thesis has, of course, been widely criticized (see Taylor-Gooby and Zinn 2005), but one reason why his thesis appears wanting, especially in the case of children and young people, is that it disregards the impact of the imbalance of power between children and adults. In part a function of their generational relationship, it is a power imbalance that rests on adult judgements about children's development and social competence. The effect of this is that, as *Every Child Matters* (hereafter referred to as ECM) clearly illustrates, far from being enabled to become reflexive and responsible individuals by the choices available within the 'risk society', children are being increasingly 'disabled' through recourse to a developmental paradigm that casts them as in need of protection *from* risk as they grow up.

Published by the Treasury in September 2003, ECM has much to say about risk and childhood. The Foreword, written by Tony Blair (indicating the importance the government attached to the document), frames the Green Paper by making reference to Victoria Climbié, a young child who was seriously abused and murdered, as an illustration of children whose lives are filled with 'risk, fear and danger'. The Foreword concludes that 'Sadly, nothing can ever absolutely guarantee that no child will ever be at risk again from abuse and violence from within their own family' (2003: 2).

ECM goes on to outline a range of measures to reform and improve children's care because, it argues, 'child protection cannot be separated from polices to improve children's lives as a whole' (para. 4). This extension by fiat of the notion of child protection from one that focuses on particular risks, for particular children, to one that embraces the lives of children and children's lives as a whole allows ECM to set out a framework for 'protective' services that cover children and young people from birth to 19 years, the aim of which is to 'reduce the numbers of children who experience educational failure, engage in offending or antisocial behaviour, suffer from ill health, or become teenage parents' (para. 4). Thus it would seem that the 'risk' from which all children are to be protected is the risk that, in the absence of such services, there will be various negative outcomes for children as they develop, which will blight their lives as future adults.

Five positive outcomes are therefore identified by ECM to underpin services for children, outcomes relating to aspects of children's physical, psychological and emotional well-being that are seen as central to their 'successful' development and which 'Everyone in our society has a responsibility for securing' (para. 1.4), as follows:

- Being healthy: enjoying good physical and mental health and living a healthy lifestyle, which will include concerns about smoking, obesity, teenage conception, suicide.
- Staying safe: being protected from harm and neglect and growing up able to look after themselves. Indicators associated with this outcome include numbers on child protection registers, numbers cautioned or convicted of an offence, victimization and domestic violence.
- Enjoying and achieving: getting the most out of life and developing broad skills for adulthood, the focus being on educational performance, truancy, children not in education or employment.

- Making a positive contribution: to the community and to society and not engaging in anti-social or offending behaviour, part of the concern being about low participation in voting by young people.
- Economic well-being: overcoming socio-economic disadvantages to achieve their full potential in life, the focus being on improving rates of employment and reducing the number of children living in low-income families.

From this list it is clear that one of the traditional authorities over childhood – the developmental perspective – far from being challenged by the 'risk society' as Beck's analysis might suggest, is being sustained and indeed reinforced. Thus, although the academy may be challenging the thrall of traditional developmental psychology over understandings of childhood, and is now arguing for models of child development that are sensitive to social context (Woodhead 1996), within the cultural politics of childhood in the UK there remains a vested interest in sustaining the traditional, more universalizing model. One reason for this may be that it is a model that justifies concerns about protection and risk, which in turn legitimates the control of children by adults.

The cultural politics of risk in childhood – discourses of control

Returning to the list of welfare outcomes identified in ECM, the juxtaposition of positive and negative potential outcomes is apparent, as is the explicit use of the language of social control. Thus, for example, in measuring the outcome of 'staying safe' – which is phrased in terms of children being protected from harm and neglect and being helped to grow up to be able to look after themselves as adults – we find the government proposing the use of indicators linked with criminal and/or anti-social behaviour. 'Staying safe' means being protected from harm and neglect; however, the proposed indicators of 'not being safe' include the number of children cautioned or convicted of an offence, as well as levels of victimization and domestic violence. This is surely an instance of gamekeeper turned poacher! The child at risk is, at the same time, also the child who can be identified as a risk to others.

Thus the notions of being 'at risk' and in need of 'protection', once central to the welfare lexicon of child abuse and child protection, seem to have become subsumed within a more embracing discourse of social control, in the best interests of the child. Thus, along the way, the meanings have subtly but substantially altered. The result of this is to minimize children's vulnerability to adult mistreatment (either by the considered actions of individual adults, as in the case of Victoria Climbié, or by the unconsidered effects of structural disadvantage) and to emphasize the waywardness of children and young people, and the responsibility that adults have to control this.

What this analysis suggests therefore, in terms of understanding contemporary childhood, is that Beck's thesis of the 'declining role of social structures and the importance of personal and active choice' (Taylor-Gooby and Zin 2005: 8) simply does not work: it cannot address the cultural complexity of the structural processes through which childhood and adulthood are currently held in tension as a generational relationship by the range of new government initiatives. Embracing both 'risky children' and 'children at risk', childhood is subject to the government's double-edged sword of care and control.

To understand fully the contemporary cultural politics of childhood, therefore, we have to address notions of governmentality that pay attention to the cultural processes and social responses that both sustain and legitimate the state's demonization of the young, through the production of new forms of 'risky 'childhood. Such an approach requires us to identify 'structures of culturally based power [that are] ... complex and intersecting, involving axes of faith, gender, employment relations, as well as property, the rule of law, particular democratic traditions and political institutions' (Taylor-Gooby and Zin 2005: 8).

One of the clearest examples appeared in March 2003, when the Home Office published a White Paper that trailed the publication of ECM, describing it as a Green Paper

> which will propose radical options to improve services for children who are *at risk* of a wide range of *poor outcomes*. These outcomes include anti-social behaviour and offending; educational under-achievement; abuse, neglect and victimisation; teenage pregnancy; and ill health.
>
> (Home Office 2003: 21; emphasis added)

In this, the government intended to set out how it would 'identify children and young people at risk'. In setting the scene for the proposals in ECM, the White Paper makes an initial passing reference to the more commonly understood construction of 'risk' by referring to young people as the *victims* of crime and anti-social behaviour (para. 2.3). However, in the context of the overall thrust and content of the White Paper this is disingenuous, since the proposals that follow are unrelated to this: children as victims of crime effectively disappear. What the White Paper actually goes on to explore are ways to manage children who offend. For example, although the White Paper states that

> a new Identification, Referral and Tracking system (IRT) is being developed across all services working with children to enable a speedier and more joined up response to problems [that will] enable all agencies to share information about young people at risk
>
> (Home Office 2003, para. 2.5)

it gives as an example someone who is *committing* anti-social behaviour, rather than an example of a child who is in need of protection as a victim or through being especially vulnerable.

Consistent with this slippage between the language of 'protection' and that of 'risk' is the proposal to use a mechanism traditionally associated with *child protection* for dealing with children's behavioural problems:

> We will be taking powers to enable intensive fostering to occur as an alternative to custody ... At the same time it is essential to work with the family to enhance their parenting skills with a view to the child returning home.
>
> (Home Office 2003, para. 2.24)

Here again protection is elided with risk: rather than foster care being a resource that can be used to protect children from abuse, it becomes redefined as an alternative to custody for children who, through their own misbehaviour, put at risk their development into adulthood. Moreover, in spite of gestures in the direction of children at risk and their need for protection, the underpinning principle of the White Paper is communitarian in that it is the *community* that is at risk from the actions of children. Indeed, this is made explicit when it is argued that 'the protection of the local *community* must come first' (para. 2.51).

This is not to say, of course, that there are no risks attached to becoming an offender, to becoming a teenage mother, to smoking, to obesity or to truancy. Nor it is to say that it is not in children's best interests to encourage them to adopt behaviours that may have less deleterious consequences: any and all of these risks can have a profound effect on a child's future as, indeed, such outcomes for children can have a negative impact on communities. It is to point out, however, that the discursive conflation of the objectives of protecting children from the risk of abuse and protecting them from the consequences of structural disadvantage is both politically convenient and disingenuous.

It also ignores evidence concerning the statistical 'normality' of offending behaviour in young people and the fact that only a small minority go on to become serious and persistent adult offenders. By focusing on such potential outcomes for *all* children, however, and by utilizing the language of risk, a discourse emerges that defines childhood itself as a problem. In turn, by relying on the rhetorical power and appeal of 'the best interests of the child', the White Paper justifies as a 'protective measure' a raft of policies that are intended to control children by rendering their childhood risk-free – to children and, importantly, to adults.

Theorizing risk in the cultural politics of childhood

To understand the complex relationship between the discourses of risk and protection that pervade current British conceptions of childhood, Mary Douglas's work proves insightful. Her cultural perspectives on managing risk and uncertainty pinpoint some of the processes at work in what she calls the social control of curiosity that underpins notions of risk. She argues that

> Most institutions tend to solve some of their organizational problems through public allocation of blame. Naturally these problems and blaming procedures vary according to the kind of organizations. Lastly, some machinery for renewing members' commitments to the institution's objectives is activated by the threat of disaster.
>
> (1986: 56)

For Douglas the allocation of blame is quite distinctive, with 'nature' being used to ensure conformity:

> well-labelled, natural vulnerabilities point to certain classes of people as likely victims: their state of being 'at risk' justifies bringing them under control. In modern, industrial society the poor are nutritionally at risk and pregnant, poor women especially so.
>
> (1986: 57)

Douglas gives as an example the theories of maternal deprivation offered by Bowlby which, through the emphasis placed on the importance of attachment, led to women staying at home for fear of 'causing their child loss of identity and incapacity to love if they persisted in what working-class mothers had long been used to doing – going out to work' (1986: 58). With respect to children, as we have seen, the emphasis on development and on children's 'becoming' represents a comparable example of the 'naturalizing' of risk. The invocation of 'nature' as a key component of social processes Douglas describes as a political act, which is enabled through the 'use of risk as a technique of coercion' (1986: 59).

As part of the strategy to deliver the five positive outcomes for every child, ECM proposes, for example, a common assessment framework to ensure that information is collected and shared across services for children. This covers special educational needs, Connexions, YOTs, health and social services. The ostensible aim is for core information to follow the child in order to reduce duplication and enable the better management of risk: 'we want to see a local information hub developed in every local authority consisting of a list of *all* children living in their area and basic details ...' (para. 4.3; emphasis added). It goes on to argue that,

> In order to capture fully the concerns of a range of professionals over time, there is a strong case for giving practitioners the ability to flag on the system early warnings when they have concerns about a child which in itself *may not be a trigger or meet the usual thresholds for intervention. The decision to place such a flag of concern on a child's record ... lies with the individual practitioner.*
>
> (para. 4.5; emphasis added)

The potential reach of such thinking is evident in such initiatives as the Pan-London Protocol for Sexually Active Under-18s (London Child Protection Committee 2005), which encouraged a range of professionals, including the police, to share information about teenagers in London who are, or are likely to be, sexually active. The protocol, drafted in response to the Bichard Inquiry Report (2004) into the double child murder at Soham, and based on the legal position that sexual activity under the age of 16 is illegal, was

> designed to assist professionals to identify where children and young people's sexual relationships may be abusive and the children and young people may need the provision of protection or additional services. It is based on the core principle that the welfare of the child is paramount and emphasises the need to accurately assess the risk of

significant harm when a child or young person is engaged in a sexually active relationship.

(para. 1.1)

The protocol went on to state that

When a professional becomes aware that a young person is, or is likely to be, sexually active, an assessment should be made of the young person's physical and emotional health, education and safeguarding needs – in the context of the sexual relationship.

(para. 2.1)

Under this protocol, assessments were required to be carried out even when a teenager is in a relationship with another young person and they are both over the age of consent.

That these guidelines have been criticized as not being in line with the recommendations of the Bichard Inquiry[1] might be taken as indicative of both the moral panic surrounding childhood and the significance of the dimension of risk in determining the social response to such issues. Moreover, although such proposals may appear well intentioned, we must also be alert to their dangers for, as Masson has recently argued,

The assessment of risk in child protection cannot be a completely objective matter. Child protection work places social workers under considerable stress, not least because of the culture of blame that has operated when mistakes are made. It is well recognised that different social workers differ in their understanding of particular circumstances ... and this leads to different responses by local authorities ... It is commonly suggested that local authorities are more likely to intervene to protect children shortly after publicity of child protection failures, such as occurred during the Climbié Inquiry.

(2005: 84)

This illustrates well Douglas's analysis of the role of blame in the organizational management of risk outlined above. In addition, the suggestion about the raising of 'flags of concern', regardless of issues concerning the criteria for and the variability of professional judgements, illustrates the core principles of a form of governmentality through which 'risk' is managed under the guise of protection. This strikes a chord with Taylor-Gooby and Zin's suggestion that, moving away from Beck's thesis, new approaches to risk are revealing the shift 'towards greater emphasis on social regulation through expectations and assumptions about individual behaviour' (2005: 11).

Indeed, ECM goes on to say that the government is 'consulting on the circumstances (in addition to child protection and youth offending) under which information about a child could or must be shared, *for preventative purposes, without the consent of the child or their carers'* and that they would welcome views on whether warning signs should include 'factors within the family such as imprisonment, domestic violence, mental health or substance misuse problems amongst parents and carers' (para. 4.6; emphasis added). This clearly suggests that children of parents who have, for example, been in prison or have had mental health problems might become the target of preventative interventions by a range of agencies. This would be on the basis of potentially highly variable professional judgements about the *risk* of a child from such a background developing such problems, regardless of whether or not there is any current evidence of problems.

What matters to children?

On a more positive note, it might be argued, not entirely without justification, that the government went to considerable lengths to involve children and young people in formulating the policies being advanced under ECM. Indeed, the government states categorically that 'children and young people have told us that [the above] five outcomes are key to well-being in childhood and later life' (DfES 2004a: para.1.1) This statement is based on a consultation process conducted between November 2001 and March 2002 in which the government spelled out its vision for all children and young people and encouraged their participation with the words 'We hope you will share it' (Children and Young People's Unit 2001b: para. 1.5) One of the key principles of this vision was that it was 'centred on the needs of the young person [and that] [t]he best interests of the child or young person should be paramount, *taking into account their wishes and feelings'* (Children and Young People's Unit 2001b, para. 2.3; emphasis added). In the consultation itself, however, those involved were asked to 'structure' their thoughts into a series of categories that bear a striking resemblance to the five outcomes that subsequently appeared in ECM, although it should be noted that issues of anti-social or offending behaviour were not brought up, either in the framing of the consultation or in the responses of those children and young people involved.

When ECM was published (containing the five outcomes that children and young people had 'told' the government were crucial), a further sample of over 3,000 responded to a consultation document aimed specifically at children and young people (DfES 2003), while others attended a series of 62 meetings across England. Their responses, which were subsequently published (*Every Child Matters – Children and Young People Responses: Analysis of responses to the consultation document.* DfES),[2] merit careful reading. Thus, for example, in response to the question 'When do you think services should talk together about a child without the child knowing or saying it is OK?' the almost immediate response from most of the groups that met was 'never'. The report goes on to note, however, that 'when pushed a little further on this', most conceded that there were circumstances when this would be appropriate.

Of the approximately 3,000 written replies to the consultation, 39 per cent said that if there was a risk of the child being in *extreme* danger, services should be able to talk about child without their knowledge. However, 24 per cent said this should never happen and that children should always be consulted; 19 per cent said children and young people should always be involved in discussions and that no decision should be made without the child knowing or giving consent; 12 per cent agreed that where possible children and young people should be involved if the child was old enough to understand; and a further 6 per cent said that every case should be treated individually.[3] Thus, over 80 per cent of children and young people indicated clearly that they thought that such issues should not be discussed without their knowledge. In a subsequent publication, however, their views were juxtaposed with those of adults who had indicated that '[w]orrying about confidentiality can stop us working together to protect children ... [i]nformation should be shared, about children and their families when it is in the best interests of the child' (DfES 2004b: 11).

The government has subsequently taken powers under the Children Act 2004 to require the establishment of a database (or databases) to enable practitioners accurately to identify a child or young person who is at risk. At this stage, the details of how such a database is to be managed and how issues of consent will be dealt with are not clear, having been relegated to secondary legislation or, more probably, statutory guidance to be issued by the Secretary of State. It remains to be seen therefore whether the concerns about the sharing of information expressed by the children and young people who participated in the consultation exercise will be reflected in whatever regulatory framework is established. As section 12 of the Act makes clear, this may include information as to the existence of any cause for concern. Here indeed are very powerful examples of the systems of internal and external control that Douglas (1986) identified in the management of risk and of the gap between the rhetoric of children's participation and its reality in the context of the cultural politics of childhood.

Managing risky childhoods?

Such policies are a clear product of the development of a political culture in which there is a highly positivistic approach to risk management, which cannot identify individuals at risk but only the probability of certain outcomes occurring within particular social categories (see also Feeley and Simon 1992, and their discussion of the new penology). As France and Utting point out, although this approach has been used in a number of fields to identify statistical 'predictors', 'these risk factors do not *predict* future behaviour in the commonly accepted sense' (2005: 79). Despite this, this culture of 'riskfactorology' (France forthcoming) is driving policies (e.g. *Sure Start* and *On Track*) and political structures (e.g. the Children's Fund, the Children and Young People's Unit and now the Children, Young People and Families Directorate at the DfES) that seek to 'manage' the risks posed to society by certain social groups, such as offenders and children (and in particular that symbolically most potent of all groups, children who offend), on the grounds of prevention.

Herein are the key components of the changing cultural politics of contemporary British childhood for, as Freeman has observed, 'prevention in these terms is a moral and political project whose definition is shaped by the prevailing cultural context in which it is considered' (Freeman 1999, cited in France and Utting 2005). In the context of the prevailing 'cultural politics of childhood', the risk and protection paradigm is integral to the government's commitment to developing an epidemiology of social problems by, in effect, 'pursuing a public health model to prevent problems at community level' (France and Utting 2005: 80) as part of its continuing but implicit commitment to the precepts of communitarianism and the Third Way.

As part of this project, ECM identifies the need to change professional and cultural barriers to information-sharing, which is central to the development of such an epidemiological approach. By way of illustration, it cites recent government guidance (*What to Do if You're Worried a Child is Being Abused*) which 'made it clear that professionals must consider the risk of not sharing information about children with other professionals, alongside concerns about respecting a child or family's right to privacy' (para. 4.8) Once again, this evidences the use of arguments that support a rationale for intervention in the name of the prevention of risk, developed in the very particular context of child abuse and protection, to justify much broader agenda for the social control of children and young people.

As France and Utting note, a number of writers 'warn that there are real dangers that the '"risk factor paradigm" can be used for anti-libertarian purposes by the state ... [and] that "high risk" populations ... may be subject to more intensive monitoring and control by the state' (2005: 81). It is interesting to note, therefore, that in a recent case (heard 20 July 2005), the High Court ruled in favour of a 15-year-old boy, who sought to challenge new police powers to detain and forcibly return home any child venturing into a designated curfew zone after 9 pm. After the hearing, in which this aspect of the Anti-Social Behaviour Act 2003 was ruled to be unlawful, the boy commented: 'Of course I have no problem with being stopped by the police if I've done something wrong. But they shouldn't be allowed to treat me like a criminal just because I'm under 16' (*The Independent*, 21 July 2005).

It is perhaps more interesting to note that the government immediately declared its intention to challenge the ruling in the Court of Appeal.

Conclusion

In a political environment such as this, the identification and allocation of 'risk' becomes a mechanism to give authority to the state to intervene in the lives of groups who are deemed to be 'dangerous', such as children. It comes as no surprise, therefore, that, as our discussion of *Every Child Matters* illustrates, such developments are taking place in the context of a raft of policies aimed at controlling children and their childhoods. Moreover, this is being pursued by a government that, as we have noted, has recently been criticized by the Council of Europe's Human Rights Commissioner (Gil Robles 2004) for its record on human rights and its illiberal policies for tackling a range of issues, including anti-social behaviour, policies that, the report warns, are criminalizing children.

Douglas writes that 'a community can take a bold public policy decision in favour of risk-seeking if it is strong enough to protect the decision-makers from blame' (1986: 61). It remains to be seen whether the government has the courage to do this. To lift the veil of protective control that surrounds risk and children, and to allow children to be individuals and to take on responsibility for the choices that they make, would seem to be too risky a venture when the state, in order to safeguard its 'future', is working increasingly in its present to demonize and thereby control children and childhood.

The moral panic that has been generated around childhood needs to be understood in this context for, as Cohen argues, at a more fundamental level

> a theory of moral panics, moral enterprise or moral indignation needs to relate such reactions to conflicts of interests – at community and societal levels – and the presence of power differentials which leave some groups vulnerable to such attacks. The manipulation of appropriate symbols – the process which sustains moral campaigns, panics and crusades – is made much easier when the object of attack is both highly visible and structurally weak.
>
> (1973: 198)

There can be little doubt that a moral crusade is being conducted by the government against the 'yob culture' and its symbols, alongside a clear sense of growing moral outrage at the lack of respect that some young people are seen to have for both for their elders and the authority they seek to wield. Indeed, it might be argued that such a crusade constitutes a key component of its aim to revitalize civic society. In this context, there is certainly a conflict of interests between adults on the one hand, and children and young people on the other, over issues such as the use of public space and of leisure time. It is also clear that the power differentials between adults and young people are considerable and that they are highly visible, whether on street corners and wearing hoodies or not, and structurally weak. Children are, therefore, as Cohen suggests, particularly vulnerable to such attacks.

Our analysis of the cultural politics of childhood in late modern Britain suggests that although our understanding of the nature of childhood has increased in recent decades and the rhetoric of children's participation trips easily off the tongues of politicians, the position of children has not improved significantly. The current moral panic is not just about a particular group of children and it is not just about crime and anti-social behaviour: rather, we suggest, it is about childhood as a category and all of its aspects, hence the strategy[4] that is emerging around the pursuit of the policies adumbrated in *Every Child Matters*. By amplifying (or not trying to defuse) this moral panic, the government is able to pursue the policies that provide the means by which children can be prevented from becoming too powerful (through the exercise of their individual rights and agency) and through which there can therefore be a re-inscription of authority through the stronger definition and regulation of childhood.

Governments stay in power by being strong, identifying risks and providing a strong response to and protection from those risks, be they terrorists or unruly children: hence the moral panic about childhood and the policy/legal measures taken in response to it. As part of this response, the government wants to enhance choice for adults but not for children. This is a means of rebalancing the power between adults and children and ensuring that adults can construct and therefore control not only present childhoods, but also future adulthoods. As a consequence of the sequestration of childhood by the state, *Every Child Matters* seems set to usher in an era in which childhood and children are ever more closely regulated, and in which the exercise of choice by children is likely to bring them increasingly into conflict with those who would deny their individuality in the name of protection and defending the child's best interests. Our concern, expressed several years ago (James and James 2001), that the net might be tightening around children and childhood seems fully justified.

Notes

1   The guidelines were criticized by Sir Michael Bichard, who chaired the inquiry, because they were not in line with his recommendation that social workers should report cases of adults having sexual relationships with under-18s to the police. In the same week, the charity Action on Rights for Children lodged a complaint with the Information Commissioner claiming that the guidelines breach the Data Protection Act 1998 (*Community Care*, 30 June–6 July 2005, 1579: 11).

2   http://www.everychildmatters.gov.uk/publications/?asset=document&id= 15513, updated 21 July 2005, accessed 21 July 2005.

3   Children were able to answer more than one question, so the percentages do not necessarily add up to 100.

4   It is important to recognize that this is, indeed, a strategy rather than a loosely related series of policy initiatives. The five outcomes for children and young people are given legal force by the Children Act 2004, whilst *Every Child Matters: Change for Children* (DfES 2004a) has spawned a series of closely related policy documents (DfES 2004c, 2004d, 2004e and 2004f). As the DfES states, their agenda for reform is nothing less than 'a ten-year programme to stimulate long-term and sustained improvement in children's health and well-being (DfES, 2004a: para. 1.5).

References

Barratt, S. (2005) Hoodies Ban Disguises a Bigger Problem. *Young People Now* 283: 15.

Beck, U. (1992) *Risk Society: Towards a New Modernity*. London: Sage.

Bichard Inquiry Report (2004) House of Commons. HC653: London.

Chief Secretary to the Treasury (2003) *Every Child Matters*, Cm 5860. London: TSO.

Children and Young People's Unit (2001a) *Learning to Listen: Core Principles for the Involvement of Children and Young People*. London: Department for Education and Skills.

Children and Young People's Unit (2001b) *Building a Strategy for Children and Young People: Consultation Document*. London: C&YPU.

Cohen, S. (1973) *Folk Devils and Moral Panics*. St Albans: Paladin.

Combe, V. (2002) *Up for it: Getting Young People Involved in Local Government*. Leicester: JRF/National Youth Agency.

Department for Education and Skills (2003) *Every Child Matters: What Do You Think?* London: DfES.

Department for Education and Skills (2004a) *Every Child Matters: Change for Children*. London: DfES.

Department for Education and Skills (2004b) *Every Child Matters ... and Every Young Person: What You Said ... and What We're Going to Do*. London: DfES.

Department for Education and Skills (2004c) *Every Child Matters: Change for Children in Social Care*. London: DfES.

Department for Education and Skills (2004d) *Every Child Matters: Change for Children in the Criminal Justice System*. London: DfES.

Department for Education and Skills (2004e) *Every Child Matters: Change for Children in Health Services*. DfES: London.

Department for Education and Skills (2004f) *Every Child Matters: Change for Children in Schools*. London: DfES.

Douglas, M. (1986) *Acceptability According to the Social Sciences*. London: Routledge & Kegan Paul.

Etzioni, A. (1996) The Responsive Community: A Communitarian Perspective. *American Sociological Review* 61: 1–11.

Ewick, P. and Silbey, S. (1998) *The Common Place of Law*. London: University of Chicago Press.

Feeley, M. and Simon, J. (1992) The New Penology: Notes on the Emerging Strategy of Corrections and its Implications. *Criminology* 30(4): 449–74.

France, A. (forthcoming) 'Riskfactorology and the Youth Question'.

France, A. and Utting, D. (2005) The Paradigm of 'Risk and Protection-Focused Prevention' and its Impact on Services for Children and Families. *Children and Society* 19(2): 77–90.

Freeman, R. (1992) The Idea of Prevention: A Critical Review. In Scott, S., Williams, G., Platt, S. and Thomas, H. (eds.), *Private Risks and Public Dangers*. Aldershot: Avebury.

Gil Robles, A. (2004) *Report by Mr Alvaro Gil Robles, Commissioner for Human Rights, on his visit to the United Kingdom, 4th–12th November 2004*, CommDH (2005)6. Strasbourg.

Home Office (2003) *Respect and Responsibility – Taking a Stand Against Anti-Social Behaviour*, Cm 5778. London: TSO.

James, A. L. and James, A. (2001) Tightening the Net: Children, Community and Control. *British Journal of Sociology* 52(2): 211–28.

James A. and James A. L. (2004) *Constructing Childhood: Theory, Policy and Social Practice.* London: Palgrave Macmillan.

James, A. and Prout, A. (eds.) (1990) *Constructing and Reconstructing Childhood.* Lewes: Falmer Press.

James, A. L., James, A. and NcNamee, S. (2004a) Turn Down the Volume? Not Hearing Children in Family Proceedings. *Child and Family Law Quarterly* 16(2): 189–203.

James, A. L., James, A. and NcNamee, S. (2004b) Family Law and the Construction of Childhood in England and Wales. In Goddard, J., James, A. and McNamee, S. (eds.), *The Politics of Childhood: International Perspectives, Contemporary Developments.* London: Palgrave Macmillan.

Kirby, P., Lanyon, C., Cronin, K. and Sinclair, R. (2003) *Building a Culture of Participation.* London: Department for Education and Skills/National Children's Bureau.

London Child Protection Committee (2005) *Working with Sexually Active Young People under the age of 18 – a Pan-London Protocol*, April. London: LCPC.

Masson, J. (2005) Emergency Intervention to Protect Children: Using and Avoiding Legal Controls. *Child and Family Law Quarterly* 17(1): 75–96.

Mayall, B. (2002) *Towards a Sociology of Childhood.* Buckingham: Open University Press.

Parton, N. (2005) *Safeguarding Childhood: Early Intervention and Surveillance in a Late Modern Society.* London: Palgrave Macmillan.

Scott, S. (2000) The Impact of Risk and Parental Anxiety on the Everyday Worlds of Children. *Children 5–16.* Research Briefing, no. 19. Swindon: Economic and Social Science Research Council.

Scott, S., Jackson, S. and Backett-Milburn, K. (1998) Swings and Roundabouts: Risk, Anxiety and the Everyday Worlds of Children. *Sociology* 32(4): 689–705.

Taylor-Gooby, P. and Zin, J. (2005) Current Directions in Risk Research: Reinvigorating the Social. *Working Paper 4*, SCARR: University of Kent.

Wade, H., Lawton, A. and Stevenson, M. (2001) *Hear by Right: Setting Standards for the Active Involvement of Young People in Local Democracy.* London and Leicester: Local Government Association/National Youth Agency.

Wyness, M. (2001) Children, Citizenship and Political Participation: English Case Studies of Young People's Councils. Paper presented at the Children in their Places conference, Brunel University, 21 June.

7

Institutional Upbringing: A Discussion of the Politics of Childhood in Contemporary Denmark

Eva Gulløv

During the last 150 years in most European societies, growing numbers of professionals have defined themselves by reference to children, drawing attention, amongst other things, to children's needs for care and education for the sake of both the individual child and society. Political concerns for children have changed accordingly as childhood has been redefined – depending on the political standpoint – as an investment in cultural and social coherence, economic development and innovation, or national security and peace. Universal institutions, such as schools and other educational facilities, day-care and health services, have been established to prepare new generations for societal challenges. Thus, with the development of modern states, the raising of children has been more and more professionalized and subject to state responsibility and authority. In this process childhood and childcare institutions have become politicized, as objects of intense discussion concerning investment and societal outcomes.

This is particularly true in Denmark where state involvement in the making of a good childhood is pronounced, not least with regard to pre-school children. The investment in public day-care institutions for pre-school children is much higher than most other countries in Europe (Bennett 2005), as is the number of children enrolled, and a growing number of professionals are employed to take care of and educate children, since the majority of pre-schoolers spend their day in childcare institutions. Thus, public care takes a high political priority and day-care institutions for children have become an integral part of society, accounting for an increasing proportion of municipal budgets (Borchorst 2000: 56).

In this chapter, I will discuss the role of the state in the making of a 'good' Danish childhood. I will do so by analysing day-care institutions as they represent state engagement and regulation, where specific notions of children, childhood and proper development are articulated. I will argue that childhood is defined through public policies, practices and ideologies and in this process, these institutions play a fundamental role. As official sites of public childcare, they greatly influence understandings of children's needs: the professional supervision and input they provide stand as a guarantee for sound child development and these institutions thus appear to be in the best interests of the child.

Characteristically, contemporary day-care institutions in Denmark, in their legal framework[1] and everyday regime, stress the notion of the child as an active and self-managing human being. In accordance with Article 12 of the United Nations Convention on the Rights of the Child (UNCRC) it is of prime importance that children are able to influence the manner and timing of their own activities, and participation in decision-making and everyday planning appear central to ideological visions of a democratic upbringing. However, the ways in which participation is understood differ among different groups, as do educational ideas of the best interests of the child. The emphasis the state places on children as competent participants, combined with an ideological concern with being Danish, have resulted in a strong focus on language abilities. Fluency in Danish has become a mark of a child's ability to participate in democratic decision-making and is thus regarded as an important vehicle for ensuring a 'good childhood'. As I will show, therefore, the 'participating child' is defined in accordance with dominant perceptions of social norms and proper language skills, which means that institutional staff do not perceive all children as capable of living up to these ideals of participation. Consequently, not all children are expected to be able to decide for themselves.

Drawing on findings from ethnographic research on ethnic minority children in two Danish day-care institutions,[2] I begin with a discussion of how childcare institutions are empowered with the right to define and control normality and the correct way of behaving. The analysis is based on seven months' ethnographic fieldwork in two pre-school institutions and their intake area. Participant observation, interviews (both formal and informal) with children, parents, pre-school teachers as well as with local authorities, provided the data.

Based on these findings, in this chapter I aim to show how institutions come to define the best interests of the child and proper childhood in accordance with current policies aimed at reinventing national culture, exemplified by legislation requiring testing of Danish language fluency levels among pre-school minority children. Testing language skills marks and defines distinctions that reinforce images of deviance that, in turn, legitimize initiatives to enrol children, specifically minority children, in childcare institutions. The testing of language can be seen as a way to define the individual needs of children in accordance with the overall demands of the state, singling out competence in Danish as an area for special educational intervention for the sake of the individual child as well as the state.

In order to understand political efforts to institutionalize childhood and control how children are brought up, it is necessary to emphasize that children are simultaneously individual subjects, with their own perspectives, interpretations and intentions, as well as being political subjects and cultural symbols, invested with different meanings by social agents in various positions. Thus, children are symbols of the caring society and a desirable future, symbols to invest in and with. The politics of childhood, including decisions made on behalf of children that organize and frame their lives, concern not just specific children but children in general, who are seen as symbolic expressions of normal development and life trajectories, social coherence, proper citizenship and visions for the future. Such ideas are constant elements in professional negotiations of what children should be like, what they can and must do and learn, and what counts as a normal childhood. To examine further the social mechanisms of political processes regarding children in Denmark, I will begin by describing the role of day-care institutions for children in contemporary society.

Early care institutions in Denmark

Early childcare in Denmark is an integral part of the institutional foundations of society. Public authorities provide childcare for children from six months to seven years of age, when compulsory education begins. The Ministry for Family and Consumer Affairs administers a system of non-obligatory, early childhood programmes, which includes *vuggestuer* – nurseries that serve children from six months to three years – and *børnehaver* – kindergartens for children between the ages of three and six or seven. These day-care institutions are publicly funded, albeit through different providers.

Municipalities regulate and fund institutions, most of which are public, but private non-profit institutions receive public funding as well (from local taxes and central governmental grants) covering approximately 67–70 per cent of expenditure, as long as they comply with regulations and standards set by local authorities (OECD 2001: 161). Fees paid by parents cover the rest – approximately 30 per cent. Over the last 30 years, the number of pre-school children enrolled in the Danish day-care system has greatly expanded: 64 per cent of all children between the age of one and three, and 91 per cent of all children between three and five (compared to 34 per cent in 1975) are enrolled in day-care (OECD 2000: 25). Almost all children are enrolled full-time, although in practice attendance varies between 5 and 11 hours a day (Winther 1999: 7). As a result, day-care institutions are a fundamental part of the lives of almost all pre-school children in Denmark.

The Danish model of childcare differs from that in most other European countries, as the market and especially the family play less influential roles in the care of pre-school children (Borchorst 2000: 55). This may be ascribed to the country's relatively long history of out-of-family care; institutional expansion began as early as the 1960s, correlating with a situation of almost full employment. Unlike most other countries, Denmark's increasing need for labour was met by women rather than by large-scale immigration, and by 1970, about half of all women of working age had entered the labour market (Borchorst 2000: 60–1).[3] The great expansion of childcare institutions during the 1960s and 1970s allowed women to fill the gap in the labour force. During this period, the status of the day-care sector changed as it became of general societal concern as part of the expanding welfare state (Kampmann 2004: 132).

Ever since the watershed law on child welfare in 1964, which turned day-care into a universal provision, the state has subsidized childcare institutions to provide pedagogically sound opportunities for all children, regardless of their parents' income. Institutions provide care free of charge for children from low-income families, whilst everybody else pays graduated, means-tested fees (up to a certain level). Thus, all families in Denmark have the option of having their young children looked after during the day by professionals. The high percentage of children enrolled in publicly subsidized day-care confirms the success of this arrangement. Mirja Satka and Gudny Björk Eydal have noted that in all of the Nordic countries, this policy is based on the strong belief that the welfare state can redress social wrongs and create equality among citizens (2004: 41).

Concurrent with the expanding day-care enrolment of pre-school children, however, new kinds of arguments concerning institutions are entering public debates. Thus, for example, Satka and Eydal argue that, by the 1990s, public day-care had come to be regarded as a child's right rather than a practical arrangement for parents (Satka and Eydal, 2004: 40–1). Concerns, common around 1970, about whether or not it was better for small children to be at home rather than in public care were, by the end of 1980s, no longer part of the mainstream debate (Jerlang and Jerlang 1996: 226–30). Instead, discourses were primarily concerned with what kinds of stimulation day-care should offer. As Jan Kampmann has argued:

> The day-care institution has become such an incorporated part of children's ordinary conditions that institutional socialization is seen as essential to a 'normal socialization' of children. This new type of 'normalization' means that it also becomes a more central state function to be actively involved in the definition of the socialization qualities of this public institution. Currently this is shown in a Danish context i.e. in the form of a considerable increased state and municipal interest in the development of national (or municipal) curricula for kindergartens.
>
> (2004: 138)

The day-care institution thus stands as society's guarantee that children will be brought up properly from the very first year of life. Whereas the debates 30 years ago concerned possible emotional distress brought on by institutionalization, often by reference to Bowlby's attachment theory, contemporary discourses reflect concerns about parental over-protection and the social under-stimulation of small children who are not in public care. As a consequence, day-care has become so much a part of the normal trajectory of the child that being at home is interpreted as potentially damaging (Gulløv 2003: 30). In Kampmann's words:

> While day-care institutions as mentioned were regarded as a 'supplement' to the upbringing in the home of the family in the 1970s, it is now clear that the socialization functions of the institutions are seen to a much greater extent as connected with the child's basic individuation process, and thereby in a more far-reaching sense in the construction of the modern child.
>
> (2004: 138)

This is particularly evident in legal definitions of the purpose of day-care as stated in the Social Services Act 2005, s. 8, which defines the needs and requirements of each child as the main focus of child-care institutions. In accordance with Article 12 of the UNCRC, it further stresses that day-care institutions are obliged to support the learning and development of each child with a special focus on developing independent children, who can take responsibility for their own lives in collaboration with others (Social Services Act, LBK nr 280, 05/04/2005). Key words in the Act are openness, tolerance and respect for others, all aspects to be considered when teaching a child to cope on its own. Creating active children, who participate in daily institutional activities and thereby contribute to their own social, cognitive and motor development, appears to be the statutory objective of contemporary childcare pedagogy. Thus, day-care is not regarded as secondary or supplementary to the home, but as an integral and necessary part of the development of every child. The day-care institution is thus a prerequisite for individuation processes, for social integration and societal coherence and for the social formation of future citizens. In some important respects, therefore, day-care institutions have taken over the task, previously the responsibility of families, of bringing up children and teaching them how to manage on their own in accordance with collectively defined behavioural norms. On the whole, institutions must endeavour to create autonomous and responsible individuals, prevent social failure and ensure homogeneity by bringing up children in accordance with dominant norms of behaviour, social responsibility and independence.

Looking in more detail at daily day-care practices, it is, however, possible to identify variations in the way children are treated, variations related not only to individual characteristics but, as Palludan (2005) has noted, also to more general aspects of class, gender and ethnicity. Day-care institutions may provide the means to individuate children but, as I will argue, staff do not consider *all* children capable of managing by themselves. With regard to children whose behaviour differs from expected and acceptable standards, institutional objectives shift – from supporting the development of 'the self-managing being' to regulating the behaviour of the 'person to become', in order to prevent any potentially negative trajectories. Support and regulation reflect the dilemma of institutional upbringing, where the desire to produce a sound democratic environment for *all* children clashes with the need to teach *some* children to express themselves and behave in ways that are socially acceptable.

Supporting and regulating thus stand as two co-existing pedagogical practices but, when carefully analysed in practice, they tend to be used in relation to different types of children. Whereas democratic engagement primarily concerns middle-class children who speak Danish fluently, regulating practices are more commonly used with lower-class children who are less articulate, particularly ethnic minority children whose parents are not in the labour market. As illustrated in the next section, the government as well as the municipality ascribes early childcare institutions a central role in the process of integrating immigrants by imbuing them with the legitimate power to socialize children in accordance with norms of dominant groups in Danish society.

Institutions as civilizing agents

In his discussion of the 'civilizing process' in Western Europe, Norbert Elias points out how the ability to control drives and emotional outbursts is 'cultivated in individuals from an early age as habitual self-restraint by the structure of social life, by the pressure of social institutions in general, and by certain executive organs of society (above all, the family) in particular' (2004 [1939]: 158). In Denmark today day-care institutions, as organs of society, have taken over the task of socializing children in some important respects by teaching them socially acceptable ways of behaving, particularly in cases where professionals doubt the socializing skills of the family. Such doubts seem to be most evident in relation to children of marginalized, non-educated and unemployed immigrant parents, which explains why these children are given priority access to day-care as early as possible.

Institutions are political mechanisms, regulated by law and instructed through political documents and debates. They are also formed and informed by social practices, through the activities of employees, municipal officials and institutional staff in their daily work in professional upbringing. As official sites of upbringing, institutions represent dominant perceptions of normality, sociality and visions for the future of society. Childhood in Denmark therefore reflects the role of institutions in negotiating and organizing children's lives, interpreting and defining norms for a proper childhood and ways of being a child, and thus their penetration into the lives of every child. This was clearly the case in the municipality where the fieldwork was carried out.

Bringing children into institutions was stated as an explicit political goal in interviews with local authorities during the fieldwork. Several officials were asked to describe the political visions for the day-care

institutions of the municipality, and enrolling children of minority ethnicity in public day-care appeared to have high political priority. The
leader of the municipality's Family Department emphasized the great
efforts being made to enrol such children in pre-school institutions,
into what she termed 'the official socializing system'. She described
how the municipality had established procedures to check automatically the ages of children in every family and, when the children reach
day-care age, to write to the families informing them of the different
institutional care and opportunities available in their district.

Health visitors, who visit all families with babies and toddlers regularly, are given the role of informing ethnic minority families of the benefits of enrolling their children in day-care, where they will have daily
contact with other children and learn to speak Danish properly.
Municipal officials are sent to families and the district's day-care centres
are also asked to inform families in the neighbourhood of the advantages of public day-care for their children. Through such efforts, nearly
85 per cent of the district's ethnic minority children were enrolled in
public child-care, and this was seen as a success.[4]

When asked why it was so important to have minority children
enrolled in 'the system', the official answered that it is meant to be supportive of the families, who 'of course, have an interest in improving the
language skills of their children'. Day-care institutions, she continued,
improve their skills in spoken Danish and, more importantly, familiarize
the children with common norms of social interaction with other people, norms they will be expected to know and practise later. The aim of
the pre-school institution is, she stated, to teach children appropriate
ways of behaving, of managing themselves and of being co-operative
and considerate towards others. Thus, language stimulation is only one
part of the municipality's desire to enrol ethnic minority children in
public day-care: from an official perspective, day-care provides normative social training that minority children do not necessarily receive at
home, training that should be undergone prior to the more intellectual
demands placed on them in schools. She stressed that knowing how to
relate to other people and behave according to group norms are by far
the most important educational outcomes of day-care and that the earlier children are enrolled, the fewer problems there are later.

The official responsible for integration within the municipality
echoed and supported these views. She anticipated that starting public
socialization at an earlier age than previously might actually prevent at
least some of the problems currently being experienced by the municipality with minority teenagers. She added that it was important to teach

immigrant children Danish traditions, such as celebrating Christmas and Easter, as well as other communal seasonal activities. From this perspective, institutions play a key role in teaching children behavioural norms and in transmitting national traditions that comprise and construct a collective system of values and reference points.

These official accounts encapsulate the role of public pre-school day-care institutions as civilizing fora. Support and regulation are tightly interconnected, since what represents the best interests of a child is politically defined. In line with the aims of these institutions, municipal objectives promote the social development of children, cultural familiarity and language skills (Social Services Act, LBK nr 280, 05/04/2005; Vejledning 2001; Integration af tosprogede småbørn) – in short, cultural hegemony. This in itself is not remarkable, since aspects of socialization are an inevitable part of the aims of any social institution. Systems of tutelage build on moral regulation, with the aim of cultivating successive generations in line with dominant understandings of traditions, values and social norms.

The statements referred to here, however, go further by giving the impression that children left in the care of their families are not necessarily in the right hands. In a radical change from earlier views on public day-care, young children who stay at home now seem to be outsiders, particularly if their parents are immigrants or refugees, uneducated, unemployed and do not speak Danish fluently. The official socializing system in Denmark is organized to teach children to 'be social'[5] in appropriate ways. The responsibility for their upbringing is therefore, at least in part, transferred to institutional settings and children not enrolled are considered to be at risk of not learning how to behave in socially sanctioned ways. The municipality's efforts to enrol ethnic minority children in day-care bear witness to the socializing power attributed to the public day-care system and the societal interests that are seen to be at stake with regard to children.

Regulating language – an example of a social policy

Being enrolled in day-care, however, is not sufficient in itself. When looking more carefully at the practices in the institutional setting, one sees a range of efforts to regulate children's behaviour. Language testing is one specific example. There is great political focus on language in day-care, as fluency in Danish is seen as a prerequisite for positive educational outcomes in school. The Ministry of Education has published a number of guidelines concerning the early language stimulation of bilingual children. One recommendation is to have a specialist visit families shortly after childbirth, to inform them about the language requirements and other challenges the child will encounter in Danish society, especially in the educational system (Ministry of Education 2000). Since 1998, it has been part of the law on compulsory schooling that immigrant children whose parents do not have Danish as their mother tongue have to be offered support to learn Danish in day-care. Children who do not attend public day-care must be enrolled in special language classes from the age of three (Law Regarding Strengthened Integration of Children of Refugees and Immigrants, LBK 486§4a). Thus, language stimulation provision for immigrant children is now mandatory and day-care institutions are one of the means by which local authorities can comply with this political priority.

The municipality in question – as in others – requires annual testing of the linguistic abilities of every bilingual child over three years of age. The term 'bilingual' refers to children who are regularly confronted with two different languages, typically because the home language is different from the official language of the host society (see Holmen and Normann Jørgensen 1993: 53; Gitz-Johansen 2004: 203–7 for a more critical discussion of the term). As discussed in more detail elsewhere, municipal authorities have issued a questionnaire to help ensure standardized testing of the children (Bundgaard and Gulløv forthcoming). In practice, the questionnaire is extensive, evaluating not just the individual child's linguistic performance and comprehension, but also his or her social and cognitive skills, as well as motor co-ordination and emotional maturity. These assessments are based on staff observation and are recorded along with more general information about the status and situation of the child and family. Institutional staff are instructed to complete the questionnaire, show it to the parents, who are expected to sign it but may refuse to do so, and then return it to the municipal authorities who, once a year, read through all the approximately 150 questionnaires submitted by the different institutions in the district.

The official responsible for these points out that their purpose is primarily to find out which institutions should be given more resources. In addition to the main funding, extra resources can be obtained if they are needed to deal with problems with specific children. Although the questionnaire is intended to provide a detailed evaluation of ethnic minority children, it also functions as an application form. When asked whether the municipality used the questionnaires to obtain a general overview of the district's minority children, the official stressed that it is primarily used for allocating resources and secondarily for estimating how many children will need special education upon entering school. Children who, according to the tests, do not speak Danish fluently enough are channelled into special reception classes.

These questionnaires are often the subject of intense negotiations between parents and staff, and to some degree between staff and local authorities (see also Bundgaard and Gulløv forthcoming). In general, minority parents complain that only their children and non-ethnic Danish children are tested. In addition, they express uncertainty and scepticism regarding the purpose of the tests and why municipality officials need to know and record tests of their children's motor development, as well as their emotional, cognitive and social skills. Some parents suspect that the real purpose is to separate their children from ethnic Danish children, since the questionnaires often demonstrate the need for special education, and that records are kept by the municipality to determine which children should be sent to special classes, fearing that such records represent a systematic way of segregating children. Others worry that the tests mark and stigmatize their children within the day-care centre itself. Staff try to convince them that the questionnaires serve only as vehicles for distributing resources, but most of the parents interviewed said that they were not convinced and do not find this a satisfactory explanation for why their children are tested, not just on their language ability, but also on other aspects like motor development.

Thus the process of documenting children's language reveals conflicting interests. Some parents refuse to sign the questionnaire; some even begin to cry when staff go over it with them. Others simply resign themselves to the process and sign, while a small group has no objection to signing. Confronting parents with the results is difficult and raises many emotions. Some staff feel so uncomfortable that they try to avoid such meetings and leave the task to their colleagues. The discomfort expressed by the most sceptical parents may be interpreted as a form of protest against the process itself as well as the fact that staff are classifying their children, and as a fruitless attempt to control the classification. Well aware of the unequal power in this situation, the most vocal parents fear that marking their children has consequences they cannot foresee: the fact that only minority children are tested makes them suspect discrimination. One young Muslim mother who spoke fluent Danish suggested, while pointing at her head: 'I don't think my boy would have been tested if I wasn't wearing the scarf.'

The example of evaluation shows how conflicting interests are at stake when it comes to the power to define children and their problems. The parents' reactions in this case may be seen as a protest against the definitions made, first by municipal officials and then by the teachers who are responsible for observing and testing the children. Negotiations, objections and refusing to sign the evaluation represent a struggle over the right to define children's needs but also over who has legitimate authority to bring up children, to intervene in their lives and to deal with any problems they may have. Parental authority has been challenged by the general institutionalization of childhood which requires sharing the responsibility of children's upbringing with professionals (and bureaucrats). Day-care professionals have the right and duty to evaluate children's competencies and development and, where there are serious problems or suspicions of neglect, they must, by law, intervene. In the worst cases, this may lead to the removal of children from their homes. Several of the parents interviewed interpreted the observations and questionnaires as a mistrust of their ability to bring up their children properly and they feared that they were losing control over their children's upbringing.

At this micro level, the language evaluation policy reveals conflicting interests and the monopoly of power that allows the municipality to disregard parental protests and authorizes staff to evaluate children in detail. Parents may complain and refuse to sign, but the questionnaire will nevertheless be returned to local authorities, stored and used in making local departmental decisions that will have consequences for both the children and their families. Struggles to challenge the legitimacy of these evaluations may be seen as a more general struggle over the right to control how children are brought up. Parents and staff, officials and politicians, take different positions and exercise different degrees of influence on the framework of childhood, and thus on children's lives.

The example of language evaluation presented here reveals an unequal distribution of influence and control over the classifications and trajectories of children, and the powerlessness felt by some parents as they confront the authority behind institutional practices. As civilizing agents, public day-care institutions are given the legitimacy to articulate children's best interests and to define proper childhood. In so far as early day-care is not obligatory, parents may withdraw their children and some do, either keeping the children at home or sending them to private institutions, thus precluding them from 'the official socializing system'. However, the majority accept the institutional project and send their children to day-care.

Problem children as a resource

This policy example illustrates that several interests intersect when problems are pointed out. On the one hand, the municipality's goal is to increase Danish language fluency among minority children before they enter school. From that perspective, language tests and evaluations are regarded as a means to educational action, to improve the linguistic competencies of minority children. On the other hand, the municipality allocates resources in accordance with the number of children with language problems in any one day-care centre. At this particular moment, with funding for day-care being routinely cut, staff are, of course, keen to obtain extra resources. As a category, the presence of 'problematic bilingual children' leads to the allocation of additional public funds and thus the identification of such children is often rewarded with extra resources. In an interview, the leader of one of the district's more economically affluent institutions speculated: 'We have more problematic children here than in any other institution in the district – I wonder how it can be?' Her puzzlement may be interpreted as a reflection of her capacity to describe problems in an adequate, recognized way. It also raises the question of whether being 'problematic' is a 'real' characteristic of the children in day-care or whether it is an element of an institutional logic that converts the category of problematic children into economic capital.

The objective of day-care institutions is to ensure each child's cultural, social and personal competencies is in line with dominant perceptions of how to behave and how to develop. This objective calls for assessments of normal and abnormal development in different areas, with specific pedagogical consequences whenever a deviation from the norm is highlighted. However, the logic of distributing day-care resources in accordance with the number of children with problems has resulted in much more explicit attention being paid to indicators of deviance than would normally be the case. The language test, for example, includes questions concerning each child's emotional, cognitive, motor, linguistic and social skills, thus detailing a range of issues and characteristics requiring staff attention. The questionnaire supposedly reflects issues defined as those most important for child development but, as we have seen, these are often also issues of greatest significance when it comes to applying for further resources.

Although it does not figure as a separate category, importance is also indirectly attached to a child's ability to 'manage oneself' in accordance with the norms of the day-care setting (cf. Ellegård 2004; Kampmann

2004). Analysis of staff comments on the questionnaires reveal that staff note when a child depends on adults' initiatives, does not join in activities with other children or is judged to have difficulties in verbal communication – e.g. in stating intentions or verbalizing emotions (Bundgaard and Gulløv 2006; cf. Nilsen, this volume). From this it follows that an unproblematic child is one that expresses its feelings and intentions in Danish, participates in negotiations over activities, and 'manages itself' properly in relation to its peers. The normal child thus participates in group play and activities in recognized ways, which means that the child is able to express clear wishes and intentions in comprehensible Danish.

That public day-care institutions aim to bring up children in accordance with the dominant society's norms is not in itself remarkable; nor is their interest in Danish language fluency, their focus on early language stimulation and on children's capabilities to engage in social interaction. The interesting aspect is their stress on and definition of *problems* – the fact that politics concerning children and childhood are preoccupied with defining and classifying different kinds of problems, diagnosing causes and proposing remedial measures. A very important aspect of the contemporary politics of childhood in Denmark thus appears to be pointing out, as early as possible, which children need help and by what means society should intervene.

Politics works through a complex set of social logics that define priorities and problems, place responsibility and distribute resources. The work of defining problems, distributing means and placing responsibility is present in all kinds of politics, but in this case it has the consequence of constituting a dominant conception of the normal child as one fluent in Danish and able to participate in activities and interactions in linguistically well-orchestrated ways. To participate 'as a child' in a Danish day-care setting requires being able to verbalize intentions and articulate viewpoints in a manner comprehensible to and recognized by the staff. Thus, it is ironic that one of the results of the effort to integrate minority children by enrolling them in the institutional system is the emergence of a definition of normal childhood that does not encompass these children. As a result, the process of allocating additional resources to the very children that the system is so eager to normalize works by identifying them as deviating from the norm.

I have argued that ethnic minority children are at once a resource and a target for Danish day-care institutions. Pointing out acknowledged problems, such as social or linguistic deviance, stresses the need for institutions, for civilizing initiatives, and helps to legitimize the official socializing system. Professionals uphold their legitimacy by indicating problems and proposing solutions, while the process of documenting the fact that problem children exist helps obtain additional resources. Socially legitimated judgements about children justify interventions in their lives by identifying the actions needed to resolve the defined problems. The politics of childhood in this context thus concerns articulating both problems and proper solutions. This practice is particularly evident with regard to well-established areas of public concern such as the integration of children of ethnic minorities. The definition of problems by those in authority leads to the construction of dominant conceptions of childhood and normalcy, the very definitions that critical parents in the above example oppose.

Childhood is defined in social struggles

It is not my intention to dispute the justice of allocating resources to children in need or to indicate that public resources are not properly distributed. Nevertheless, the case presented here illustrates how the different interests of parents, staff and the municipality intersect as a result of the structural logic of allocation procedures. Different interests reflect the range of social positions from which people interpret and define children's best interests. Children are therefore embedded not only in societies with specific historical ideas about childhood and the proper treatment of children, but also in fields[6] of social relations, where agents in different positions try to consolidate their own status and influence. The politics of childhood is thus the outcome of social struggles over the right to define problems and distribute resources, and therefore over the right to define the best interest of the child.

The social world is comprised of relations; it is a configuration of relations between objective positions that define the possibilities and influences of the agents (Bourdieu 1996: 84). In any given social field, influence and power are distributed differentially among such positions, so that various statements and definitions do not have the same impact or importance. Dominant conceptions of childhood reflect the distribution of power and dominance between the positions in the field; it is through the struggles over these positions and their legitimacy that children and childhood are defined. Day-care settings, institutional practices, political attempts to enrol children in kindergarten and mandatory language questionnaires, may all be seen as outcomes of negotiations (institutional, verbal or practical) among agents seeking to sanction their viewpoints and their right to define childhood.

In this sense, perceptions and definitions of childhood and children's best interests are the result of social processes, where some understandings have gained influence over others. Thus, to be raised at home with unemployed immigrant parents is not perceived as appropriate for a child. The outcome of social struggles over influence has turned institutions into political solutions as places for raising children of families not regarded as appropriate. The social construction of childhood is the result of a process of dominance where power relations among different social actors have an important say.

Enrolling children in day-care and testing their emotional, cognitive, social and linguistic skills with regard to a specific standardized scheme may be interpreted as a means of control, and as a political strategy at once legitimized by and legitimizing positions of influence. Defining aspects of children's lives as problematic, deciding on interventions and allocating responsibilities are fundamental aspects of the politics of childhood, and thus form part of the social struggle for legitimate social positions and authority. Institutional settings are important forms of sociality and can be seen as battlefields in the social struggles over the upbringing of children, visions of the future and social positions related to children. The quest for civilization is part of a social game over influence – one which, in the case of contemporary public institutional upbringing, produces a paradoxical result: children are characterized in terms of problems and childhood becomes a highly politicized project.

Day-care institutions in Denmark have a long tradition of emphasizing tolerance and social responsibility in conjunction with the development of the individual child. Democratic values have a key place in public upbringing and the Social Services Act stipulates that children in day-care shall participate and share the responsibility for their own lives (Social Services Act, LBK no. 280, 05/04/2005, section 4, §8; Vejledning om dagtilbud m.v. til børn1998). More recently, this emphasis seems to have been overshadowed by another agenda: in a political climate in which dominant groups, in reaction to global influences, argue for the reinvention of national culture, ethnic minority children are legitimate targets for particular Danish civilizing initiatives. Although it is beyond the scope of this chapter to go into further detail here, this re-invention has manifest consequences for the childcare sector in the form of curriculum change, more emphasis on Danish language skills, quotas for ethnic minority children in various institutions, and revised ways of allocating resources. The politics of childhood reflects the power relations at play among different social groups in society with the result that institutional civilizing programmes are explicitly directed at ethnic minority children.

In this discursive atmosphere, ethnic minority children become 'others', as children and as ethnic outsiders, and as such are considered obvious objects of nationalized institutional upbringing. Thus, analysis of the practices related to ethnic minority children within institutional settings sheds light on the dominant notion of a proper childhood in contemporary society. In general, stress is placed on the 'participating child', who is able to exert an influence on the kind of activities he or she engages in. Children who deviate from expected linguistic and behavioural standards are thought to need more specialized training. Being 'others' in relation to ethnic Danish children means becoming the object of educational interventions, and not being left to 'manage oneself' (Ellegård 2004; Palludan 2005). To sum up, ethnic minority families are pressured into enrolling their children in pre-school institutions, so that in these settings they can experience how to 'be social' in ways considered proper by the groups empowered to decide what this means.

Conclusion

Over recent decades, the raising of pre-school children in Denmark has changed. Whereas this used to be principally a family concern, it has developed into a responsibility shared between families and childcare institutions. In accordance with the general move of mothers and primary caretakers out of the home and into the labour market, pre-school institutions have become an intrinsic part of a normal childhood, simply because no adults are at home during the day to look after the young. In the process, institutions have taken on some of the civilizing duties and rights, including the right to intervene in families who are not bringing up their children according to acceptable norms.

Although parents can reject institutional socialization by withdrawing their children, overall institutions play a central role in the daily lives of children. Although peripheral oppositional voices occasionally argue that the family is the right place for children, the dominant role of institutions is rarely discussed in this social climate. Thus, most children aged 3–6 spend the day in institutions, while children not in care are closely watched by local authorities, especially if their parents are not in the labour market and are not fluent Danish-speakers. This is the situation for some of the ethnic minority families followed in this study. Parents who, for various reasons, are not in the labour pool and therefore do not need day-care are currently contacted by the local authorities who try to persuade them to enrol their children in pre-schools.

Public day-care institutions have an important say in the organization of pre-school children's lives in Denmark. The fact that more than

90 per cent of children aged between 3 and 6 spend their day in out-of-family care makes such institutions an important starting point for an analysis of contemporary childhood. Day-care institutions regulate children's daily lives and, as official sites of public upbringing, greatly influence conceptions of children's needs and development. Childhood is defined through public policies, practices and ideologies – what I have termed the politics of childhood – and in this process, these institutions play a fundamental role.

It has not, however, been my intention to postulate that childhood is undisputed or unequivocal. Rather, I have tried to argue that struggles between social agents – especially various kinds of professionals – result in dominant understandings, expressed in the legal and political initiatives that frame institutional practices. It is, for example, not necessarily the teacher's personal conviction that it is important to test and evaluate minority children on a variety of criteria, but the logic of the dominant belief system makes it necessary to do so, whatever the individual teacher may think. The politics of childhood is an expression of social dominance, of the struggles among various professionals, resulting in dominant definitions of childhood. Institutions reflect the politics of childhood as the dominant notions and visions are implemented in the statutory objectives of pedagogical work. The juridical and political injunctions and definitions therefore clearly and explicitly frame the institutional practices and express dominant notions of proper childhood. Childhood cannot be reduced to structural logic or system definitions, but analysing institutional upbringing is an attempt to indicate the social forces at play in the social construction of childhood.

Notes

1   Day-care institutions are regulated under the Social Services Act, and are formulated in accordance with the principles laid down in the UN Convention on the Rights of the Child.
2   The project was based on seven months' ethnographic fieldwork from August 2002 to February 2003 in two pre-school institutions and their intake area in a suburb of Copenhagen. The fieldwork was conducted with Associate Professor Helle Bundgaard, of the Institute of Anthropology, Copenhagen.
3   In 1994 Denmark had the highest rate of all European Community (EC) countries of working mothers with young children – approximately 79 per cent (Stenvig, Andersen and Laursen 1994).
4   About a quarter of all ethnic minority children in Denmark aged 0–2 years have a place in a day-care facility. In the 3–6 age group about 65 per cent have a place. The percentage for all children in this age group is 90 per cent (OECD Background Report 2000: 39).

5   'Being social' is a widely used expression in the data covering the ability to behave well and show consideration for other people's viewpoints and feelings.

6   With inspiration from the work of Pierre Bourdieu I use the notion of field as a structured space of positions determined by the distribution of different kind of resources. See Bourdieu (1991: 229–31) for a definition of field.

References

Bennett, J. (2005) *Where Does Denmark Stand?* Paris: OECD/BUPL.

Borchorst, A. (2000) Den danske børnepasningsmodel – kontinuitet og forandring. *Arbejderhistorie* 4: 55–69.

Bourdieu, P. (1991) *Language and Symbolic Power*. Cambridge: Polity Press.

Bourdieu, P. (1996) *Symbolsk makt*. Oslo, Pax Forlag A/S.

Bundgaard, H. and Gulløv, E. (2006) Children of Different Categories. Educational Practice and the Production of Difference in Danish Daycare Institutions. *Journal of Ethnic and Migration Studies* 32(1). Brighton: Centre for Migration Studies, University of Sussex.

Bundgaard, H. and Gulløv, E. (forthcoming) Targeting Immigrant Children. Disciplinary Rationales in Danish Pre-schools. In Dyck, N. (ed.), *Exploring Regimes of Discipline*. New York: Berghahn Books.

Elias, N. ([1939] 2004) *The Civilizing Process*. Oxford: Basil Blackwell.

Ellegård, T. (2004) Self-Governance and Incompetence: Teachers' Construction of 'the Competent Child'. In Brembeck, H., Johansson, B. and Kampmann, J. (eds.), *Beyond the Competent Child. Exploring Contemporary Childhoods in the Nordic Welfare Societies*. Roskilde: Roskilde University Press.

Gitz-Johansen, T. (2004) The Incompetent Child: Representations of Ethnic Minority Children. In Brembeck, H., Johansson, B. and Kampmann , J. (eds.), *Beyond the Competent Child. Exploring Contemporary Childhoods in the Nordic Welfare Societies*. Roskilde: Roskilde University Press.

Gulløv, E. (2003) Creating a Natural Place for Children: An Ethnographic Study of Danish Kindergartens. In Fog Olwig, K. and Gulløv, E. (eds.), *Children Places*. London and New York: Routledge.

Holmen, A. and Jørgensen, J. N. (1993) *Tosprogede born i Danmark. En grundbof.* København: Hans Reitzels Folag.

Integration af tosprogede småbørn i dagtilbud, vejen til integration i det danske samfund. Socialministeriet Departementet, 2001.

Jerlang, E. and Jerlang, J. (1996) *Socialisering og habitus*. København: Munksgaard-Rosinante.

Kampmann, J. (2004) Socialization of Childhood: New Opportunities? New Demands? In Brembeck, H., Johansson, B. and Kampmann, J. (eds.), *Beyond the Competent Child. Exploring Contemporary Childhoods in the Nordic Welfare Societies*. Roskilde: Roskilde University Press.

LBK no. 280 af 05/04/2005 – Social Service Act. The Ministry of Social Affairs.

Ministry of Education (2000), Vejledning om sprogstimulerende tilbud for tosprogede børn. http://pub.uvm.dk/2000/tosprog/5.htm.

OECD (2000) *Background Report: Early Childhood Education and Care Policy in Denmark*. Copenhagen: The Ministry of Social Affairs.

OECD (2001) *Starting Strong. Early Childhood Education and Care.* Paris: OECD Publishing.

Palludan, C. (2005) Når børnehaven gør en forskel. PhD dissertation. Copenhagen: Danish University of Education.

Prout, A. and James, A. (eds.) (1997) *Constructing and Reconstructing Childhood: Contemporary Issues in the Sociological Study of Childhood.* London: Falmer Press.

Satka, M. and Eydal, G. B. (2004) The History of Nordic Welfare Policies for Children. In Brembeck, H., Johansson, B.and Kampmann, J. (eds.), *Beyond the Competent Child. Exploring Contemporary Childhoods in the Nordic Welfare Societies.* Roskilde: Roskilde University Press.

Stenvig, B., Andersen, J. and Laursen, L. (1994) Statistics for Work and the Family in Denmark and the EC. In Carlsen, S. and Larsen, J. E. (eds.), *The Equality Dilemma: Reconciling Working Life and Family Life, Viewed in an Equality Perspective.* Copenhagen: Danish Equal Status Council.

Vejledning om dagtilbud m.v. til børn efter lov om social service af 6. marts 1998, Socialministeriet.

Vejledning om ændring af vejledning om dagtilbud m.v. til børn, Socialministeriet, 14. juni 2001.

Winther, Ida W. (1999): *Småbørnsliv i Danmark – anno 2000.* København: Danmarks Pædagogiske Institut.

8
Education and the Cultural Politics of Childhood in Cyprus

Spyros Spyrou

Introduction

Political entities such as nation states must, if they wish to reproduce themselves and maintain control over their subjects, find ways to inculcate in children understandings of the meaning of 'good' and 'proper' citizenship, in order to produce the kind of citizen who will believe in the state's ideological legitimacy and who will work towards serving its interests. The formal education of the young is the primary way by which states seek to inculcate in children those virtues and values that are deemed necessary for becoming a good citizen, a process of social and cultural reproduction that is much more tightly controlled in divided societies such as Cyprus, in which political realities often give rise to specific political and ideological agendas that are promoted through public education.

This chapter is concerned with educational policy and practice at the primary school level in Cyprus and the tensions that arise when ideas of a 'good' childhood and citizenship that are presented to children through educational practices are responded to in different ways by children. This encounter provides us with insights into the ways in which culture, politics and childhood intersect in the contemporary world.

The ethnographic data presented in this chapter come primarily from two periods of fieldwork. The earlier, year-long study (1996–7) examined ethnic identity construction among Greek Cypriot elementary school children in two communities, one urban and one rural. Much of the data came from participant observation in classrooms, school playgrounds and neighbourhoods as well as in-depth interviews with children, parents and teachers. The more recent study was carried out in 2004 and included three months' fieldwork in Greek Cypriot schools attended by Turkish-speaking children, which focused on identifying the educational needs of these children. The data of this study also mainly came from participant observation in schools and interviews with children, teachers, school administrators and government officials.

I first turn to the earlier piece of fieldwork in order to discuss how educational policy and practice shape children's school lives and experiences and how the children themselves respond in their everyday worlds.

The cultural politics of childhood in Cyprus: an ethnographic example

On 15 November 1996, as on every other day of the school year, I arrived early at the school where I was carrying out my fieldwork to make sure I did not miss anything that took place. My research focused on Greek Cypriot children's constructions of ethnic identity and though I was interested as much in the mundane, everyday aspects of the process of identity construction, I knew very well that that day was not like any other day[1] because it was the anniversary of the declaration in 1983 by the Turkish Cypriot authorities of the Turkish Republic of Northern Cyprus (TRNC) as an independent state. Greek Cypriots refer to the TRNC as a pseudo-state, for not only do they not recognize it, no other country (apart from Turkey) recognizes it as a state either.

Every year on 15 November demonstrations are organized by Greek Cypriots to denounce the declaration, and schools often organize their own activities in support of this. The first activity organized by the school I was attending was the creation of a banner by the children bearing slogans against the declaration of the TRNC; one could see children writing 'We don't want the Turks in Cyprus', 'Cyprus is and will remain Greek', 'NO, to the Pseudo-state', 'I want Cyprus to be free', and so on. While the children were making their banner, I saw two boys in the school playground who were in the 1st grade of secondary school and who had graduated from elementary school the previous year. I asked them whether they were going to the demonstration organized by their own school, but they said they would not because there might be 'troubles'.

A few minutes later, I noticed another group of children (two boys and one girl, all of whom also attended the 1st grade of secondary school and were graduates of my field site school) walking past the school. Each of them was holding and waving a Cypriot flag. They told me they were going to demonstrate at Ledra Palace, a landmark on the buffer zone where many demonstrations take place. They told me that while secondary schools were meeting elsewhere, the three of them decided to go to Ledra Palace where it was mainly adults who would be demonstrating. A little later, I saw two of the children from my field school, a 4th grade boy named Stathis who was carrying a big Greek flag on his shoulders and Elena, a 6th grade girl. They joined the three secondary school children and then all left together. As they passed the school, Elena and Stathis broke into a run so their teachers would not see them, since their decision to demonstrate at the Ledra Palace meant that they did not intend going to school that day. Elena, however, made a point of attracting my attention and making sure that I noticed her.

As I discovered later from the teachers, other children did not attend school that day because they (or their parents) feared that it would be dangerous for them to attend the demonstration. One of the teachers told me that a 6th grade boy who had not come to school had actually called other children the day before and tried to discourage them from going to the demonstration because of the risk of violence. The rest of the children proceeded to the Statue of Liberty,[2] however, where the school principal read out the customary message from the Minister of Education; they then recited poems, sang patriotic songs and placed a laurel wreath at the foot of the statue. Their demonstration ended with singing the national anthem. They then returned to school.

The particular incidents I describe here, and my focus in this chapter, are illustrative of what James and James (2004) call the *cultural politics of childhood*, a conceptual area of inquiry in childhood studies which the two authors attempt to theorize by engaging productively with what social scientists have been debating for a number of decades – the tension between structure and agency. For James and James, the cultural politics of childhood is concerned with the processes of continuity and change we see in childhood and with 'both the many and different cultural determinants of childhood and children's behavior, and the political mechanisms and processes by which these are put into practice at any given time' (2004: 4). At the same time, they argue, the cultural politics of childhood takes seriously the role children themselves play in the construction of childhood, irrespective of whether the outcomes of their actions are intended or unintended. In that sense, the cultural politics of childhood is centrally concerned with the implications that particular social constructions of childhood have on children themselves and with the various responses that children have to these constructions and structures which control and constrain them (James and James 2004: 12–13; see also Coles 1986; Stephens 1995).

Ideas of a 'proper' or 'good' childhood require that children become particular kinds of children, 'proper' and 'good' being defined by the state's political and ideological agendas. Children, as members of society, are embedded in these kinds of understandings, which seek to shape them as future citizens. But in reality, ideological prescriptions rarely result in unproblematic adherence and full support. Hence, the tension between officially sanctioned ideas of childhood and children's lived, everyday experiences. What children actually do may end up reproducing these ideas, but it may also help reconstitute them since children, as members of families and other social units, have their own agendas and interests that they might choose to pursue even when these oppose or contradict official notions of 'proper' and 'good' childhood.

Returning to the events surrounding the 15 November anniversary, I suggest that what we see here is the cultural politics of childhood at work. On the one hand, the entire structure and emphasis of the school programme on that day is primarily the outcome of the larger educational policy of the Republic of Cyprus, which seeks to inculcate in the younger generation the need 'to fight for the liberation of their half-occupied homeland'. This necessitates shaping their education in such a way that they can grow up with this aspiration in mind. On the other hand, what really happens on that day is not entirely predictable, simply and precisely because children have agency and sometimes choose to exercise it, even if this happens in relation to the constraints of the school that they happen to attend. What the specific example also illustrates is that children manage to act on their worlds through their own initiative, even in relation to the school setting, which is a tightly adult-controlled context and which largely constrains what a child can be and do. Thus, the fact that some children chose not to attend the demonstration while others chose to attend an alternative one suggests that children (and their parents in the case of the former) did not passively accept the school's programme but rather responded to it. The children who did not attend chose not to do so because they (and their parents) interpreted it as being potentially risky. The children who attended the demonstration at Ledra Palace, however, also responded to the school's programme, but for a very different reason: they wanted to participate in a more dynamic demonstration where they would be able to express their national identities in a new and, for them, more appropriate fashion than the rest of the children would be able to do with the school.

Elena, for example, explained to me later that she preferred to go to the Ledra Palace because she would have the opportunity actually to go to the buffer zone. On their way there, she said, they shouted slogans like 'Cyprus is Greek!' and 'Attilas, Out of Cyprus!' although they also shouted other slogans that she admitted she could not understand. This is how she described what they did at the demonstration:

Elena: First, we threw pepper at the policemen.

Spyros: Why?

Elena: I don't know. Because they would not let us go in [i.e. enter the buffer zone]. They told us that we could not go in – to go through the buffer zone – and because someone [a demonstrator] wanted a lot to go through, he attacked them, and he said to the policemen: '*You* will tell *me* where to go? I will go to my village,' he told them. And there was a quarrel there and things like that. But they were peaceful. Just some fights.

Spyros: Did you want to pass through [the buffer zone] and go [to the other side]?

Elena: Yes.

Spyros: 'Why? The policemen were saying 'No'!

Elena: Eh, I wanted to go and see my mother's village.

As the daughter of refugee parents, attending a demonstration against the pseudo-state was an important event for Elena. Her participation was motivated by her status as a refugee and by her desire to see her mother's occupied village. She hoped that she could do so by attending this alternative and, in many ways, more passionate demonstration, which took place right on the buffer zone, rather than going to the school demonstration which was much more closely monitored by the teachers and relatively predictable. Her defiance of the school and her pursuit of an alternative course of action allowed her to construct and express her identity in a context of her own choosing, from which children of her age were mostly absent. Elena reflected and acted upon her world; she worked around the constraints associated with her status as an elementary school child essentially to increase her social age by participating in a predominantly adult event (see Solberg 1990).

The children who stayed at home because they or their parents feared that it was too risky to take part in the school demonstration similarly resisted the school's agenda. They juxtaposed their own agendas and interests with those of the school and also made their own choices; their decision to stay at home was also expressive of their agency, their ability to reflect and act upon their worlds.[3]

'The best interests of the child' and the dominance of the Cypriot family

The state in Cyprus treats childhood as a category that is subsumed in its entirety under the institution of the family. Following Makrinioti's (1994: 268) argument in relation to more general processes, what we see in Cyprus is children's familialization, whereby childhood becomes fused with or subsumed under the institution of the family to such an extent that to talk about children is really to talk about families. In this way, children's particular needs and interests are defined as coterminous with those of the family; the state only intervenes when the family is seen to be failing to perform its proper role in relation to children. State laws are one clear and powerful way through which this particular discourse on childhood finds expression in Greek Cypriot society.

Consider three of the most important laws concerning children: the Parents and Children Relations Law 1990; the Violence in the Family Law 1994; and the Adoption Law 1995. All three frame children's rights in relation to the family and thus indirectly reinforce the boundaries between childhood and adulthood. At the same time and in line with the UNCRC, these laws stress the importance of taking into account the best interests of the child. Thus, for instance, the Parents and Children Relations Law changed the law, giving responsibility for supporting the child to the father, to the current provision in which both parents are given the right and responsibility for providing for and supporting the child, bearing in mind the best interests of the child. In cases of divorce or separation, the courts decide which parent will gain custody of the child, having taken into account 'the best interests of the child' as well as the child's opinion.

In the educational context, similar declarations, at least in principle, are made to pinpoint how Greek Cypriot society is aligning itself with the globalization of child law and the provisions of the UNCRC, which help reconstitute the notion of childhood at a global scale (James and James 2004: 215). In a circular sent by the directors of primary, secondary and vocational education (12 October 2005), school principals were encouraged to organize celebrations on 20 November, the day of the UN Convention for the Rights of the Child; among other things, the circular notes the importance of giving primacy to the child's interests when decisions affecting the child are made.

Thus although adults and parents in particular have jurisdiction over their families (i.e. they are responsible for the welfare of their children), it is the state that ultimately takes responsibility if parents fail to perform their duties in relation to their children. The state's intervention in the case of Cyprus ranges from giving advice to parents on how to provide proper parenting to removal of the child from the family. In such cases, when the state considers it necessary to protect the child from the family, the Department of Social Welfare Services intervenes. Similarly, in cases of adoption the court appoints an officer from the Department of Social Welfare Services whose task is to make sure that during the court proceedings 'the best interests of the child' are served.

Although the above changes in the law, which undoubtedly bring it more in line with the principles of the UNCRC, are intended to provide for the best interests of the child, it is adults such as parents and Welfare Department officers who are expected to ensure that the decisions made actually provide for the children's best interests. And although some of the laws take into account children's opinions when reaching decisions that affect them, it is adults who ultimately enforce these provisions. As Kouloumou (2004: 637) argues, in Greek Cypriot society, 'cultural values designate adults as experts in decision making even on issues that affect directly children'. It is not surprising, therefore, that one of the concerns expressed by the UN Committee that monitors the implementation of the UNCRC, in their response to the Greek Cypriot report in 1999, was that the state was not doing enough to ensure the participation of children in decision-making processes affecting them, including decisions taking place in the family, in schools and in courts (Report of Cyprus to the UN Committee for the Implementation of The Convention for the Rights of the Child 1999: 105). It is paradoxical therefore that, through this formulation, children's best interests seem to be 'served' without their input on how this can be done. As James and James (2004: 211) have aptly put it: 'As a giver of rights, it [the law] *does* have the potential to acknowledge the child as a social actor, a person with agency, although as a provider of protection, it can also deny that agency.'

The tensions outlined above between the UNCRC's provision for the best interests of the child on the one hand, and the dominant role that the family plays in terms of giving substance to the 'best interests' principle on the other, are illustrative of the larger tensions that come about as a result of the globalization of childhood and its simultaneous continuing shaping by local, cultural forces. Formal education, as a key institution in constructing citizenship, exhibits similar tensions between ideology and praxis and it is to the role of educational policy and practice that I now turn in order to discuss how they help constitute each other.

An education in nationalism

Despite Cyprus's entry into the European Union in 2004, the education of Greek Cypriot children remains highly nationalistic. Although the ethnocentric focus of educational policy and practice is problematic, it is not difficult to understand why it is the dominant ideological frame on the island: Cyprus is a country that is politically divided between the occupied north (where Turkish Cypriots reside) and the south, where Greek Cypriots live and which is under the official control of the Republic of Cyprus. The recent history of Cyprus, revolving primarily around the ethnic conflict that erupted between Greek and Turkish Cypriots in the 1960s, as well as the coup and the Turkish invasion of 1974 which resulted in the *de facto* partition of the island between north and south, created a climate of opposition and enmity between the two major communities on the island, something which is clearly reflected in their respective educational systems.[4]

In this section, I shall examine how children and childhood are conceived through educational policy and practice at the elementary school level in the Greek Cypriot community of Cyprus. More specifically, and of especial interest, is how a particular kind of child is constructed through educational policy and practice – the national citizen – who will develop a strong sense of national identity that will serve to sustain both the state and the Greek nation at large. At the same time, however, it is important to consider how children themselves contribute to, and shape, the process of the cultural politics of childhood; how, in other words, they both help to produce and *re*produce what it means to be a national citizen.

The public educational system of Cyprus is highly centralized and both curriculum and textbooks are centrally prescribed for all schools. This highly centralized educational system implies that educational policies are national and all children who attend public schools in Cyprus will be educated in the same way. As in so many other educational contexts, what we see in Cyprus is a process which more or less aims to provide the same to all. To summarize Qvortrup (1994: 10), through a process of *institutionalization* (i.e. putting children in schools) and the accompanying *individualization* (i.e. regarding children as individuals rather than as representatives of other groups), we get the *individuation* of children (i.e. the means by which all children are treated the same way *because they are all children*, and in order to bureaucratically control them).

The school in many ways complements the family, as an institution that supplements and extends the control of society on children and further contributes to the separation between childhood and adulthood. But unlike the family, which serves its own agenda, the school becomes a 'state apparatus', to use Althusser's (1971) terminology, for the effective transmission of ideology on children. In this way, the school helps to produce the kind of citizen who will sustain the legitimacy of the nation-state. Though the extent of control used in schools does vary, it is deemed necessary that the school exercises sufficient control to ensure the production of the right kind of child who will become the right kind of citizen.[5]

In such a regimented and tightly controlled environment, children's agency is quite limited. The power of adult authority constrains the extent to which children themselves can work to produce new meanings within the conceptual space of the school; instead their role is deemed successful to the extent that they manage to reproduce its ideologies. Ideological reproduction is achieved through the right kind of learning – in this case, largely nationalistic learning – and the right kind of development, maturation and discipline, which guarantee that the child is above all a Greek, irrespective of whatever else she or he may be (James, Jenks and Prout 1998: 38; see also Levinson and Holland 1996). This, to the extent it is successful, ultimately allows nationalism and the nation state to reproduce and sustain themselves in the long run.

Constructing the national citizen: the curriculum as ideology[6]

As Bourdieu and Passeron (1977) and others have shown, schools are not neutral grounds for the objective transmission of knowledge, but rather institutions set up to reproduce the privileges of certain groups. School curricula are similarly selective constructions of the world, the aim of which is also to legitimate the otherwise subjective knowledge and interests of certain privileged groups and to objectify what is socially constructed. Thus schools are implicated in questions of power and identity, through making assumptions about children's development and potential; ultimately, they are about producing the proper kind of children and the proper kind of childhood, as defined by the state (James, Jenks and Prout 1998: 41–2; see also Apple and Weis 1983; Apple and Christian-Smith 1991; Mayall 1994; Reed-Danahay 1996; Luykx 1999).

In her prologue to the curriculum guidelines (1994), which are still in use, the then Minister of Education, Claire Angelidou, stressed the important role of education in 'our half-occupied homeland which is struggling today to preserve its Greek and Christian roots, under such adverse conditions'. She proceeded to emphasize the need to instil in children 'the will for freedom and return to our occupied territories'. In his introductory note to the volume, the General Director of Elementary Education stated that one of the main objectives of Greek Cypriot elementary education is to help in

> the establishment of national and cultural identity and of the feeling of belonging, both to the state of the Republic of Cyprus as well as to the broader Hellenism,[7] to preserve unquenched the memory of our occupied territories, and to prepare [students] for struggles of vindication.

The minister's message emphasizes the ideology of Hellenism [(i.e. that Greek Cypriots are above all else Greeks) while the General Director's message incorporates elements of both Hellenism and Cypriotism – i.e. we are Greeks who live in an independent country, the Republic of Cyprus (see Mavratsas 1997). Yet despite the difference in emphasis, this is broadly speaking the educational ideology of citizenship: largely Greek-centred, with Cyprus being an integral cultural segment of Hellenism, whilst also being politically independent. To the extent that the particularities of Cyprus are emphasized, it is within the larger framework of the Hellenic world. Thus, despite the re-evaluation of the nationalist model of education following the 1974 war, education remains essentially nationalistic, at least in the sense that its primary emphasis is on a strong identification with the Greek nation. As Persianis (1981: 81–2) pointed out several years ago, in an observation that still holds true today,

> National instruction continues to be the most important educational duty of the primary and secondary school teachers. This is stressed not only by the circulars of the Educational Authorities but also by the oath which all teachers take in a special ceremony shortly after their appointment. In this oath they make a solemn promise that in the practice of their teaching profession they will 'remain faithful to the Christian and national ideals of Greek people as these have been shaped through the religious and national life'.

This ideology constructs citizenship primarily on two categorical ascriptions of belongingness: our *Greek* identity and our *Christian Orthodox* identity. In this formulation, to be Greek necessarily implies being Christian Orthodox and thus a main goal of Cypriot education is the preservation of the national, religious and cultural traditions of the island. The anomaly created by the Turkish invasion of 1974, however, necessitates a more firm ideological position: children need to learn about 'our enslaved land' and 'to preserve the memory of our occupied territories' and what is more important, to realize their duty towards 'our Turkish-held homeland', which basically means doing all they can for the application of human rights in Cyprus so that one day it is liberated from Turkish rule (Curriculum Guide 1994: 19, 20).[8] At the same time, the curriculum encourages the development of 'democratic' and 'autonomous citizens' – that is citizens who are immersed in the European orientations of education,[9] whose lives are directed by universal values, and who can function in a continuously changing world (Curriculum Guide 1994: Message of Director of Primary Education).

Although it is curriculum guidelines and textbooks that outline the official ideology on citizenship, this is not to suggest that there is one monolithic ideology that is promulgated in a uniform fashion; in fact, there may be several official ideologies, expressed through a variety of state agents. Nevertheless we may, in broad terms, identify some basic themes that constitute an official position on citizenship and which are frequently and repeatedly encountered in the official documents of state education, such as curriculum guidelines and textbooks. The official position on identity can be briefly outlined as follows:

We are essentially Greeks though we reside in Cyprus which happens to be an independent state. This means that we share Greek culture and history with the rest of the Greeks. We are one people and all the historical evidence points to that. We have an ancient civilization which the whole world looks up to. Though we have been repeatedly enslaved by multiple conquerors we have managed to preserve our identity – as Greeks of Cyprus and as Orthodox Christians – unchanged through the centuries. As Greeks we are peaceful and civilized people, but we also love freedom and will do everything possible to remain free. As Greeks of Cyprus we are an integral part of the European civilization to which Hellenism has contributed immensely. Currently, we are in danger of disappearing as a people because of Turkish aggression and occupation of Cyprus. It is imperative, therefore, that we preserve our national identity. We must remember our occupied territories, teach the younger generations about them, and do everything possible to return to them one day. With half of our homeland under Turkish occupation, the current situation is unacceptable. We refuse to give up our homeland to the Turks and we will fight until all the refugees return back to their homes.

We have lived for centuries in peaceful coexistence with Turkish Cypriots and desire to live peacefully side-by-side with them once again. But not with the Turks who have no right to be in Cyprus and who have proven to be the most barbaric people of all. History proves that the Turks have always been our enemies and the present situation is another example of that.

But what kind of child-student and future citizen does the curriculum wish to construct? The Curriculum Guide imagines the child at the centre of the educational process: 'the child reflects, asks questions, thinks, experiences and acts'; 'whatever is carried out at school must be for the benefit of the child and take place with his/her own free and willing participation and personal effort' (Curriculum Guide 1994: 27).

In its outlining of the basic principles of learning and development, the Curriculum Guide explains that children differ because of different degrees of biological maturity, different experiences due to family, socioeconomic and other environmental factors, and the degree of support and encouragement that children receive from adults, as well as idiosyncratic differences, differences in intelligence and differences in other abilities. It goes further to explain that there are differences even within the same age category and explains that it respects each child's uniqueness (Curriculum Guide 1994: 21). Nevertheless, it proceeds to outline Piaget's stages of cognitive development, focusing on their age parameters and the associated abilities that children are expected to have during each stage.

To sum up, one detects in the curriculum a clear effort to promote a Greek-centred education and to help children become loyal members of the Greek nation while at the same time, there is an effort to promote broader European and global values and principles. Similarly, the curriculum encourages teachers to see the uniqueness of each child, while at the same time the assumption is that children will develop in more or less the same way. Such contradictions bring into sharp focus the problem of aligning identities operating at different levels (e.g. a local Cypriot identity, a national Greek identity and a European or global identity) and with diverse value orientations (e.g. nationalism vs. multiculturalism/interculturalism).

The power and the limits of the curriculum

In such a context, a key issue when examining the cultural politics of childhood in relation to educational policy is how children react to the curriculum. Is it a curriculum that determines what kind of children they are and what kind of adults they become? Is it a curriculum that serves its intended purpose, which is to craft the next generation of citizens of the Republic of Cyprus who will also, but above all, be loyal to the Greek nation and the Greek Orthodox religion?

To start with, it is important to understand that educational policies are implemented by educators who act as mediators between the policies and the children, and that the extent to which they do this influences the extent to which such policies ultimately affect children. When, in the course of conducting fieldwork during 1996–7, I asked the teachers to reflect on the official curriculum, they responded in a variety of ways. In general, the most of them did not disagree with the ideology outlined in the curriculum and although some were critical of the implications of such an ideology, which emphasizes homogeneity and excludes difference, most did not feel constrained by the curriculum. Rather, they saw it as flexible 'guide' offering suggestions, which they could decide whether to use or not. They pointed out that they felt free to work creatively within the general framework provided by the curriculum. Thus, with regard to the emphasis placed on remembering the occupied territories, one teacher said:

> In a circular, the Ministry [of Education] says that emphasis should be put on this objective. But from there on, how you work, in which way you work, how you pursue it, what actions, what activities, and so on [you carry out], is up to the school, it is up to the teacher. It is a general objective for the children to get to know the occupied territories, to not forget them.

Although some teachers mentioned that they frequently consulted the Curriculum Guide, the majority said that they did so only occasionally; some followed it only for certain subjects, others only with regard to the very general guidelines outlined in it, while others never consulted it at all. Some of the latter explained that they preferred to focus on the book and the teacher's guide (for the particular course they taught) rather than the general Curriculum Guide. Added to this is the whole set of factors that constitute each and every teacher's identity and which, in turn, influence what she or he ends up selecting or emphasizing from the curriculum – in other words, what they decide to do with it. To illustrate by reference to one key variable – a teacher's political loyalty (i.e. with which political party she/he identifies) – we may say that a right-wing teacher is much more likely to favour and emphasize Hellenism and nationalistic ideas, drawing a sharp distinction between 'us' and 'them' when teaching, compared to a left-wing teacher, who is much more likely to favour and emphasize Cypriotism and the need for coexistence with those who are different from 'us'. From my classroom observations, I noticed on several occasions that certain teachers either played down or emphasized certain aspects of the curriculum in line with their ideological preferences and political affiliations.

Returning to the role of children themselves in the cultural politics of childhood, we should not underestimate the larger ideological constraints that limit the extent to which children can exercise their agency in relation to the school. After all, the school is a privileged social space for the systematic transmission of ideology; it is an institution that is often credited with knowledge and authority, and with the legitimate right to impart to children society's values. It is therefore no accident that although we often hear people criticizing the educational institution for its ineffectiveness in doing what it is supposed to do, we rarely hear criticisms about its right and legitimacy to carry out its educational role.

As part of the state apparatus (Althusser 1971), the school seeks to implement educational policy and to construct and reproduce the state's own ideas of 'good' childhood, which will uphold its agendas and interests and sustain its ideological legitimacy in the long run. Children's own responses – whether accepting, rejecting or negotiating (see Hall 1980) – to educational policy give rise to a more complex and dynamic encounter between policy and practice, and often a less determined outcome. Here, however, the focus will be on one particular aspect of educational policies – the emphasis given to nationalistic constructions of 'self' and 'other' – in order to illustrate not only the extent to which policies constrain the construction and expression of children's identities, but also the fact that children's identities are never totally determined and that children are able to find ways to exercise their agency and escape, even temporarily, the constraints imposed on them.

During both lessons and other school-related activities, most teachers from my observations resorted to an 'us' vs. 'them' frame – Greeks vs. Turks – to explain the past, present and future of Cyprus (see Spyrou 2006). In these formulations, the teachers spoke most of the time with the authoritative voice of nationalistic discourse: *the Turks have always been our enemies, they have always been barbarians, and nothing will change their future behaviour.* Consider the way one teacher from a geography class with the 5th and 6th grades frames this understanding of the Turks in a way that ultimately leaves children with little room to dissent:

> From what we read, were they [the Egyptians] people with a civiliza-
> tion? Were they – let's put it this way – barbarians like the Turks, the
> Ottomans, who have always been barbarians?

On countless occasions, I have heard teachers ask children questions
that would confirm for everyone in the class the very well-known and
understood cultural assumptions about the inferiority of the Turks as a
people and, by implication, 'our' superior nature. All questions that
affirmed the existing nationalistic framework were rewarded by the
teacher, and in fact many children played a key role in reproducing
such understandings. Thus, when children contributed to class discussions with alternative understandings that challenged nationalist
assumptions, the teachers dismissed such opinions as invalid. Consider
the following example from a religious instruction class with the 6th
grade, where a teacher readily and decidedly rejects a child's input
because it challenges the patriotic ideal of fulfilling one's duty to the
homeland:

Nikiforos: Sir, what about the children and the women if there is
war?
Teacher: We said that only those who can fight will fight in a war.
Marinos: Adults say that if war takes place they will go and hide.
[Here, the student is referring to cynical statements occasionally made by men about their disillusionment with
politics and their unwillingness to fight for their country.]
Teacher: Marinos, you should not listen to what they say in the
neighbourhood.

In this case, the teacher defined the classroom as a setting where only
certain kinds of knowledge are appropriate, a setting in which personal
knowledge is inappropriate: it is seen as inferior and potentially harmful
because it contradicts the 'right' kind of attitude towards the homeland,
namely, that one should be ready to die for it whenever called on to do
so. The teacher refuses to allow a change in the use of speech genres
from an instructional, patriotic genre, which is authoritative and clear
in its declarations (e.g. 'one should fight and if necessary die for the
homeland'), to one based on personal (and hence defined as non-
authoritative) knowledge, which seeks to challenge the clear injunctions
of the former. In the end, as James and James (2004: 136) aptly put it,

'any difference risks reconstruction as deviance'; the resolution is simply to dismiss the personal in preference of the collective.

However, this emphasis on nationalism – on 'our' Greekness, 'our' Greek identity – worked against other stated goals of the educational policies, such as the need for children to develop a sense of belonging and loyalty to the Republic of Cyprus and a desire to live peacefully with Turkish Cypriots. Thus my classroom observations revealed that although teachers talked to the children about Turks all the time, they rarely talked to them about Turkish Cypriots, with the result that only a small minority of children actually knew who Turkish Cypriots are.[10] This certainly makes problematic the development of a civic identity and the possibility of finding a solution to the Cyprus problem that will reunite the island, by bringing Greek and Turkish Cypriots under one political roof.

But there were also occasions, which were certainly fewer but nevertheless important, when children actively reflected on the curriculum they were confronted with and challenged its nationalistic framework.[11] Thus when, in a 4th grade history class, the teacher celebrated the heroic patriotism of the Spartan women who, according to legend, threw their disabled babies over a cliff 'so that only strong and healthy children who could become warriors would be raised', one of the girls challenged the teacher by pointing to one of the integrated special needs children in the classroom saying, 'If they continued to be like that, some children like Makis would not be alive.' The student in this case identified the conflicting set of values included in the curriculum – the value of commitment to the nation and the value of commitment to one's family and children in particular – and openly challenged the teacher, who was herself a mother, leaving her with little room to respond (see Spyrou 2000).[12] What might have gone unnoticed in another classroom setting became an issue for critical reflection for this classroom and for penetrating, however minimally, the established nationalistic common sense. Thus, despite their common experiences in the face of adult authority, children's experiences in school result in a diversity of lived childhoods which, over time, contribute in their own way to discontinuity and ultimately change (see James and James 2004: 47; see also Giddens 1979: 72; Shilling 1992: 79).

Discussion

Cultural discourses of childhood are often informed by, and overlap to some extent with, other discourses, be they local discourses on the family or global ones about children's rights, like the UNCRC. As discourses, they are part of a process; they have pasts, presents and futures. They are therefore implicated in both the continuity and change of childhood as an institution and play a key role at any particular time in defining (sometimes clearly, sometimes contradictorily) what kind of children the society wishes to have (James and James 2004: 74). Educational policies, explicated principally through school curricula, play this role in relation to formal schooling and through the process of educating (or more appropriately, *socializing*) children. By regulating and controlling children and their experience of schooling, educational policies seek to produce the kind of adults that the state desires, or, as James and James (2004: 115) put it, 'the state's current interest in childhood is very much out of self-interest'.

The process of educating children in Cyprus, as in so many other parts of the world, is one of exerting symbolic violence on them, to use Bourdieu's (1977) term. Contrary to official declarations about the liberating role of education and students' participation in the educational process, children are, more often than not, told what and how to think, what kind of children they should be in the present and what kind of adults they should grow up to be (Bourdieu 1974; James and James 2004: 124). Yet, change is as much a characteristic of this process as continuity.

In 2004, a report was issued by an Educational Reform Committee, appointed by the Ministry of Education and Culture, to analyse the educational system and to make proposals for its reform. The report argued that there was a need for a fundamental reform of the educational system of the country, by incorporating new trends in education and by moving away from the Greek-centred approach, which it characterized as 'narrowly ethnocentric and culturally monolithic' (Report 2004: 4). The report recommends that the teacher becomes a professional and democratic pedagogue who will educate citizens rather than a labour force, while it recommends that the system as a whole must work to cultivate respect for diversity and pluralism and develop a European outlook. In line with this, the report recommends the reinforcement of the civic education course and the formation of a team of scientists to rewrite school history texts. Similarly, the report recommends cooperation with Turkish Cypriot schools, common teacher training for Greek and Turkish Cypriots, and the implementation of anti-racist educational programmes.

A careful survey of the circulars sent to all primary schools by the Ministry of Education and Culture since 2004 reveals a definite turn towards a more inclusive, less nationalistic and more open educational system. This can be seen, for example, in a circular dated 2 January 2004, in which the Director of Primary Education outlines in detail the various approaches to democratic citizenship that primary education must follow. He lists and analyses five such approaches: education for human rights; civic education; intercultural education; global education; and peace education. It is no coincidence that these ideological changes have coincided with Cyprus's recent entry into the EU (May 2004, and the accession period preceding that) and with the declared objective at all levels to become fully integrated into the 'European family'. This integration process implies also the adoption of policies that reflect the multiculturalism and interculturalism of the EU as an institution.

The arrival in Cyprus of large numbers of immigrants during the last 10–15 years has also confronted schools with a new reality, which has forced the educational authorities to rethink their policies. The new 'European family', which Cyprus entered in 2004, has had to confront the challenge of cultural 'otherness' in education for a lot longer than Cyprus has, and although the directives of the EU on education distinguish between citizens of EU Member States and third country nationals (demanding more integrative measures in the case of the former), they nevertheless exert pressure on Member States to confront the issue and take steps to address it. Greek Cypriot public schools are no longer mono-cultural; they are increasingly heterogeneous and demand transformation to a more open, multicultural European outlook which will, at least in principle, cater for the educational needs of all children and not just Greek Cypriots.

The assimilationist and exclusionist model used by the state since its establishment in 1960 has come under a lot of pressure as more and more students from different cultural and linguistic backgrounds have entered the republic's schools, and the system has not been able to accommodate them successfully. In a study of schools attended by Turkish-speaking children carried out in 2004 (including Turkish Cypriot children residing in the south, as well as other Turkish-speaking children such as Roma and Kurdish), I identified a range of serious problems encountered by these children, their parents and teachers, and the educational authorities of the schools in question. The inability of the system to integrate these children successfully has meant that most of them were simply incorporated into the appropriate grade for their age, irrespective of their knowledge of Greek, in the hope that they would eventually be assimilated. Most of these children were, as a result, unable to communicate in Greek and thus to participate in their classes, many of them failing to attend school, and those who did show up often resorted to disruptive behaviour in the classroom. The study also revealed that conflicts and other forms of tension arose during particular lessons when the Turkish-speaking children reacted to what was being taught. As one teacher explained to me:

> Sometimes in the history class for the 6th grade, as I am teaching, the Turkish Cypriots react when they hear the word 'Turk'. History for the 6th grade is the history of the Greek revolution of 1821 [against the Ottomans who are however referred to as 'Turks' in Greek Cypriot school texts]. I face this issue every day. They tell me: 'You should be afraid of the Turks.' When I talk about Athanasios Dhiakos [a Greek national hero], who was skewered [by the Ottomans], they tell me: 'He deserved it.'

Some teachers also felt that the education of Greek Cypriot children was suffering as a result, since they could not give them sufficient time to cover the syllabus, whilst others felt that they lacked adequate materials (e.g. materials in both Greek and Turkish or with appropriate translations, or materials that could support intercultural education, such as books and videos) that would be appropriate for the Turkish-speaking students and their particular needs. Prejudice and racism expressed by Greek Cypriot children towards them has also, in many cases, resulted in aggression and violence between the two groups.

For this reason, as well as a result of the pressure exerted on the educational system from the country's integration into the EU, the educational authorities have developed programmes to address these changes. One of these developments has been the establishment of 'Educational Priority Zones', whose overall aim is to help underprivileged students and to bring about more equality in education. The main criterion used to designate such a zone is the low socioeconomic level of the community, which in many cases goes hand-in-hand with the high concentration of immigrants in the area. Consequently, to note one policy change since March 2004 that is illustrative of the changing climate in education, Turkish-speaking children are now offered Turkish language classes when the rest of the Greek Cypriot children attend [Greek] history and [Greek Orthodox] scripture classes.

Like their Greek Cypriot counterparts, who engage with the curriculum they are presented with through their relationships and interactions with their teachers and peers, immigrant and minority children came to constitute and reconstitute educational policy and practice, thereby indirectly contributing to both their reproduction and change (James and James 2004: 57). The influx of children from immigrant families and their reactions to a closed, nationalistic system of education that could not accommodate them successfully has resulted, albeit unintentionally, in changed notions of childhood among the adults involved in the educational process and has ultimately resulted in new policies aimed to address the issue of diversity in education (James and James 2004: 105). These policy changes reflect a stark contract to the way that public elementary schools operated during the 1990s, when the cultural homogeneity of schools was taken more or less for granted. Ideas of Cypriot childhood are therefore being reconstituted through changes in educational policy and practice, changes to which children have also contributed, not through any formal consultation or right to participation but through the exercise of their own agency.

Notes

1 Ethnographic fieldwork for this project extended from September 1996 to August 1997 and was carried out in two communities, one urban near the buffer zone in Nicosia and one rural to the south-west of Nicosia. The project examined both the school processes involved in children's ethnic identity construction and extra-educational processes taking place in other contexts such as the home, the neighborhood and the playground (see Spyrou 1999).

2 The Statue of Liberty is a monument which consists of the statues of those who fought for the liberation of Cyprus from the British during the 1955–59 anti-colonial war.

3 Of course, when the decision to stay at home was primarily the parents', the constraints normally placed on the children by the school were simply replaced by those of the home.

4 In 1960 Cyprus gained its independence from the British following five years' anti-colonial guerrilla warfare by Greek Cypriot nationalists. The last official census of the entire population of the island showed that Greek Cypriots accounted for 80 per cent and Turkish Cypriots for 18 per cent of the total population.

5 The fact that education is mandatory (until the age of 15) rather than voluntary implies that the state is not strictly speaking serving children, but is also serving its own goals, though no one would deny the benefits accruing to children (see Qvortrup 1994: 9–10).

6 All my references to the Curriculum Guide are with regard to the 1994 issue which is still in use.

7 *Broader Hellenism* refers to Hellenism or Greek culture wherever it is found, whether in mainland Greece, the Greek islands, Cyprus or anywhere else where one finds the Greek diaspora.

8 Many messages sent to elementary schools by the Minister of Education and Culture end with the minister's conclusion that the children, as the new generation, are the hope for the future who will continue fighting for the liberation of Cyprus from Turkish occupation.

9   In recent years, following Cyprus's application for full membership of the European Union and its subsequent entry, a so-called 'European orientation' is evident in education. Such an orientation implies the adoption of what are seen as European standards, values and mentality. The EU ideology, which aims to establish a European identity among member countries, emphasizes the need to preserve the traditions and identity of the various peoples that comprise it while at the same time encouraging communication, understanding and co-operation. In Greek Cypriot elementary education, European civilization is presented as a continuation of Greek civilization. The implication, of course, is that since Cyprus is part of Greek civilization it is also part of European civilization. Europe has played a civilizing role in the history of human kind and continues to be the center of intellectual and cultural development. European countries are highly developed and what is of great importance, they are democratic countries. Cyprus, as a member of the EU is part of this European civilization (see Philippou 2005).

10 Many children offered fanciful explanations when I asked them to explain who they thought Turkish Cypriots are (see Spyrou 2001).

11 Prewitt (1970: 619), in his study of political socialization among African schoolchildren, has warned against the tendency to make inferences about children's values by analysing the content of educational policies.

12 See Billig et al. (1988) who rather than viewing ideology as coherent and internally consistent wholes, have argued for a view of ideology as essentially inconsistent and made up of contrary themes which give rise to dilemmas and dialogue (see also Giroux 1983: 285).

References

Althusser, L. (1971) Ideology and Ideological State Apparatuses. In *Lenin and Philosophy and Other Essays* (pp. 127–86). London: New Left Books.

Apple, M. and Christian-Smith, L. K. (1991) The Politics of the Textbook. In Apple, M. and Christian-Smith, L. K. (eds.), *The Politics of the Textbook* (pp. 1–21). London and New York: Routledge.

Apple, M. and Weis, L. (eds.) (1983) *Ideology and Practice in Schooling.* Philadelphia: Temple University Press.

Billig, M. et al. (1988) *Ideological Dilemmas: A Social Psychology of Everyday Thinking.* London: Sage.

Bourdieu, P. and Passeron, J.-C. (1974) The School as a Conservative Force: Scholastic and Cultural Inequalities. In Eggleston, J. (ed.), *Contemporary Research in the Sociology of Education* (pp. 32–46). London: Methuen.

Bourdieu, P. and Passeron, J.-C. (1977) *Reproduction in Education, Society and Culture.* Trans. R. Nice. London: Sage.

Coles, R. (1986) *The Political Life of Children.* Boston and New York: The Atlantic Monthly Press.

Committee on Educational Reform (2004) *Manifesto of Educational Reform.* Nicosia: Ministry of Education and Culture.

Cyprus Ministry of Education and Culture (1994) *Curriculum Guide for Elementary Education.* Nicosia.

Giddens, A. (1979) *Central Problems in Social Theory: Action, Structure and Contradiction in Social Analysis.* Berkeley and Los Angeles: University of California Press.

Giroux, H. (1983) Theories of Reproduction and Resistance in the New Sociology of Education: A Critical Analysis. *Harvard Educational Review* 53(3): 257–93.

Hall, S. (1980) Encoding/Decoding. In Hall, S., Hobson, D., Lowe, A. and Willis, P. (eds.), *Culture, Media, Language* (pp.128–39). London: Hutchinson.

James, A. and James, A. (2004) *Constructing Childhood: Theory, Policy and Social Practice.* Palgrave Macmillan.

James, A., Jenks, C. and Prout, A. (1998) *Theorizing Childhood.* New York: Teachers College Press.

Kouloumou, T. (2004) Children's Welfare and Everyday Life in Cyprus: A Family Affair with Intergenerational Implications. In Jensen, A. et al. (eds.), *Children's Welfare in Ageing Europe* (pp. 591–647). Trondheim: Norwegian Center for Child Research.

Levinson, B. and Holland, D. (eds.) (1996) *The Cultural Production of the Educated Person: Critical Ethnographies of Schooling and Local Practice.* New York: SUNY Press.

Luykx, A. (1999) *The Citizen Factory: Schooling and Cultural Production in Bolivia.* New York: SUNY Press.

Makrinioti, D. (1994) Conceptualization of Childhood in a Welfare State: A Critical Appraisal. In Qvortrup, J., Bardy, M., Sgritta, G. and Wintersberger, H. (eds.), *Childhood Matters: Social Theory, Practice and Politics* (pp. 267–83). Aldershot, Brookfield, Hong Kong, Singapore and Sydney: Avebury.

Mavratsas, C. (1997) The Ideological Contest Between Greek-Cypriot Nationalism and Cypriotism 1974–1995: Politics, Social Memory and Identity. *Ethnic and Racial Studies* 20(4): 717–37.

Mayall, B. (1994) Children in Action at Home and School. In Berry M. (ed.), *Children's Childhoods: Observed and Experienced* (pp.114–27). Lewes: Falmer Press.

Persianis, P. (1981) *The Political and Economic Factors as the Main Determinants of Educational Policy in Independent Cyprus (1960–1970).* Pedagogical Institute of Cyprus. Dissertation Series 1. Nicosia.

Philippou, S. (2005) Constructing National and European Identities: The Case of Greek-Cypriot Pupils. *Educational Studies* 31(3): 293–315.

Prewitt, K. with Okello-Oculi, J. (1970) Political Socialization and Political Education in the New Nations. In Sigel, R. (ed.), *Learning About Politics: A Reader in Political Socialization* (pp. 607–21). New York: Random House.

Qvortrup, J. (1994) Childhood Matters: An Introduction. In Qvortrup, J., Bardy, M., Sgritta, G. and Wintersberger, H. (eds.), *Childhood Matters: Social Theory, Practice and Politics* (pp. 1–23). Aldershot, Brookfield, Hong Kong, Singapore, Sydney: Avebury.

Reed-Danahay, D. (1996) *Education and Identity in Rural France: The Politics of Schooling.* Cambridge: Cambridge University Press.

Report of Cyprus to the UN Committee for the Implementation of the Convention for the Rights of the Child (1999). Nicosia.

Shilling, C. (1992) Reconceptualising Structure and Agency in the Sociology of Education: Structuration Theory and Schooling. *British Journal of Sociology of Education* 13(1): 69–87.

Solberg, A. (1990) Negotiating Childhood: Changing Constructions of Age for Norwegian Children. In James, A. and Prout, A. (eds.), *Constructing and Reconstructing Childhood: Contemporary Issues in the Sociological Study of Childhood* (pp. 118–37). Lewes: Falmer Press.

Spyrou, S. (1999) Small Ethnic Worlds: Identity, Ambiguity, and Imagination in Greek Cypriot Children's Lives. PhD Dissertation. Binghamton: Anthropology Department, State University of New York.

Spyrou, S. (2000) Education, Ideology, and the National Self: The Social Practice of Identity Construction in the Classroom. *The Cyprus Review* 12(1): 61–81.

Spyrou, S. (2001) Those on the Other Side: Ethnic Identity and Imagination in Greek Cypriot Children's Lives. In Schwartzman, H. (ed.), *Children and Anthropology: Perspectives for the 21st Century* (pp. 167–85). Westport, CT and London: Bergin & Garvey.

Spyrou, S. (2006) Constructing 'the Turk' as an Enemy: The Complexity of Stereotypes in Children's Everyday Worlds. In Theodossopoulos, D. (ed.), *When Greek Think About Turks: The View from Anthropology* (pp. 95–110). London and New York: Routledge.

Stephens, S. (ed.) (1995) *Children and the Politics of Culture*. Princeton, NJ: Princeton University Press.

9
Children's Culture, Cultural Education and Policy Approaches to Children's Culture: The Case of Germany

Heinz Hengst

This chapter deals with the processes of the 'de-schooling of learning', or what might be called a 'de-schooled learning', that have occurred within and outside the school in Germany during the past 35 years, the period to which many social and cultural theoreticians refer when analysing the impact of modernization. The specific focus of this chapter is on developments in the Federal Republic of Germany in a field that encompasses culture, aesthetics, 'cultural pedagogics', cultural work with children, cultural education and 'artistic education', and what work in this field reveals about our understanding of childhood and 'the child'.

The concept of cultural pedagogics is closely related to the German concept of *Bildung*,[1] namely that cultural-aesthetic processes are at the same time 'educational' (in the sense of *Bildung*). It is implicitly assumed that anyone speaking of *Bildung* is also, and has always been, speaking of aesthetics. In Germany, this notion has been manifested in the focus placed on aesthetics in art education, following Friedrich Schiller, and in the debates and controversies surrounding children's and youth culture since the first art educationalist conferences and educational reform movement of the early twentieth century. As this chapter argues, the same idea appears in the updated and revised educational concepts that have been dominant in Germany since the early 1970s.

In the decades following the Second World War, the humanities, educational sciences and educational policy-makers were unable to formulate an up-to-date and rational German school system, based on a central educational authority. At the same time, traditional youth association work and extra-curricular work with young people lost some of its *raison d'être*. It was possible, therefore, for a new form of cultural education to emerge from this 'educational vacuum'. This aspired to the more general educational nature and qualities provided by voluntary and informal cultural activities and thus aesthetic experiential environments became increasingly important for extra-curricular (educational) work with children and young people. In the case of Germany, the special importance attached to the extra-curricular domain is linked to the fact that German children and young people, unlike their peers in virtually every other European country, attend school for half the day only and therefore have a relatively large amount of free time at their disposal.

In exploring these issues about art, education and German childhood, this chapter illustrates how this cultural pedagogical field has developed outside the school, and explores its impact on our ideas of children's culture, cultural education (a term often used in Germany synonymously with cultural work and cultural pedagogics) and children's cultural policy more generally. Here, cultural policy is understood to comprise the mix of laws, programmes and activities that are legitimated by adopting educational and social policy objectives, as a form of policy-making that is broadly similar to educational policy. Taking 'de-schooled' cultural education as its specific focus, the chapter explores the implications that processes of democratization, and cultural democratization in particular, have had for the conceptualization of children as subjects and targets of cultural policy and government initiatives. It also considers the opportunities for participation that this process has given children with regard to shaping their own lives, and also for their participation in the public sphere. Attention is centred on the representations of 'the child' invoked in these processes and on the social frameworks to which these representations relate, including the semantic significance of concepts such as self-determination, co-determination, self-responsibility, self-assistance and self-help.

For the period up to German reunification (from the late 1960s until 1989), the analysis presented in this chapter relates to trends in West Germany only, since in the former GDR, 'cultural pedagogics' was unknown. After reunification it was simply exported, at first as a term and then as a discipline and a field of work, usually without reference to anything analogous. Although in eastern Germany there were indeed examples of expert cultural educational praxis, these were hierarchically structured, with doctrinaire norms and objectives dictated by the state. However, after unification 'cultural education' and 'socio-culture' became keywords and fields of work in the new *Bundesländer* as well. This was both a pragmatic response to problematic areas of regional support, and a conceptual bridge aimed at preventing everything from the old regime being simply thrown overboard.

Since the early 1970s, other countries in north-western Europe have been working systematically at establishing children's culture in a de-schooled sense.[2] Policy programmes and measures therefore aimed at providing a range of cultural activities and infrastructures outside school and, from a very early stage, a common element in these political initiatives was the development of a separate policy-making field relating to children's culture. A key concern of children's culture policy was, and continues to be, that children should be encouraged to play an active cultural role outside the family and the school. This emphasizes the importance of the traditional institution of 'childhood' as a separate social space, while also reflecting a feature characteristic of children's culture policy in the Nordic countries – that child policies are designed as policies of equality and pursued with the intention of enabling children to live independently of their parents' economic and cultural resources and as citizens enjoying equal rights.

While national policies on children's culture with a shared basis in egalitarian policies ('egalitarian individualism'; cf. Therborn 1993) can be identified in the Nordic countries (cf. Hengst 1995), however, it is much more difficult to identify and reconstruct anything typically 'German' in the comparable programmes, intervention schemes and institutions found in Germany. The field of activities is more heterogeneous and in many respects more confusing since, in contrast to Scandinavia, it has to a significant degree developed organically, out of everyday practice. That said, it is possible, nonetheless, to identify typical discourses and intervention strategies in the fields of cultural policy and education, especially during the 1970s and 1980s, which address the same problems and activities as in the Nordic countries and which are framed by similar social challenges.

A *fin-de-siècle* mood in education: 1960s–1970s

In order to explain the cultural climate in which children's culture policy developed in the Federal Republic of Germany, I would like to begin by briefly describing the situation and 'images' of education and culture in the 1970s. Two things are worthy of note as far as education was concerned: first, a trend towards anti-authoritarianism in children's education and upbringing, with elements of a children's rights movement emerging; and second, anti-pedagogical mentalities in 'virtually all practical fields and areas of life' (Zinnecker 1996: 45).

The critique of education and schooling was expressed in both theoretical terms and in practical activity. Referring to the 'children's centres' (*Kinderläden*) and 'schoolchildren's centres' (*Schülerläden*) set up in the late 1960s – self-governing units conceived of as a radical alternative to conventional facilities and dominant educational thinking – the educationalist Klaus Klemm spoke in terms of a new 'participatory political culture' (2003: 52).[3] The children's and schoolchildren's centres were supplemented in the early 1970s by a wave of newly established alternative schools, characterized by an anarchic scepticism towards dominance, state authority, centralism and bureaucratic organization. Alternative schools (some of which still exist), which aimed at achieving an element of Utopia – 'to live and not be schooled' (Klemm 2003: 79) – were another product of the children's centre movement.

'Childrearing's great turn away from schools' (von Hentig 1971: 13) was accompanied in the late 1960s and early 1970s by Cuernavaca and CIDOC (*Centro Intercultural de Documentacio*). The latter, founded by Ivan Illich in Mexico in 1960 as a centre for training aid workers and missionaries for work in South America, became the epicentre of a global debate on de-schooling. For the first time, this centre reflected systematically on the idea of de-schooling and endeavoured to debunk the 'central myth-forming ritual of industrial society' (Illich 1972: 11). Books like Ivan Illich's *Entschulung der Gesellschaft* (*De-schooling of Society*) (1972) and *Schulen helfen nicht* (*Celebration of Awareness*) (1970) became much-debated bestsellers, in (West) Germany in the early 1970s and, indeed, elsewhere. Paulo Freire's *Pädagogik der Unterdrückten* (*The Pedagogy of the Oppressed*) (1971) was greeted with similar acclaim.

A specifically German phenomenon, however, albeit heavily influenced by the children's rights movement in the US, was *Antipädagogik* (anti-pedagogics). This term encompasses all the initiatives whose central aim was to overcome educational relations based on the traditional model of *homo educandus* – that is to say, it was a rejection of the education system *on principle*, by anti-educationalists. Their concern was not to devise an educational alternative to conventional pedagogics, but to abolish them entirely in order to achieve a fundamental change in generational relations.

Democratizing educational relationships

By the beginning of the 1980s, the theoretical concept behind anti-pedagogics, as presented to the educational public in the second half of the 1970s (Braunmühl 1975, 1978), had been developed into a practical philosophy for everyday life (Schoenebeck 1982, 1985). The core postulate of this philosophy is an 'everyday life free of education' and the encouragement of a 'post-educationalist' quality of life in which everyone, children and adults alike, is conceived of as a 'person responsible for him- or herself'. The ealier ambiguous term 'anti-pedagogics' was replaced, accordingly, by 'post-pedagogical' (Schoenebeck 1992).

This description could also be applied to a more general tendency in Germany during this period which has been outlined by Jürgen Zinnecker (1996). In an attempt to explain the crisis afflicting the socialization paradigm in Germany, he referred (among other things) to 'deep currents of anti-pedagogical mentality … [that] have been affecting virtually all practical fields and areas of life since the historical watershed of 1968' (1996: 45). Zinnecker provides a number of examples: hitherto acknowledged models of socialization have lost their significance and there is now less confidence in the idea that children 'learn by example; parents today prefer to 'live with children' rather than educate them; to an increasing extent, it is not adults who are deemed to have the skills necessary for the future, but adolescents and young people (e.g. in media or in relation to environmental issues); and there is a public debate over 'educational objectives and methods'. Zinnecker summarizes these developments as follows:

> 'Anti-pedagogical' mentalities determine first of all … everyday life and everyday practices; this is especially true for the privileged educational elites in urban centres. Mediated through this social group, corresponding mentalities penetrate into (social) scientific discourses and programmes. This mostly occurs unawares, meaning the collective carriers of such mentalities do not usually understand themselves as anti-educationalists …
>
> (1996: 45)

An idea of the (perhaps) specifically German aspects of the changes that have been taking place since the early 1970s can be obtained when one considers how differently the French translated into practice the desire, common after 1968, to reform the education system. Beatrice Durand (2004), an expert in cultural studies who is well acquainted with the trends in Germany and France, has emphasized that in the 1970s and 1980s efforts in Germany were focused primarily on democratizing educational relationships. She points out, explicitly, that experiments 'at the periphery of state schools' contributed to changes in teaching styles in the schools themselves as institutions, whereas the reforms taking place at the same time in France were aimed at a different form of democratization. Getting rid of the old authoritarian style of teaching was not the primary aim in France, but rather establishing equality of opportunity by abolishing traditional schools, which merely reproduced and reinforced the social stratification of society. Durand refers to the marginalization of experiments like Freinet pedagogics,[4] which were used as pilot projects. However, she also notes that democratization in France (compulsory education in standard schools until the ninth form, doubling the percentage of baccalaureate candidates) has something to do with the *retention* of authoritarian styles of teaching and education. In describing the paradoxical result, she identifies these styles as being a result of *social* democratization (Durand 2004: 66ff.).

My argument in the next section is that anti-educationalist emotions and mentalities, in the sense described by Zinnecker, became established to a certain extent in the discourses, programmes and practices relating to children's (culture) policy and cultural work with children in Germany, and that they found a new home there for a period during the 1970s and 1980s. This was possible because the *fin-de-siècle* mood in education in Germany coincided with the heyday of the cultural. As I shall argue, however, since the 1990s there has been an observable reversal in these trends, with a modified attitude towards the school as an institution in political discourses and practices, a trend that is associated with a new framework that locates 'the school' within a 'culture of growing up'. Thus the importance of de-schooling has become less important.

The heyday of the cultural: 1970s–1980s

The 1970s and 1980s saw a new interest in culture at both the national and international levels. It had become apparent that economic and ecological developments were difficult to control (see e.g. Meadows et al. 1973). Faced with this situation, many, politicians among them, hoped for a cultural contribution to solve the 'great challenges of our time' and for 'coping with the world's problems' (cf. Kramer 1988: 65). In Germany, commentators noted a growing interest in culture and observed that the drivers of social change had become a renewed focus of attention, but that there had been a shift in emphasis. The line of argument was that, although the fostering of technology and technology transfer had not really been played out to the full, the process of modernization was also cultural, requiring support from and through culture.

Kurt Biedenkopf, a leading CDU (Christian Democrat) politician, appealed for 'broad and unregimented support for all cultural areas, initiatives and institutions – with no exclusion of 'dreamy Utopianists' (1986: 19). Lothar Späth, prime minister of Baden-Württemberg and also a member of the CDU, until then a pioneer of technology promotion, demanded not only basic research but above all, support for creative and artistic development. Jürgen Möllemann, the German Minister of Education and an FDP (Freie Demokratische Partei – Free Democratic Party) politician, wrote, in 1987, that he considered the 'free cultural education' work being performed in socio-cultural centres to be a 'key integrational factor in our society' (cf. Treptow 1988: 82). And the former Austrian Chancellor, Fred Sinowatz, a Social Democrat, provided perhaps the clearest expression of the cultural understanding on which (new) cultural policy was to be based. For him, cultural policy was the 'generic term for all political activity', something that was aimed at 'the sum total of life references, ideas and facts in this life, the standard and quality of life, welfare and well-being' (Sinowatz 1987: 308).

The flourishing of cultural policy in West Germany has been addressed by sociologists such as Gerhard Schulze, who drew attention to the special situation in German cultural policy. He emphasized that, although 'the aura of grand politics' was (still) absent and that remote academic conferences and publications were still the only places where an integrational debate relating to the whole of society was taking place, it was also a fact that, 'despite its confinement to the local community, the increased importance and institutionalisation of cultural policy is a phenomenon affecting society as a whole, and one requiring sociological analysis' (Schulze 1992: 495).

Schulze reconstructed the history of cultural policy thinking in the Federal Republic using a typology of cultural policy motives that also aids understanding of the enhanced importance of policies for children's culture, work in children's culture, cultural pedagogics and cultural education. He distinguishes (in ideal-typical terms) among several basic or guiding motives in the cultural sphere that appeared successively in post-war West Germany: the 'high culture', 'democratization' and 'socio-cultural' motives, and a secondary, 'economic' motive (Schulze 1992: 499ff).

The *high culture* motive dominated the period immediate post-1945 until the 1960s. The aim of the policies based on this particular *leitmotif* was the preservation and safeguarding of high culture: 'the policy goal of guaranteeing art's existence is complemented by the educational goal of making people capable of 'high culture' (Schulze 1992: 499). The *democratization* motive (emerging in the 1960s), on the other hand, signifies a departure in the sense that it resulted in policies that marked a transition from a compensational cultural policy aimed at workers and the 'small people' in favour of a cultural policy for all. This implied that more social groups should be involved, including children and young people, and, at the same time, the idea of a compensatory cultural policy was incorporated in the all-embracing notion of an *equal* cultural policy. Thus, alongside the compensatory variant of the equality postulate – cultural policy compensating for social inequalities – there was a needs-based variant: something for everyone (or for every social group).

Since the 1970s the *socio-cultural* motive has signalled increasing attention to a cultural critique of the problems of everyday life that result from the expansion of the consumer society. Here the focus has been on the social milieu with the aim of bringing people driven by individualization back to communicating: 'in place of the pedagogical idea of the educated person in the high culture approach, the sociocultural approach applies the pedagogical idea of the self-realising person' (Schulze 1992: 500). The socio-cultural motive is thus closely associated with self-help and self-determination. It takes its subjects' cultural interests and forms of expression seriously and seeks to assist cultural self-help by means of establishing specific initiatives and projects. Characteristic features of its political intentions are the key terms self-determination, decentralization and co-operation. They indicate that the goals of socio-culture are the further democratization of society through culture (Wiepersdorfer Erklärung 1992: 7ff).[5]

Establishing children's culture as a distinct field of political intervention and activity in Germany from the 1970s to the 1990s (something which Schulze himself does not discuss) coincides in time and content with the assertion of democratization and socio-cultural motives. Indeed, children's culture was part of the cultural boom. For example, protagonists of the new departures in cultural education noted in 1988 that 'culture is booming' and referred to the phrase coined by Hilmar Hoffmann (at the time, cultural secretary of Frankfurt) that begins his foreword to the second edition of a much-discussed and cited book, *Kultur für alle* (Culture for All) (1979): 'even children's and youth culture are booming' (1988: 11).

The term 'children's culture' (always used by advocates in conjunction with youth culture) serves to bracket many schemes, activities and fields of practice that were established at the time. The following definition can be found, for example, in a publication by the Federal Association for Cultural Education of Youth on 'Planning Children's and Youth Culture':

> Children's and youth culture work refers here to all activities aimed at extensive aesthetic and creative experience with the aid of various artistic means (e.g. theatre, music, dance, literature, play, graphic arts, film, photography, video). At the same time, they reflect and include the social and political conditions for the everyday life of children and youths.
>
> (Kolfhaus 1992: 9)

What this definition makes clear is that work with children and young people was conceived of as an open and autonomous field of experience, within everyone's range, occupying a place 'between school and social work, art education and youth associations'(cf. Zacharias 2001: 76). The practice is not confined to art, the spectrum of activities reaching from theatre, music and museum projects to environmental projects, community work and historical learning. Art is understood as a special case, however, and again and again it is a highlight of cultural work with children. Cultural pedagogy aims at forging links between art and (social) life.

Despite the authority in cultural matters that the different federal states (*Länder*) in Germany wield, some key programmatic and organizational steps in the field of children's culture policy were effected at the national level. Mention should be made, for example, of the 'central lobby' provided by the Federal Association for Cultural Education (*Bundesvereinigung kulturelle Jugendbildung* – BKJ), set up in 1963, and the Society for Cultural Policy (*Kulturpolitische Gesellschaft*), both of which became driving forces behind the development of cultural pedagogics with their congresses, conferences and publications. Another strong partner was the German Culture Council (*Deutscher Kulturrat*), which presented concepts for cultural education (using the term *kulturelle Bildung*) in 1988, 1994 and 2005.

In work aimed at developing this field, reference is repeatedly made to a document issued in 1977 by the *Bund-Länder* Commission for Educational Planning and Research Promotion, entitled the *Supplement to the Education Plan*. This document was a co-ordinated government recommendation intended as a guideline for national, regional and local government bodies regarding the fostering of cultural education. One special aspect was that the *Supplement* proposed an organizational concept for cultural education at the local community level. The prime task of the cultural education services (the cross-cutting coordination units in local government) was, first and foremost, to develop concepts and programmes that would ensure cooperation not only between cultural and educational institutions, but also with youth and leisure facilities. The aim of these services was to broaden the scope and impact of cultural events and facilities, and to improve interdisciplinary skills among those working in the cultural education field in various institutions (see e.g. Eichler 1988: 110ff.).

Culture with children, based on the culture of children

The growing importance attached to culture and the reorientation of cultural work with children in Germany, from the 1970s to 1990s, was ultimately connected to the search for 're-integration' (Ulrich Beck's term, cf. Beck 1986), given the breakdown in both sense and meaning that had affected traditional social institutions. What used to confer identity – family, work, social morals, school and the education system – had largely lost self-evident cultural meaning. Children's culture too could no longer be confined to its conventional products, places, expressions and activities. Instead, greater significance was attributed to its redesign, mainly through emphasis being given to the importance of the 'social'. Thus, the idea of cultural work at this time departs from the cultural sector in its narrow sense, and acquires key significance for the entire lifeworld. People planning or doing cultural work with children and young people now saw their contribution as a largely de-traditionalized enterprise that took place outside school. Above all, their work could no longer be reduced to the unilateral transmission of culture from adult to child. Adult culture was no longer deemed to be a 'guide' to be emulated. Instead, children's creativity had to be valued in its own right.

This approach is informed by an understanding that children are (and have always been) autonomous participants in the cultural process and that they develop specific ways of appropriating culture that can be cultivated or wither away. Thus, 'this normative definition surmounts the notion of a culture merely *for* children, in favour of cultural work with children that is based on the culture *of* children' (Klein 1993: 163). It links into the arguments of the children's rights debate, according to which children have their own worth as human beings, not some abstruse, derived kind of rights. It asserts that children have a right to develop their personality, a right that they must also exercise in their own interest. Children's weaknesses and need for protection are not denied, but the 'onus of proof' is reversed. It is not children's lack, which has to be dismantled by adults in a protracted education process, that defines childhood – for in this view, entertained by adults, the decision as to what is in the best interests children must be taken *in advance*. Instead, children are assumed from the outset to be independent, and questions then centre on where their independence is suppressed, restricted, prevented or obstructed. This position thus emphasizes the rights of children to their own cultures. Another basic assumption is that children have a potential for creativity that is unique to them. The point is to explore that potential with sensitivity and commitment, 'without projecting specific characteristics into childhood from a romanticised, utopian perspective based on semi-ontological images of children' (Klein 1993).

For those who planned and framed cultural work outside the school, it was considered important to be on an equal footing with those they addressed. A key principle they propounded, therefore, 'proximity' to the everyday routines of children, who are themselves to be accorded the space and the time needed for the formation of self. Within this approach, representative symbols are the main tools (unlike in school, where the discursive dominates), the aim being to help create meaning through the sensuous (*Sinn durch Sinnlichkeit*).

The emphasis on socio-culture can thus be summarized as an effort to establish contexts and milieux that generate or at least foster children's participation. As far as the de-hierarchization of the inter-generational dimension is concerned, the appeal of cultural pedagogics is thought to consist not only in its being able to link into the real interests and needs of children and young people, but 'that the field is also appealing to adult experts, because they have usually chosen their occupation due to precisely such interests and they have developed their occupational identity from that field' (Fuchs 2002: 114). Compared to the usual debates about childhood, in which the convergence of legal and economic options are foremost, the particular benefits and opportunities of focusing on cultural education processes are seen in the fact that they are very powerful in helping individual sensitivities express themselves, and in fostering in children and young people a conscious relationship to their own person, biography and future. Strengthening the self-experience and self-awareness of children and young people in this way is seen as essential to the assertion of independence in a pluralist society, with its diversity of potential identifications, and is also necessary for standing up effectively for one's own rights.

The culture of the self – 1990s to the present

The pedagogical idea of the 'self-realizing human', which Schulze identified as a *leitmotif* of the socio-cultural approach of the 1970s, can be said to be *the* idea informing cultural pedagogics and education in Germany to this day. It is an idea that centres on what I call the 'culture of the self' (in the sense of *Selbstbildung*, formation of the self) and the social framework within which such processes of 'self-realisation' and the 'culture of the self' are conceived in cultural policy discourses is marked by conceptual terms such as 'individualization', 'reflexive modernity', 'second modernity' and 'postmodernity'. Moreover, ideological backing for this expanding activity in the field of children's and youth culture pedagogy in Germany (evident in the congresses, conferences and publications of the respective lobbies) comes from analyses of society that reflect a gradual shift in interest in the social sciences since the 1970s. There has been a move away from the classical theories of social inequality towards culturally based concepts centred on terms like 'everyday life', 'lifeworld', 'lifestyle', milieu and – later – the 'art of living'. This trend, ushered in by the turn to theories of everyday life, makes the focus of interest 'one's own life project'. The assumption is that individuals are bombarded by new challenges, against a background of extensive and intensive de-traditionalization processes and, by asserting a trend towards 'individualized forms and situations of existence that compel people to make themselves the centre of their own life planning and way of life', Beck (1986: 116ff.) defined the paradigm that was, and still is, important for the (broad) debate on lifestyle.

The *Bundesvereinigung Kulturelle Jugendbildung* (BKJ – Federal Association for Cultural Youth Education) deserves particular mention in this context since it focused intensively on the importance of children's and youth culture work for the development of individuals' control over their lives. Their *Lernziel Lebenskunst* ('art of life as a learning objective') was a Federal pilot project and, in an overview of the new cultural pedagogics in Germany, the 'art of living' (*Lebenskunst*) is described as a 'paradigmatic buzzword'. The issue or goal is 'education through self-aware control of one's life' (Zacharias 2001: 219).

Thus, for instance, one of the conferences that the BKJ organised in 2000 in connection with this project was entitled 'Participation – Education – Art of Living. Models of Participation in Cultural Youth Education'. The proceedings of the conference give a good impression of the special role to be played by children's 'participation in cultural education' and reference is made to the model provided by the *Lernziel*

Lebenskunst project. The proceedings clearly showed that the conference was not about participatory projects in the field of political involvement, or pursuing specific interests – for example, in relation to the residential environment of children and young people, in which discussions with politicians, children's centres and local government officials responsible for children's affairs are key mechanisms. Rather, the point was to demand, and actively promote, opportunities and ways to ensure participation and independent action by young people beyond any political framework in the narrower sense. There are, nonetheless many points of contact.[6]

Participation and exclusion

Work on the *Lebenskunst* concept is being done at a time when poverty is again becoming the subject of public debate, and many studies are being published on childhood poverty in Germany (see, in particular, the anthologies on children and poverty by Klocke and Hurrelmann 1998; 2001; Mansel and Neubauer 1998; Butterwegge 2000; Butterwegge and Klundt 2002).

Moreover, it is occurring at a time when German sociology is drawing attention to the fact that, although the social climate is characterized by conflicts of interest and rivalry, society is not being torn apart and it is precisely this ability of society to incorporate and integrate that which threatens it that is brought into focus by the concept of exclusion, a term imported from debates in France and England (see e.g. Bude 2004). This term functions as a counter-concept to participation, describing the slow or sudden falling through the social safety net, and the isolation and inaccessibility of those excluded in this way. Eliminating the internal and external restraints and barriers with which people seeking upward mobility are confronted was one of the principal motives of social and education policies in the 1960s. The goal of equal opportunity always related to an essentially open space. By contrast, the term 'exclusion', characteristic of the 1990s onwards, centres not on upward, but on downward mobility. It not only focuses (in respect of poverty and homelessness, for example) on ways that the 'majority society' shields itself against 'losers', it also highlights the risk of dropping out of society, as fundamental within mainstream society. It is becoming clear, therefore, that 'the fat years' turned Germany into a 'trade union and social welfare state for the middle classes' and in the debate about the old and new mechanisms of a class society, the question of interrelationships between economic, social and cultural capital is one that is acquiring new and explosive relevance. It is education policy that is treated as the most important area for intervening in these interrelationships.

This analysis implies a twin challenge for the idea of cultural work outside school: one the one hand, it reinforces doubts that such work can to reach everyone; and on the other, it raises the issue of how such work can accept the cultures of those who pursue *self*-exclusion through their cultural interests and activities. In the 1990s, as outlined above, criticism was increasingly voiced against the concept of cultural work which, as an extra-curricular endeavour, competed from the outset with social work, where reservations were expressed from the beginning.

As far as the first challenge is concerned, protagonists of cultural pedagogics have emphasized repeatedly that focusing purely on the supply side and the provision of participatory options is not sufficient to get all social groups involved. The results of empirical studies on stratum-specific perception of infrastructural provision can be applied without difficulty to cultural participation. As regards the second challenge, reservations about cultural work have always been voiced by the social work camp, which has pointed to 'preferences in taste specific to the underclass', preferences that lead to exclusion of various kinds as soon as aesthetics come into play (cf. Treptow 1988: 89f.). Culture workers have countered this by saying that all people have capacities for cultural expression, but these are neglected if we concentrate on their problems and disadvantages. They argue that selectively looking at deficiencies and limited competencies blocks the very de-stigmatization that helps to achieve integration and that this is the core issue. I do not wish to examine these problems further here, but would merely conclude that, however one conceives the tension or polarity between the social and the cultural, it is at this juncture that the limited scope of pedagogics outside school becomes apparent.

Departing from the primacy of the extra-curricular

Since the 1990s – and especially since German schoolchildren performed so poorly in international comparisons[7] – extra-curricular pedagogics has been at risk of being isolated and ignored even though it has been assigned great importance in Germany until now (as already mentioned) because of the tradition of the half-day school. This has led to a relatively well-developed range of schemes outside school that perform educational tasks in the wider sense. Besides the (new) cultural pedagogics, on which this chapter focuses, there are youth associations, sports, Church-based and environment activist organizations, all of which compete for the leisure time of children and young people. The Youth Welfare Act, in force until 1991, signified a commitment as early as 1922 to institutionalize social and extra-curricular pedagogics. The law which succeeded the Youth Welfare Act, the Children's and Adolescents' Aid Act 1991 (*Kinder- und Jugendhilfegesetz*), reiterated this commitment.

Social and cultural pedagogics – the former traditionally dealing with the problems and deficiencies, a sort of societal repair company, the latter intending to realise cultural and social education for all – have in common the fact that they both define themselves in opposition to school. To that extent they are called into question by current efforts in Germany to establish all-day schools (like those which have existed almost everywhere in Europe for decades), but also ultimately because of their specific understanding of pedagogics, the roots of which reach back far into the past. Max Fuchs (2005: 215) identifies the extended influence of a highly reformist approach to pedagogics outside school, as characterized by the certainty that one is pursuing (only fitting) real, child-related pedagogics.

The relationship of both institutions (cultural and social pedagogics outside school) to school is, therefore, undergoing a remarkable change of perspective. It is claimed, for example, that the theory and practice of work outside school must align with schools, in contrast to the initially necessary distance maintained by play- and culture-based initiatives and projects in the 1970s and 1980s (with the exception of schools of music and art for the young): 'cooperation and networking with everyday schooling and school culture, as well as holistic and life-world approaches to everyday life and the aesthetic and cultural learning of children and youths is sorely needed and necessary' (Zacharias 2001: 162). Collaboration between cultural education and schools is demanded by the German Cultural Council in its 'Concept for Cultural Education' (1994). *Kultur macht Schule* is the title of a national assessment of co-operation and networking of school-based and cultural pedagogical learning with artistic and aesthetic goals.

Indeed, the Federal Association for Cultural Education of Youth organized a dialogue on this issue between schools, cultural education workers and youth workers, with the aim of exploring 'general education' at a variety of levels (BKJ 1997: 15ff). In contrast to the earlier approach, representatives of cultural education now emphasize with increasing frequency the common characteristics of school *and* cultural pedagogics: shared target populations, shared conditions and problems of growing up, a shared social context in which pedagogics takes place, in school and outside school; and shared responsibility for supporting people in their education. Efforts are made to generate scale and synergy effects by linking school practices and cultural pedagogics. But it is emphasized that co-operation with schools makes sense only on the basis of differences, because it is the differences that form the real basis for co-operation. The desired partner is a school that, in the words of the chairman of the German Cultural Council, 'is at the centre of education for adolescents, but strives for fair cooperation with other venues of education as part of a broader educational network' (Fuchs 2005: 236).

Thus, the broadly defined concept of culture in the 1970s and 1980s has been replaced by a 'broadly defined concept of education' (in the sense of *Bildung*) 'that respects the fact that very many more competencies, skills and attitudes are needed than are addressed by concentrating on the purely cognitive' (Fuchs 2005: 245). This is bound up with the acceptance that other agencies and venues are needed besides school. Under such conditions, a school can be well integrated into a local educational network in which various bodies take responsibility for different educational tasks. However, this requires 'a major internal reform of school' (Fuchs 2005: 245). Reference is also made in this connection to 'schools centred on the social space' (Fuchs 2005: 246). 'The agenda includes qualitative control over the *development of a local educational infrastructure* in the sense of a local educational landscape' (Lindner 2004: 8ff.). Such an approach demands, and fosters, co-operation between the various players in child and youth aid in the locality, and the forms of participation they practise. The realization, long present and implemented among representatives of cultural pedagogics, that participative cultural work depends on decentralized schemes based on social space, is now embracing school as well.

The expectations that cultural and social pedagogists have of schools being partners in Germany are, however, limited. Radical critics of neoliberal tendencies in education reform preach caution when assessing the merits of all-day schools. Bernhard, for example, after an ideological critique and review of learning cultures as recommended by neoliberals, recommends that the intensive linking of school pedagogics and social work be 'reflected upon anew, instead of devaluing its usefulness for emancipatory action with the killer argument that it installs total educational control' (Bernhard 2004: 321). Equally, the cultural pedagogics side is dominated by scepticism towards the changes that will occur in the relationship between cultural work (outside school) and school practice, if school and education policy-makers in Germany take steps to establish all-day schools. Scepticism is expressed regarding the likelihood that a school, which is primarily concerned with its own affairs and has other concerns, will start opening itself up to more social issues during this radical change.

Likewise, teachers are expected to have other priorities than co-operation with those in the field of cultural work with children and youths. Recent empirical studies (Behr-Heintze and Lipski 2005) show that, so far, co-operation on the part of schools has mainly been concentrated on services that address problems or deficiencies – parental counselling, general and occupationally related social work, educational psychology services. Despite this bad starting point and a framework in dire need of improvement, Lindner (2004) calls on those doing cultural work with children and young people to focus on pragmatic co-operation with schools – even to accept half-baked compromises.

In the 1970s and 1980s, 'culture is booming' went unquestioned in Germany. Ever since the results of the first PISA study were announced, however, it would now be more accurate to say that '*Bildung* is booming' – in public discourse at least. In his address to a conference entitled '*Bildung* is More! The Significance of Different Learning Venues' (2002), the Mayor of Nuremberg said, 'this conference is being held at a time in which – if we ignore football – there is only one topic, and this is unusual: the topic is *Bildung*' (Förther 2003: 23).

This does not mean, though, that culture is no longer playing a role in public discourses or politics. Indeed, German cultural policy even experienced a boost in the late 1990s.[8] Representatives of the SPD and the CDU/CSU (the two largest political parties) have, for example, emphasized that future culture policy will attach considerable importance to the cultural education of children and young people. If the term 'cultural education' (in contrast to children's culture, cultural work and cultural pedagogics) has become largely established in more official documents and announcements (and in the ever more frequent opening addresses – the symbolic expressions of support – by ministers and other politicians), then one can view this as an indication that the field has gained in importance.

A revaluation of culture applies also to new emphases in policy programmes concerning children. For example, in the 10th Children and Youth Report (BMFSFJ [Federal Ministry for Family, Senior Citizens, Women and Youth] 1998), which is also designated as the first children report of the Federal Republic of Germany, a *culture of growing up* is defined as the *political objective*, the intention being to ensure that children, and the task of taking care of them, are considered to be a primary social obligation. Childhood is not understood in a familialistic manner, but as embedded in a social network and in the culture of growing up, a culture that promises support for the respective individual education and development processes of children. It is conceptualized as a culture where the individualism of children and diverging development have their place, just like frictions, conflicts and crises, because children also develop through conflicts and crises. The culture of growing up is evidence for the image of the child as a 'self-active, individual subject'.

Cultural education, circular subjects and the primacy of the *Eigenwelten*

At conferences and in publications about culture policy, in the sense used in this chapter, the work performed to date is also analysed and evaluated. It is pointed out, for example, that since the cultural upswing in the 1970s, efforts to expand supply-side provision and to improve the broader conditional framework have been very successful. Christina Weiss, the Federal Government Commissioner for Culture and Media, said in her opening speech to the 3rd National Culture Policy Congress on the topic *publikum macht kultur* (the public makes culture) that '"Culture for All" is a reality. The financial and ritual barriers to access have been ground down' (Weiss 2005: 32). The conclusion she drew generally applies equally to the younger generation. If one compares the results of the 'Youth Culture Barometer' for 2004 with a study dating from 1973, what we find is not a decline in the participation of young people in art and culture, as was feared, but a trend towards greater participation (cf. Keuchel 2005: 12ff).

However, if we look more closely, we find that the positive results relate only to a small section and that not even 8 per cent of schoolchildren in or leaving secondary school take advantage of aesthetic and cultural projects and schemes. Even when it comes to informal activities like graffiti spraying and the like, the proportion of young people with minimal school education joining in is a mere 18 per cent. Thus, what the PISA study discovered for school-based education – namely a blatant lack of equal opportunity – applies equally to cultural activities outside the school. But what the Youth Culture Barometer also shows clearly – which the advocates of a new form of cultural pedagogics, who are critical of schooling and teaching, had assumed and that greatly inspired their efforts – is that school has little success in awakening children's cultural interests using the tools of conventional art and music classes. This holds true even when lessons are enjoyed by the children concerned.

One aspect that is at least as important as the non-participation of the socially disadvantaged is a change in cultural interests, not only among social groups with less education but also among relatively well-educated households – i.e. those who still make use of available cultural offerings more or less as a matter of course. Such a finding is all the more noteworthy in that the conditions for cultural participation have not only improved considerably as a result of the disproportional increase in cultural offerings in recent decades, but also due to more leisure time, greater purchasing power and higher levels of formal educational attainment.

Conclusion

In discourses on the cultural education of children and young people in Germany today, arguments dating from the 1970s and 1980s continue to play a major role. Since the 1990s, culture and cultural education have also been viewed as an instrument against economization and the neoliberal *Zeitgeist*, and are still under discussion as a vehicle for re-integration.[9] The spectrum of co-existing and competing aims, motives and approaches is likely, therefore, to be greater in Germany today and, indeed, is matched by a broadening of the field of activity, such as the various initiatives and projects, run in some cases by schools and teachers, that extend into the leisure time of children and youths.

What is noteworthy here, as far as basic and guiding motives are concerned, is that the critique of the 'high culture' motive has virtually faded away. Anti-authoritarian and other perspectives critical of education have also evaporated, at least from public discourse. This does not signify, however, any relapse into authoritarian patterns of thinking in general. Rather, it is assumed that anti-authoritarian currents and informalization tendencies have (finally) become established in everyday culture. Moreover, the greater the distance from the intense de-traditionalization arguments of the 1970s, the more clearly the consequences for everyday life and habitus, which arise from welcome gains in liberalization, are articulated in public discourse.

The cultural capital that contemporaries in general, and young people in particular, are injecting into (cultural) learning processes is likewise viewed more sceptically (and is seen more in need of cultivation than in the 1970s and 1980s). Schulze (1999) coined the term 'circular subject' to illustrate his view that cultural perception, and perception of the world in a very general sense, is adjusted to the subjective spectacles of one's own world, or *Eigenwelt*. Thomas Ziehe (2005) describes these *Eigenwelten*, constructed under a fusion of normal everyday life and popular culture, as 'relevance corridors' that are no longer niches like the *Eigenwelten* of previous generations of youth, and which no longer have to be defended against the demands of the environment. They are perceived instead as 'the mental centre of one's own way of life'; they radiate into all spheres of life and give them a specific hue; and therefore they are not only a socially accepted parallel world, but have become a genuine 'leading culture' (Ziehe 2005: 202).

It is only logical, therefore, that when Ziehe demands the 'decentring of *Eigenwelten*' he is asking that the search for a reality beyond one's own horizon be made a core issue in learning and cultural work. So it is no coincidence that, in critical contributions to the practice of cultural work, there is more emphasis on the argument that the aesthetic does not gain its real significance in affinity but in opposition to everyday culture and everyday life (see e.g. Jäger and Kuckhermann 2004). Generally, the authors adhere to the necessity of subject orientation in (cultural) learning processes but simultaneously emphasize the Janus-faced character of this orientation; under the conditions of neoliberalism and globalization, educational options that aim at strengthening subjectivity are always in danger of being undermined.

Participating in the consumption of their everyday worlds, it is argued, they have the chance to shape their subjectivity, but not at all in the sense of the formation of the self (*Selbst-Bildung*). But there are also more structurally-oriented critics in current educational discourses who register a cult of self-learning as a reflex of modernization imperatives, which represent an invitation to a 'laissez-faire-attitude' (Bremer 2004: 195ff.). Such critics complain that the emphasis on self-learning and informal learning outside educational institutions shifts attention away from how education is framed – for instance, from the institutions of education, from the structural conditions and the teaching personnel – to the cultural actors as constructors of their own educational biographies (*Bildungsbiographien*). What is demanded instead of mainly short-term and often one-off measures are 'reliable', 'consistent' and 'long-term' educational offerings. These would need to be accompanied by cultural-political curricula and programmes considering especially the requirements of open all-day schooling and following an integrated (school- and culture-) pedagogical approach. They would also need to be built in the developing 'culture of growing up'.

Notes

1 *Bildung* (education in the formative, cultural sense) is a very complex term confined to the linguistic regions of Germany and Scandinavia. In German, it has a specific relationship with the concept of *Erziehung* (education in the

sense of upbringing and rearing). In German, a distinction is made between *Erziehung* and *Bildung*, two terms with different connotations that are subsumed in English under the single term 'education'. One characteristic feature of *Bildung* is the autonomy of the educational subject. *Bildung* is understood to be a process involving the self-formation of personality. This self-formation is not directed at any materialist objective, but occurs for its own sake. Wilhelm von Humboldt believed that the need to 'form' or educate oneself (*sich zu bilden*) is inherent in people and need only be wakened. According to Humboldt, education in the sense of *Bildung* is the stimulation of all of people's energies in order that they develop and unfold through mental appropriation of the world and progress to a self-determining individuality and personality. The modern, holistic concept of *Bildung* (education in the formative sense) stands for a never-ending process in which people expand their intellectual, cultural and practical skills, as well as their personal and social competencies.

2   Vinterberg (1985), for example, has pointed out that the first reference in the Danish language to 'children's culture policy' was in 1971, both in the public debate and at ministerial level. It was Scandinavians who brought children's culture as a topic and political task into the European debate (cf. Liljestrøm 1980). The importance to be attributed to Danish policies on children's culture can be seen in the fact that, through its foreign embassies and consulates, the Danish Foreign Ministry disseminates fact sheets in several languages on 'Danish themes', one of which is about 'Children's culture in Denmark'. The authors explicitly identify with the work programme of the Nordic Council of Ministers, thus underlining the supranational basis of these children's culture policies. The Swedish Institute (Svenska Institutet), a government institute assigned the task of informing people in other countries about Sweden, has published a paper entitled 'Swedish Children's Culture' as part of its 'Culture in Sweden' series. To quote from that paper (February 2002): 'The right of Swedish children to have culture and access to culture has become fully integrated with the concept of childhood.'

3   *Kinderläden* (literally children's shops, so called because they were often set up in empty shop premises) are self-organising, self-governing ('alternative') kindergartens or day centres, attended by children of pre-school age (between about 3 and 6½ years). By self-governing is meant that the 'children's shops' were totally unregimented at first, then later organized by small, not-for-profit associations comprised of the parents and in many cases the teachers (*Erzieher*). These associations are largely self-governing. However, although they operate along self-governing lines, and it is possible for children's parents to become directly involved, the supervisory authority is the same as for conventional kindergartens, namely the Youth Office (*Jugendamt*). The specific tasks and responsibilities discharged by parents and teachers/educators differ from one 'shop' to the next. Administrative and maintenance work is usually done on a voluntary basis. As far as cooking, cleaning and deputizing for personnel on sick leave is concerned, there are almost as many models as there are children's centres. The voluntary commitment of all those involved makes it possible for the children to be assured a more individual form of care in these relatively small children's centres than is the case in larger institutions. The form of

education striven for aimed at freedom from repression. The aim and intention was that children should develop their own independence, critical-mindedness and creativity at as early a stage as possible. The same principles of organization, management and education applied in 'schoolkids' shops' (*Schülerläden*) as in 'children's shops': small, self-governing centres for schoolchildren, mostly run by private associations. Primary school children go to such centres after school (which can be any time from 10 or 11 in the morning until late in the afternoon).

4   Célestin Freinet wanted to reform the school system from within. Based on his work and experience as a teacher, and on the reformist educational ideas and ideals of 1920s reformers, he developed a concept of schooling now referred to as 'Freinet education'. The basic principles of Freinet's educational philosophy include the free development of personality, critical interaction with the environment, children's self-responsibility, as well as cooperative learning and shared responsibility. In Freinet education, teacher-controlled lessons are replaced with self-determined lessons by and for the schoolchildren themselves. Classes are organized as cooperatives that are self-governing in every respect. Schoolchildren and teachers each have one vote in the governing body, the Class Council. The children decide for themselves, by and large, what they want to learn, and arrange among themselves who they want to work with and what objectives they will pursue. They report to the class as a whole on the work they have been doing. Key techniques and methods of Freinet education are the school printing press (documentation of work performed, free expression, class newspaper, demystification of the printed word), correspondence, free work, class councils (allocation of posts, drawing up work schedules), exploration and trips outside the classroom.

5   A statement made in 1991 in favour of 'Structural Assistance for Socio-culture' declared that the new political and economic freedom in the eastern states of the Federal Republic needed fields of cultural experimentation so that involvement, commitment, creativity, imagination, the ability to engage in discourse and tolerance could develop as essential resources for building a democratic society and for meeting the challenges that lay ahead. 'Socio-culture' also provides a programme and tested practices that are flexible enough to be adapt changing social conditions (see Zacharias 2001: 84f.)

6   Children and young people's participation in decision-making concerning themselves has been on an upward trend in the FRG for several years and is now embodied in the KJHG (Children and Youth Welfare Act). Early in the 1990s, participation was talked about as a 'primary cultural technique' (cf. Wiebusch 1991). In recent decades, numerous forms and methods of participation have been tried and practised at various levels. In this connection, special mention should be made of local politics where children's interests get a hearing and young people learn about democratic structures at an early stage (not least) in order to participate actively in social processes in the future. Participation includes children's parliaments, children's hearings and special consultation hours for children with local politicians; exploration of interests, town planning, development of playgrounds and the residential environment have become established areas. There are many points of contact with activities within the scope of cultural work in a narrower sense. Moreover, both areas have been inspired by the children's rights movement

and the 1989 UN convention. Many participation projects are located in the field of political co-determination and enforcement of concerns relating to the environment of where children and young people live. Discussions with politicians, children's offices and child commissioners in communes are important.

7   After the publication of the results of the PISA (Programme for International Student Assessment of OECD) 2000 study even the general public knew what had been well known to experts for many years: the German school system is suffering from a striking lack of quality, an extreme lack of motivation and an excessive amount of injustice (cf. Deutsches Pisa-Konsortium 2001). PISA 2000 is part of a project, divided into three four-year research cycles, which ran from 1998 to 2007. During the first cycle (1998–2001) literacy, mathematics and the natural sciences were tested. Of the 180,000 15-year-old male and female pupils from 32 countries, 5,000 came from Germany. Germany came almost at the bottom (20th out of 21 places), far behind the Scandinavian, Anglo-Saxon and some Asian countries.

8   In 1998, Chancellor Schröder's Social-Democrat/Green Party coalition government created the post of Federal Government Commissioner for Culture and Media, and parliament established the Committee for Culture and Media. In addition, the Enquete Commission on 'Culture in Germany' proposed anchoring culture as a state goal in the Basic Law or constitution of Germany. The intention here is to make it the state's duty to protect and promote culture as a constitutional principle, and so put culture on a par with other state goals.

9   Renate Schmidt, Federal Minister for Family, Senior Citizens, Women and Youth, wrote in a statement setting out the reasons for youth-cultural competitions: 'Especially under conditions of social change – where points of orientation cease to exist – culture, as a sense and direction, becomes more and more important and supports imagination, creativeness, sensitivity and identity, critical faculties and commitment to a vision of a better world. The youth-cultural competitions are a reflection of these cultural education offers' (Schmidt 2005: 29). She points out that it is indispensable for a vibrant democracy to give children and young people a platform where they can present themselves and express their points of view.

References

Beck, U. (1986) *Risikogesellschaft*. Frankfurt: Suhrkamp.

Behr-Heinzte, A. and Lipski, J. (2005) *Schulkooperationen. Stand und Perspektiven der Zusammenarbeit zwischen Schulen und ihren Partnern. Forschungsbericht des DJI*. Schwalbach/Ts.: Wochenschau Verlag.

Bernhard, A. (2004) Neue Lernkultur und die marktkonforme Zurichtung der Bildung. *Das Argument* 44: 311–24.

Biedenkopf, K. (1986) 'Kultur für alle'. Kommunalpolitische Vereinigung der CDU. In Nordrhein-Westfalen (ed.) *Der Mensch lebt nicht vom Brot allein. Kultur für alle oder Träume von Spinnern*. Düsseldorf: 11–32.

Braunmühl, E. von (1975) *Antipädagogik*. Weinheim: Beltz.

Braunmühl, E. von (1978) *Zeit für Kinder.* Frankfurt: Fischer.

Bremer, H. (2004) Der Mythos vom autonom lernenden Subjekt. Zur sozialen Verortung aktueller Konzepte des Selbstlernens und zur Bildungspraxis unterschiedlicher sozialer Milieus. In Engler, S. and Krais, B. (eds.), *Das kulturelle Kapital und die Macht der Klassenstrukturen. Sozialstrukturelle Verschiebungen und Wandlungsprozesse des Habitus.* Weinheim and München: Juventa: 189–213.

Brenner, G. (2005) Bildung und Lernen. Anmerkungen zur Ambivalenz der Subjektorientierung. In Hafeneger, B. (ed.), *Subjektdiagnosen. Subjekt, Modernisierung und Bildung.* Schwalbach/Ts.: Wochenschau Verlag: 223–49.

Bude, H. (2004) Das Phänomen der Exklusion. Der Widerstreit zwischen gesellschaftlicher Erfahrung und soziologischer Rekonstruktion. *Mittelweg 36* 4/2004: 3–15.

Bundesvereinigung Kulturelle Jugendbildung e.V. (ed.) (1997) *Kultur macht Schule.* Remscheid: BKJ.

Bundesvereinigung Kulturelle Jugendbildung e.V. (ed.) (2000a) *Kulturarbeit und Armut. Konzepte und Ideen für die kulturelle Bildung in sozialen Brennpunkten und mit benachteiligten jungen Menschen.* Remscheid: BKJ.

Bundesvereinigung Kulturelle Jugendbildung e.V. (ed.) (2000b) *Partizipation und Lebenskunst.* Remscheid: BKJ.

Bundesvereinigung Kulturelle Jugendbildung e.V. (ed.) (2002) *Kultur leben lernen. Bildungswirkungen und Bildungsauftrag der Kinder- und Jugendkulturarbeit.* Remscheid: BKJ.

Butterwegge, C. (2000) *Kinderarmut in Deutschland. Ursachen, Erscheinungsformen und Gegenmaßnahmen.* Frankfurt and New York: Campus.

Butterwegge, C. and Klundt, M. (eds.) (2002) *Kinderarmut und Generationengerechtigkeit.* Opladen: Leske & Budrich.

Deutsches PISA-Konsortium (ed.) (2001) *PISA 2000. Basiskompetenzen von Schülerinnen und Schülern im internationalen Vergleich.* Opladen: Leske & Budrich.

Durand, B. (2004) *Die Legende vom typisch Deutschen. Eine Kultur im Spiegel der Franzosen.* Leipzig: Militzke.

Eichler, K. (1988) Alles nach Plan – Möglichkeiten und Grenzen der Kulturentwicklungsplanung. In Müller-Rolli, S. (ed.), *Kulturpädagogik und Kulturarbeit. Grundlagen, Praxisfelder, Ausbildung.* Weinheim and München: Juventa: 105–18.

Förther, H. (2003) Die Gestaltung einer Bildungslandschaft als kommunalpolitische Aufgabe. In Prölß, R. (ed.), *Bildung ist mehr! Die Bedeutung der verschiedenen Lernorte. Konsequenzen aus der PISA-Studie zur Gestaltung einer kommunalen Bildungslandschaft.* Nürnberg: Emwe-Verlag: 23–6.

Freire, P. (1971) *Pädagogik der Unterdrückten.* Rowohlt: Reinbek.

Fuchs, M. (2002) Kulturelle Bildung in der Jugendhilfe. In Münchmeier, R., Otto, H.-U. and Rabe-Kleberg, U. (im Auftrag des Bundesjugendkuratoriums) (eds.), *Kinder- und Jugendhilfe vor neuen Aufgaben.* Opladen: Leske & Budrich: 107–17.

Fuchs, M. (2005) Kulturpädagogik und Schule im gesellschaftlichen Wandel – Alte und neue Herausforderungen für die Theorie und Praxis von Bildung und Erziehung. Ein Versuch. In Deutscher Kulturrat (ed.), *Kulturelle Bildung in der Reformdiskussion. Konzeption Kulturelle Bildung III.* Berlin: Deutscher Kulturrat: 155–276.

Grüneisl. G. and Zacharias, W. (1988) *PA. Die neue Kinder- und Jugendkulturarbeit. Kulturpädagogisches Lesebuch IV, Teil 1–3.* München: Pädagogische Aktion.

Hengst, H. (1995) Von und mit Kids – Aktive Kinderkultur in Westeuropa. *Kunstschule im Kontext. 10 Jahre Landesverband der Kunstschulen Niedersachsen e.V.* Hannover: Landesverband der Kunstschulen: 56–65.

Hentig, H. von (1971) *Cuernavaca – oder: Alternativen zur Schule.* Stuttgart: Klett.

Hoffmann, H. (1979) *Kultur für alle.* Frankfurt: Fischer Verlag.

Illich, I. (1970) *Schulen helfen nicht.* Rowohlt: Reinbek.

Illich, I. (1972) *Entschulung der Gesellschaft.* Rowohlt: Reinbek.

Jäger, J. and Kuckhermann, R. (2004) Ästhetische Praxis im gesellschaftlichen Kontext. In Jäger, J. and Kuckhermann, R. (eds.), *Ästhetische Praxis in der Sozialen Arbeit. Wahrnehmung, Gestaltung und Kommunikation.* Weinheim and München: Juventa: 249–80.

Keuchel, S. (2005) Kunst und Kultur im Aufwind? Ergebnisse aus dem Jugend-Kulturbarometer 2004. *Infodienst Kulturpädagogische Nachrichten* 3: 12–13.

Klein, A. (1993) *Kinder, Kultur, Politik. Perspektiven kommunaler Kinderkulturarbeit.* Opladen: Leske & Budrich.

Klemm, U. (2003) Zur Relevanz und Rezeption antiautoritärer Erziehungsmodelle und der Antipädagogik für die Bildungsreform. In Bernhard, A., Kremer, A. and Rieß, F. (eds.), *Kritische Erziehungswissenschaft und Bildungsreform. Programmatik – Brüche – Neuansätze. Band 1. Theoretische Grundlagen und Widersprüche.* Baltmannsweiler: Schneider Verlag Hohengehren: 50–82.

Klocke, A. and Hurrelman, K. (eds.) (1998/2001) *Kinder und Jugendliche in Armut. Umfang, Auswirkungen und Konsequenzen.* Opladen: Westdeutscher Verlag.

Kolfhaus, S. (1992) Kinder- und Jugendarbeit als Querschnittsaufgabe. In Bundesvereinigung kulturelle Jugendbildung (ed.), *Kinder- und Jugendkulturplanung.* Remscheid: Akademie Remscheid: 9–15.

Kolland. D. (2005) Kultur gegen Armut und Ausgrenzung. Über eine Europäische Initiative zur gesellschaftlichen und kulturellen Teilhabe. *Kulturpolitische Mitteilungen* III: 72–3.

Kramer, D. (1988) Zum Kulturbegriff der öffentlichen Kulturarbeit. S. Müller-Rolli (ed.), *Kulturpädagogik und Kulturarbeit. Grundlagen, Praxisfelder, Ausbildung.* Weinheim and München: Juventa: 65–79.

Landesarbeitsgemeinschaft Spiel- und Kulturpädagogik Bayern (ed.) (1990) *Kinder- und Jugendkulturarbeit in Bayern.* LAG Werkstattbücher Nos. 1–3. München.

Liljestrøm, R. (1980) *Children and Culture.* Strasbourg: Council of Europe.

Lindner, W. (2004) 'Genug ist nicht genug'. 12 Anmerkungen zu Stand und Perspektiven der Kooperation von Jugendarbeit und (Ganztags-)Schule. http://kultur-macht-schule.de/.

Mansel, J. and Neubauer, G. (eds.) (1998) *Armut und soziale Ungleichheit bei Kindern.* Opladen: Leske & Budrich.

Meadows, De., Meadows, Do., Zahn, E. and Miling, P. (1973) *Die Grenzen des Wachstums. Bericht des Club of Rome zur Lage der Menschheit.* Reinbek: Rowohlt.

Schmidt, R.. (2005) *Infodienst Kulturpädagogische Nachrichten,* 3: 29.

Schoenebeck, H. von (1982) *Unterstützen statt erziehen.* München.

Schoenebeck, H. von (1985) *Antipädagogik im Dialog.* Weinheim: Beltz.

Schoenebeck, H. von (1992) *Die erziehungsfreie Praxis.* Münster: Votum.

Schulze, G. (1992) *Die Erlebnisgesellschaft. Kultursoziologie der Gegenwart.* Frankfurt and New York: Campus.

Schulze, G. (1999) *Kulissen des Glücks. Streifzüge durch die Eventkultur.* Frankfurt and New York: Campus.

Sinowatz, F. (1987) Das Alltägliche ist die Heimat. In A. Wiesand (ed.), *Kunst ohne Grenzen? Kulturelle Identität in Europa.* Köln.

Therborn, G. (1993) Children's Rights since the Constitution of Modern Childhood. A Comparative Study of Western Nations. In Qvortrup, J. (ed.), *Childhood as a Social Phenomenon. Lessons from an International Project.* Vienna: European Centre: 105–38.

Treptow, R. (1988) Kulturelles Mandat. Soziale Kulturarbeit und kulturelle Sozialarbeit. In Müller-Rolli, S. (ed.), *Kulturpädagogik und Kulturarbeit. Grundlagen, Praxisfelder, Ausbildung.* Weinheim and München: Juventa: 81–103.

Vinterberg, S. (1985) Kinderkulturforschung? Kann man das essen? Ansätze zur Diskussion der Kinderkulturforschung in Dänemark. In Hengst, H. (ed.) *Kindheit in Europa.* Frankfurt: Suhrkamp: 280–301.

Weiss, C. (2005) Das Publikum ist die Macht der Kultur. *Kulturpolitische Mitteilungen,* III: 32–4.

Wiebusch, R. (1991) Mehr Politik für Kinder wagen? – Perspektiven einer Politik für Kinder, mit Kindern und für Kinder. In Aktion & Kultur mit Kinder e.V. (ed.), *betr.: Kindheit '90.* Düsseldorf: Akki: 61–76.

Wiepersdorfer Erklärung (1992) *Forderungen und Empfehlungen für eine Strukturhilfe Soziokultur in den neuen und alten Bundesländern.* Dortmund et al.

Zacharias, W. (2001) *Kulturpädagogik. Kulturelle Jugendbildung. Eine Einführung.* Opladen: Leske & Budrich.

Ziehe, T. (2005) Schulische Lernkultur und zeittypische Mentalitätsrisiken. In Hafeneger, B. (ed.), *Subjektdiagnosen. Subjekt, Modernisierung und Bildung.* Schwalbach/Ts.: Wochenschau Verlag: 193–222,

Zinnecker, J. (1996) Soziologie der Kindheit oder Sozialisation des Kindes? Überlegungen zu einem aktuellen Paradigmenstreit. Honig, M.-S., Leu, H. R. and Nissen, U. (eds.), *Kinder und Kindheit. Soziokulturelle Muster – sozialisationstheoretische Perspektiven.* Weinheim and München: Juventa: 31–54.

10
Work and Care: Reconstructing Childhood through Childcare Policy in Germany

Michael-Sebastian Honig

The Federal Republic of Germany and the German Democratic Republic were not only two opposing political systems; pre-school childcare and education in the two states were also based on opposing beliefs. In West Germany there was traditionally little support for the idea that childcare should be provided for by the state. However, since German reunification in 1989 the 'old federal states' in West Germany have been undergoing a quantitative increase in institutional pre-school care, which would have been unthinkable during the Cold War years. Today, virtually every child attends pre-school, at least in the year prior to school enrolment. However, this development is not so much due to the appeal of the East German model; more important are the cultural and economic changes in West German society itself, in particular the growing number of women, including mothers, in paid employment, as well as a diversification of family types.

What is more, this change is to no small degree a result of political action, motivated by concerns about demographic changes, which aims to facilitate the decision to have children and in particular highlights the significance of the pre-school years in promoting child development. The traditional idea that institutional pre-school childcare education performs only a supplementary support function to the family is thus being eclipsed. Educational institutions for children between 3 and 6 years of age (kindergartens) are being called upon to re-examine their traditional self-conception as a 'world of the child', in order to enable mothers and fathers to combine family and work as well as to promote the social and cognitive development of children. The pedagogical quality of these institutions is subject to scrutiny and assessment, and quality management is important. The transition from pre-school to elementary school has also considerably increased in importance and parents are now expected to participate in the work of pre-school institutions.

Whilst these changes are the subject of lively and controversial debate in Germany from a number of perspectives, their effect on children, and on childhood as a structural element of society, is rarely discussed. My argument, explored in this chapter, is as follows: not only is the quantitative increase and changing pedagogical nature of non-family-based pre-school childcare and education important in terms of the development and welfare of children, but a reconstruction of childhood is also in progress, a process that is involving a re-contextualization of childhood in terms of the relationship between family, market and state (Honig and Ostner 2001).

In this context, the term re-contextualization refers to the reconstruction of childhood as an *institution*, which is leading to a more flexible categorization of 'child' and 'family' and redefining the responsibilities of the state and the family towards children (Honig and Ostner 2001: 294; cf. Brannen and O'Brien 1996). Public pre-school childcare is, however, not the only relevant arena here. For example, what lies at the heart of the widespread discussion concerning child poverty in Germany at present? Reference to children and child poverty reflects, I suggest, a new approach to social policy that sets out to readjust priorities: for instance, from compensation to prevention, from passive finance to active measures, from the assignment of privileges to certain groups in the labour market to a redistribution of employment opportunities. 'The child' has now become an age-differentiated status where rights and responsibilities are subject to more detailed regulation than in any other phase of life; Nauck 1996: 26; (Proksch 1996) and in the process, new collective patterns of childhood have evolved.

Such changes comprise a new development – what I term a sociogenesis of childhood. This chapter therefore deals with the processes through which a new definition of childhood is being institutionalized by asking how childhood is changing as a result of childcare policy in Germany. What are the principles of a 'good childhood' and how are 'the child's best interests' being addressed? These issues will be explored by placing the main elements of the argument in an institutional-theoretical context: outlining the empirical changes in institutional childcare in Germany that have given rise to these reflections; providing a more concrete description of childcare arrangements based on institution theory; considering empirical findings from my own research; and summarizing the results and drawing conclusions in terms of future tasks for research.

Theoretical framework: the institutionalization of childhood

'Childhood' offers the ideal starting point for a readjustment of social benefits since, by definition, in a Western European context, childhood is a phase of life in which there should be no need for paid employment. It therefore attracts welfare benefits. Indeed, the twentieth century was the age in which childhood and childcare became 'welfarized'. For this reason, any analysis of the reconstruction of childhood must begin by examining the mobilization of adults' earning potential.

The reconstruction of childhood occurs at two levels, which can be illustrated by means of two triangles (cf. Honig and Ostner 2001). The first is the well-known welfare triangle of market, state and family, which represents the framework of social policy in relation to a child's living conditions and development. This triangle allows us to show the readjustment of responsibilities towards children. I call the second triangle the 'children's well-being triangle'; its poles are the child's degree of freedom, vulnerability and development. This second triangle represents the normative standards of care between adults and children and it can be used to show readjustment in the mode of social integration of childhood. The welfare triangle and the children's well-being triangle are in a state of mutual dependence determined by the tension between a childhood which is at risk from society and in need of protection on the one hand, and a childhood which is dangerous to society and in need of control on the other (Donzelot 1980). The re-contextualization of childhood as an institution can be analysed as a process of shifts within and between these two triangles.

Adopting such an approach, I will trace the re-contextualization of childhood as an institution in Germany by focusing directly on the process of institutionalization itself, while illustrating the flexible categorization of 'child' and 'family' in line with the current political trend towards a redistribution of responsibilities between state and family. The current reconstruction of childhood in Germany can be explored by asking three general questions that relate to these processes:

1. What criteria are used to determine the expenditure of taxpayers' money to be spent on children? (Which children in which families should receive funds? Under what conditions? How much? For how long? And in what form?)
2. What should parents – or rather mothers and/or fathers – be expected to 'deliver' for 'their' children?
3. What can legitimately be expected of children themselves?

Such an approach allows a child-oriented position and a structural perspective to emerge that treats children as a social category. In the context of the question of childcare, therefore, the term 'institutionalization' is not being used to refer to the act of putting children in institutions or facilities created by adults, supposedly in the best interests of the child. Though this is what the concept of institutionalization is often taken to mean, this narrow interpretation reduces schools or preschool institutions to their organizational function and sees them as 'containers' for children. Rather, in this context 'institutionalization' is used, following a long sociological tradition, to capture the dynamic processes involved in the creation, shaping and continuing development of social orders. Social orders are a rational form of social relationships characterized by a tendency towards maxims and rules (Walter 1999). Processes of institutionalization are thus processes by which social orders are formed on the basis of value orientation; an example is Leena Alanen's (2001) school-forming concept of generational ordering. To consider schools and pre-schools as 'institutions' in this sense means seeing them as social arenas of 'childhood' rather than as places where children go. In this sense, then, 'the child' is not institutionalized; instead, childhood is itself an institution, a particular kind of social order (cf. James and James 2004).

This conceptualization of the process thus provides the insight that childhood is no longer automatically, and naturally, institutionalized by what Zinnecker (2000) has described as 'the pedagogical moratorium'. Pedagogical moratoriums are preparatory arenas that implement a principle of integration by means of separation (cf. Herrmann, 1986). Thus, younger members of society are liberated from their obligation to reproduce (via both a ban on child labour and the cult of 'innocence') which allows them to learn. For Zinnecker, the concept of pedagogical moratorium describes an historical process that initially was no more than a utopia, but later became a privilege, and by the twentieth century was established as the typical pattern of childhood, a process that involves the principle of achieving the social integration of children by separating them from adults.

The moratorium concept can be seen, therefore, as a special case of generational ordering, embedded within a specific generational relationship, which is itself structured by substitutional inclusion (cf. Baecker 1994) – a concept originally derived from systems theory and applied to generational orders. Thus, it is pedagogical experts (teachers or parents) who interpret the distinctive qualities of their novices, conveying the adult world and its cultural traditions to them. In the twentieth century, family and school were the most important agencies of substitutional involvement of the next generation in the social system, which are assigned to specific phases only in the lives of young people.

The greater the increase in the significance of formal institutions of care and education for the reproduction of society, the more these are extended in individual biographies. Thus the pedagogical moratorium provides children and teenagers with a space for self-regulation, although this space is also determined by structural ambivalence. After all, the principle of 'integration through separation' bears within it the contradiction between institutionalized immaturity and independence. Substitutional inclusion is thus manifested, historically and empirically, just as much in measures for protection and advancement as it is in strategies for the disciplining and standardization of children and young people (cf. Herrmann 1986). Structural ambivalence is responsible for the extension of institutional moratoria, which now face a powerful tendency towards erosion; not only young people but children too are acquiring the status of citizens and consumers. In Germany, child policy has responded to this with a participation debate; markets and the media target children as independent consumers and emancipate them, albeit with some ambiguity, from their traditional status as novices in adult culture (cf. Hengst 1996).

Development trends in institutional childcare and education in Germany

When the subject of pre-school childcare outside the family is debated in the German context, the theoretical and historical background – whether consciously reflected or not – is not necessarily shared by the US, Britain or the Nordic countries. In contrast to social policy research and research on educational systems, comparative research on the various structures of non-familial institutional care for young children is underdeveloped, despite some important studies (cf. Lamb et al. 1992; Roßbach 2005; Einasdottir and Wagner 2006); there is thus very little comparable data. This applies especially to comparative research from the perspective of systematic theory as would have been necessary for the line of enquiry pursued in the present study.

From an historical point of view, pre-school childcare in Germany is inconceivable without the influence of the British social reformer Samuel Wilderspin and his conception of 'infant schools'. From the mid-nineteenth century, however, it was Friedrich Fröbel's idea of a 'kindergarten' ('children's garden') which became so universal that the word 'kindergarten' is still in use beyond the German-speaking world.

Nonetheless, it has very varied associations. Fröbel's core idea was that he recognized the importance of early childhood for overall development. He elaborated a theory of early childhood which aimed to stimulate the development of human potential in a comprehensive manner. In the tradition of Fröbel, the kindergarten was always a 'child's world' – a concept expressive of the unity of care, education and personality development. In the Anglo-Saxon discussion, a combination of the twin concepts of 'early education' and 'care' would come closest, perhaps, to defining the all-embracing nature of the kindergarten and the 'best interests' of the 'good childhood' that it embodied.

However, Fröbel's ideas had only a limited effect on the social reality of institutional childcare. The latter was in reality determined by a dual motive: in terms of social policy, the aim was to prevent poverty, while the goal in terms of educational policy was to promote child development. This is not to say that the two motives were equally weighted; from a conceptual point of view, they were not explicitly related to one another until the so-called *Volkskindergärten* (people's kindergartens) were established at the turn of the twentieth century, and legally anchored in the social legislation of the Weimar Republic. Gertrud Bäumer, a leading figure in the fledgling German welfare state, emphasized in a famous essay (Bäumer 1929) that this fulfilled not only the right of the child to education but also the right of society to well-educated offspring. Bäumer's point implicitly raises the question of who bears responsibility for infant education, thus accentuating a line of conflict that is equally characteristic of the German tradition as Fröbel's unity of care, education and personality development – the tension between family and state.

While this was initially characterized by class differences, after the experience of National Socialism it acquired a clearly anti-totalitarian tendency. The family policy of the young Federal Republic of Germany may seem conservative or patriarchal today, but in the 1950s and 1960s the autonomy of the family was regarded as fundamental to a free society. Only a third of children aged between 3 and 6 attended a kindergarten, and institutions for children aged under three (crèches) hardly existed in the 1950s–1970s. Children attended kindergarten during the morning but attendance was, and remains, voluntary and parents pay fees which are means-tested and vary by region. All three elements distinguished West German pre-school infant education fundamentally from school.

From the educational reform of 1970 onwards, however, kindergartens have fulfilled something of a hybrid role. They were to support, or at least supplement, family care on the one hand, yet at the same time act as the elementary stage of the educational system. Since the 1970s, day-care institutions for children have evolved from providing this kind of supplementary pedagogical support to the family to becoming part of a more general infrastructure for families and children, while at the same time adopting an increasingly educative function. In the former East Germany, priority has been given to enrolling women in the labour force and therefore a nationwide system of all-day care and education was provided for children aged 0–6 (i.e. from birth until school enrol-ment) and what is more, the kindergartens came under the responsibil-ity of the Ministry of Education.

German unification was a landmark. The Children and Young People Support Act 1990 laid down the unified principle of care, upbringing and education as the task of day-care institutions; it is a federal law, although all 16 states must pass their own regulatory statutes on labour and material resources, for example. Although it is the municipalities that are responsible for providing the institutions, they do not determine what happens in them: this function is per-formed by publicly accredited private associations, from local parental initiatives to large-scale, ideologically-based welfare associations. Since 1992, characteristically in the context of a reform of abortion legislation, every child in Germany aged between 3 and 6 has had the right to a kindergarten place, although even during the decade prior to this, the percentage of children attending kindergarten had increased to over two-thirds. Today, virtually every child attends a kindergarten, at the very latest one year before entering school, and there are as many specialist staff employed in day-care institutions for children as in primary schools.

The publication of the PISA studies in 2000 provided a powerful impulse for the reform of the educational system in Germany, but although considerable forces have been mobilized to reinforce the sig-nificance of the kindergarten as a preparation for school, at the same time the service function of the kindergarten has been emphasized. The aim is to make it easier for mothers and fathers to be in paid work, reflecting the fact that the mobilization of female labour and concerns about a rapidly ageing society are currently powerful driving forces behind childcare policy in Germany. One cannot fail to notice, however, that the old conflict between the various functions of the kindergarten – in relation to family, social and educational policy – remains potent. The key question is: what happens in these institutions? The latest develop-ment is an initiative by the Federal government to increase the avail-ability of institutional care for children aged between 0 and 3 from around 5 per cent to 20 per cent in five years, by means of a major injection of financial resources; at the same time the Federal government and a number of state governments have made concrete decisions to make day-care institutions for children free to parents.

Consequently, the role played by day-care institutions in the life of children has changed considerably; when virtually every child attends kindergarten, childhood as a phase of life takes on a new quality, whilst the merging of the service-oriented and educational functions of the kindergarten (Joos 2002) has made institutional pre-school childcare an agent of the 'de-familialization' (Huinink 2002) of childhood. The various strategies of 'cash for care', 'parental leave' and 'institutional care' promoted by family and social policy currently also being pursued create a range of options which exercise a significantly differentiating influence on the patterns of a child's everyday life and on the ideas of what is 'childlike' and on what a 'good childhood' is, including the role of family, peers and professional educators.

Conceptual elements of a description of care arrangements

In order to analyse these developments in educational and social policy in Germany as processes of the re-contextualization or institutionalization of childhood, the thesis of the erosion of the male breadwinner/female homemaker family is helpful (Janssens 1998). In very simple terms, it is as follows: the *male breadwinner family* secures care and support for the children and adults by releasing women from paid employment so that they can devote themselves to childcare: the woman and children are supported, in return, by a working husband. In comparative social policy research, it is generally recognized that the male breadwinner norm is particularly strong in Germany (see Ostner 1998). The premise of the male breadwinner family as both the norm and an empirical reality has not been considered in terms of childhood theory, even though this family type provides the institutional framework for childhood as pedagogical moratorium. If the model of the male breadwinner/female homemaker family loses its normative force and significance in everyday life, however, this must have consequences for childhood as a moratorium. These consequences can be studied empirically by looking at changes in the care arrangements for children.

What makes this change significant beyond changes in the circumstances of children's lives is the fact that the male breadwinner model is a specific solution to the problem (from the parental perspective) of securing a living by means of paid employment and looking after children at the same time. That is to say, the male breadwinner family was determined by the necessity to combine two different forms of work – the need to secure material subsistence and the need to care for those who are not yet or no longer able to work. The logic of the labour market and the requirements of family welfare production do not supplement each other harmoniously, however; on the contrary, employees face the dilemma of not jeopardizing their chances of employment due to their obligations to provide care for the children or the elderly. The male breadwinner/female homemaker model offers a solution. However, this is at the expense of women's opportunities to secure their own living – a price which has found less and less acceptance in Germany since the 1980s. However, this raises the question of who looks after children and old people, since a family in which both parents are in gainful employment offers no answer to the question (the so-called care crisis; cf. Michel and Mahon 2002). Instead, the answer comes from social and family policy, although here the concern is less with gender equality than with demographic development: it is the extension and qualification of institutional care and education of children at preschool age. The attribution of childhood – especially early childhood – to the family therefore becomes looser, while the structural position of children within the family, and as citizens within society, is changing, becoming more dependent on changes in the labour market.

Seen in this light, a theory of changing childcare arrangements is a theory of how structural incongruities are overcome. The model of the two triangles ('welfare', 'children's well-being' – see above) helps us to analyse such changes in terms of which protagonists and which normative standards these processes involve: in other words, it provides an instrument to describe processes of the institutionalization of childhood. In what follows, the focus will be on a specific aspect of this process, namely on the question of what values mothers and fathers themselves seek to implement when they attempt to overcome these structural incongruities, and what the consequences for children and childhood are.

A study by Jane Lewis gives rise to a provocative theoretical idea. Lewis analysed strategies in British social policy, because in her view the care crisis demands a response in terms of the welfare state and socio-ethics (Lewis 2001). She notes that British social policy has responded to the change in economic conditions that sustained the male breadwinner model by changing the model to one that demands paid employment for men and women, fathers and mothers. However, the reality – parents' coping strategy in these changed economic circumstances – is different: it is more like a 1½ worker model – at least in Britain. Lewis found six patterns of male and female paid work and arrangements for care (Lewis 2001: 157; for Germany, see Wieners 1999). She proposes that the reality of the range of family responses that has emerged following the erosion of the male breadwinner model is not simply a phenomenon of inequality or due to the fact that women have simply not yet caught up, so to speak. Instead, she sees these varied forms as differential manifestations of an unavoidable relationship between processes of family care and those of work. This suggests that families, and parents in particular, are subject to a moral economy of work and care, which is difficult to restrict solely to a microeconomic common denominator of optimized individual benefits (Huinink 2002). The issue here is not simply a lack of facilities and the need for measures to reduce the compatibility costs of work and care to parents: it also refers to the aspirations parents (and the state) have for the creation of a 'good childhood' and a life with children.

In order to describe the institutionalization of childhood empirically, we must focus on care arrangements and the relationship between action orientation and coping strategies, childhood norms and sociocultural reproduction, since care arrangements are social practices that set out to solve the problems caused by the structural care dilemma for parents. Returning to the example of the male breadwinner model, what becomes clear is that this is not an ideal type but rather a normative construct that influences reality to varying degrees. At the empirical level it is, in effect, a *patterned solution*.

Thus, any analysis of the dimensions of care arrangements needs to take cultural indicators into account as well as socio-economic ones: that is to say, it needs to take account not only of the legal and economic determinants of children's position, but also the wider socio-cultural milieu that determines children's potential experience and scope for action. Beyond any pedagogical programme, care arrangements thus fulfil a cluster of societal expectations. The debate on educational policy highlights the educational aspects of such arrangements; in terms of economic and labour market policy, however, the priority given to the provision of childcare reflects the need to bring more women with children into the labour market. But in terms of social, family and women's policy, the focus is on how child day-care facilities create more equal opportunities in life and work (Honig, Joos, and Schreiber 2004).

This approach goes beyond exploring a narrow pedagogical concept of care in relation to the institutionalization of childhood, to consider the specific dimension of children's everyday living conditions. Here it is important to distinguish between care arrangements in a narrower sense and care milieus. The concept of care arrangements in this sense does not just refer to statutory care facilities, though these may be an element of such arrangements. Instead, care arrangements can include the social network of the family (especially relatives, neighbours, friends), the recreational facilities market (clubs, groups, classes) and care provided by domestic staff and other paid individuals (the care market; Schreiber 2004b). Moreover, while care arrangements are generally made by parents/guardians, at the same time as making these arrangements, they also create the settings within which children grow up – children's everyday life contexts.

The multifunctional nature of care arrangements finds its match in the perspective of care milieus (Joos and Betz 2004) by revealing a tension between ideas and behaviour, and focusing on the meaning of social relationships. In an extension of Bourdieu's class concept in socialization theory, Betz depicts this as follows:

> It is essential to the milieu concept ... to map the interweaving economic, cultural and social structural inequalities and unequal socialisation contexts onto their corresponding socialisation and education processes, i.e. to match up the differences in the practices of families and children.
>
> (Betz 2004)

Mothers and fathers cope with the structural care dilemma by working out particular types of care arrangements, and milieus manifest themselves in these solutions; they become determined by the values on which parents base their actions, by professional attitudes/expertise and milieu-related 'subjective' orientation of day-care professionals, as well as the care policies of the welfare state itself. Unlike the expression 'care arrangements', the term 'care milieu' emphasizes the fact that the description of childcare, from the point of view of childhood sociology, shows that in the arrangements made for care, both in and outside the family, child-rearing and education are linked within a social structural and socio-cultural context whereby the child's life is embedded in arenas of experience and life opportunities that provide milieu-specific structures and norms. Care arrangements and care milieus thus create the matrix for the central elements of young children's life situation. In the morphology of a child's everyday life, childhood patterns emerge that are created by the daily routines of care arrangements, as experienced and co-determined by children. In the next section, some aspects of these considerations will be underpinned with empirical findings in relation to care arrangements in Germany.

Re-contextualization of childhood – empirical findings

Tietze and Rossbach (1991) published a pioneering study on the care of pre-school children. The categorization of care types upon which they based their study are 'core family', 'social network', 'paid persons' and 'institutions', reflecting the classic structure of childhood distributed between family, relatives and institutional care.

According to the findings of the German Youth Institute's (Deutsches Jugendinstitut – DJI) longitudinal study on the current care situation, only 4 per cent of children aged 5–6 do *not* attend kindergarten. This is quite well known, but what is surprising is the finding that parents actively seek a *mix* of care arrangements themselves which links private and public services. In addition to the parents and the kindergarten, there is an astounding variety of care arrangements. Almost one in four children receive care from three people in addition to parents and a kindergarten (cf. Alt, Chr. nd). This 'care mix' refers to a multiplication of classic family and institutional forms of care described by Tietze and Roßbach (1991).

Schreiber (2004b) subjected these data to a more detailed analysis and has been able to show that parents actually look beyond relatives and neighbours and use the *services of the leisure market* to a significant extent in providing care for their children, although the leisure market does not refer to paid entertainment for children in this context. Similarly, in a parent survey conducted in 2001, we found that the emphasis was on sporting activities. According to our survey, 61 per cent of kindergarten children (3–6-year-olds) take part in organized leisure activities after kindergarten:

> The parents questioned reported the following organized activities in which their 3–6-year-old children were involved: ballet, child–parent groups, recorder, foreign languages, early learning, football, piano, riding, swimming, play group, dance, therapy, tennis, gymnastics. Programmes offered by aid organizations for children were also mentioned (e.g. fire service).
>
> (Schreiber 2004b: 5)

While the data of our parent survey relate to Rhineland Palatinate and Saarland, Schreiber based his typology of private care arrangements on the data of the first and second wave of the DJI longitudinal study, which has been available since 2004. According to this, private care of 5–6-year-olds generally falls into four categories:

1. 31 per cent of parents use *social networks and leisure market offerings in addition to the core family*;
2. 23 per cent of parents care for their child *mainly themselves* and use the *offerings available in the leisure market*;
3. 21 per cent of parents organize private child care solely via *social networks*; and
4. 21 per cent of parents *do not use any other care services apart from the core family* (Schreiber 2004b: 21f.).

These findings reveal that the significance of the leisure market in terms of children's care has been considerably underestimated. Thus care arrangements for children can only be accurately described if use of the leisure market is included. The leisure market as a form of care did not feature at all in Tietze and Roßbach's study and children's networks were also virtually ignored as forms of care by that study. At the same time it is obvious that the function and significance of care must be redefined to do justice to these changes. Not only has care left the traditional settings of the pedagogical moratorium, it also includes an element of the agency of children.

From such data it is clear that multidimensional patterns of childhood are generated by the functional, normative and interactive dimensions of care arrangements. These create different arenas of experience and life chances for children. From the child's point of view, care outside the family is not an isolated phenomenon but interacts with changes in other areas of the child's living context, including changes in family life; children move between the worlds of family, day-care and child culture. From a child's perspective, care institutions fit into the general horizon of a broader living context, the quality of which would be better described as a cultural moratorium rather than a pedagogical one (Bundesministerium für Familie 1998). Dencik (1989) formulated a concept of dual socialization in this connection, attaching key importance to the duality of family and public education for the experience of growing up in postmodern societies.

But what do these findings signify in relation to the re-contextualization of childhood as an institution? First, they provide a strong indication that the childhood moratorium is open to non-familial and non-institutional determinants, even at pre-school age. Indeed, it is the parents themselves who play an active role in this process: mothers in particular make use of the afternoon to supplement their children's development with programmes on offer in the leisure market. This does, however, require investment of money and personal effort in terms of transport. Here we see an important change in the aspirations of significant numbers of parents in relation to child support, as well as higher aspirations in relation to their own role as the educators of their children. This, therefore, qualifies the significance of day-care institutions in children's everyday lives and the attitudes of parents towards institutional facilities since the data cited indicate that the structure of care arrangements and socio-cultural patterns of what comprises a 'good childhood' are linked. Clearly, ideas about what a child *needs* or what additional support children *ought* to be given within certain social milieus are also highly significant, which is an indication that care milieus are acting as a normative influence in children's care arrangements.

Findings relating to the need for *all day* care also reflect how important parental values are for the structuring of care arrangements. The Trier study attempted to depict care as (among other things) a parental demand for institutional childcare (see Schreiber 2004a). However, here, a careful distinction was drawn between the current *need* for public childcare and the *desire* for such care. Of the 3,300 families questioned, 90 per cent gave precise details of the times at which they required childcare outside the family and only 18 per cent said they required continuous care from the morning through the afternoon. This group generally wanted closing times of 4 or 5 pm, and in most cases a hot lunch for their child. Surprisingly, only 60 per cent of women working more than 40 hours a week claimed to want all day care: exactly 41 per cent of mothers with a 40-hour week required all day care. Clearly most families surveyed are able to resolve the problem of child-care with half-day public facilities, even where the mother (or father) works eight hours a day.

One might criticize these results by saying that they describe a condition in which mothers' desire for paid employment is not explored, a criticism that is relevant to the linking of care needs with value-based ideas regarding life with children. However, the Institute for Labour Market and Occupation Research of the Federal Employment Office (IAB) carried out a representative survey on this subject in 2000 (Beckmann and Engelbrech 2002). This showed that the majority of mothers with children requiring care in the new and old federal states of Germany are in favour of a model in which women reduce their professional commitments temporarily for the purposes of child-rearing; these results are reminiscent of Lewis's study.

Thus, if the many mothers not working today because of the lack of available jobs were able to fulfil their wish to work part-time, our findings indicate that there would be no significant increase in the demand for all day childcare facilities; and that if the structural care dilemma were merely a problem of the costs of having children, both parents – particularly women – would want all day care and there would therefore be a demand for the relevant facilities. According to our data, however, this is not the case. What is more, all day care would by no means be the only option for many families, even if availability in Germany were to be increased. Thus, the demand for all day public care probably depends to some extent on how well it fits in with the private care arrangements and care aspirations of the families concerned and more public childcare during the afternoon would especially benefit children who are not able to take part in organized leisure activities due to a lack of financial resources, since these incur additional costs.

Conclusion: the social value of children – research perspectives

The aim of this study is to analyse the major expansion of the system of publicly organized care and education of pre-school age children, which has been taking place in Germany since the 1980s, from the point of view of whether or not it has brought about a change in the definition of childhood. The theoretical framework of this analysis is provided by the idea that work and care are mutually dependent within the context of family welfare production and that the institutionalization of childhood is significantly influenced by the way in which this relationship is organized. The argument is derived from the idea that the erosion of the patriarchal family model has brought about a recontextualization of childhood. A model is proposed which attempts to describe this change, allowing for a realignment of responsibilities for children and a readjustment of the mode of social inclusion of children.

The decline of the male breadwinner/female housekeeper model of the family confronts parents with a structural dilemma: how can they combine family life, including responsible care of children, with the need to secure their material existence, at the same time as realizing equal life opportunities for father and mother? The structural dilemma facing parents in paid employment thus encourages parents not to have children at all – an option being chosen by increasing numbers as the significant drop in Germany's birth rate testifies.

In contrast to the 1970s, when childcare outside the family was criticized as being disadvantageous to children's development, the expansion of institutional care for infants is now in vogue in Germany in terms of family policy, social and educational policy. Empirical findings on value orientations practised by mothers and fathers in organizing extra-familial care show that a large proportion of those who have children expend significant resources in terms of finance and time to provide their children with a diverse and stimulating world of experience. They make use of the infrastructure provided by the state to organize extra-familial care for their children independently. One might describe this paradox by concluding that many parents pursue pedagogical motives in taking their children beyond the limitations of the traditional pedagogical moratorium.

The ideas of the value of a child reflected here deserve closer study. How are these ideas formed, and how important are they in regulating relationships between the generations? Are these ideas connected with notions of a 'good childhood'? Do they go hand in hand with investments in 'cultural capital', representing a strategy which has a long tradition among the middle class? Whatever the answer to these questions is, the care arrangements for children are a focus of change in which the relationships between family, childhood, market and state are being redefined, opening up new worlds of experience and options to children which 35 years ago would have been regarded as 'inappropriate' for the child.

References

Alanen, L. (2001) Explorations in Generational Analysis. In Alanen, L.and Mayall, B. (eds.), *Conceptualizing Child–Adult Relations* (pp. 11–22). London and New York. Routledge/Falmer.

Alt, Chr. (nd) Erste Befunde des DJI-Kinderpanel. Präsentation beim Parlamentarischen Abend des Deutschen Jugendinstituts. Berlin.

Baecker, D. (1994) Soziale Hilfe als Funktionssystem der Gesellschaft. *Zeitschrift für Soziologie* 23(2): 93–110.

Bäumer, G. (1929) Die historischen und sozialen Voraussetzungen der Sozialpädagogik und die Entwicklung ihrer Theorie. In Nohl, H.and Pallat, L. (eds.), *Handbuch der Pädagogik. Fünfter Band: Sozialpädagogik* (pp. 3–26). Langensalza. Beltz.

Beckmann, P. and Engelbrech, G. (2002) Vereinbarkeit von Familie und Beruf: Kinderbetreuung und Beschäftigungsmöglichkeiten von Frauen mit Kindern. In Engelbrech, G. (ed.), *Arbeitsmarktchancen für Frauen* (pp. 263–81). Nürnberg. Institut für Arbeitsmarkt- und Berufsforschung der Bundesanstalt für Arbeit.

Betz, T (2004) Bildung und soziale Ungleichheit: Lebensweltliche Bildung in (Migranten-)Milieus. Universität Trier, Zentrum für sozialpädagogische Forschung, Arbeitspapier II-16.

Brannen, J. and O'Brien, M. (eds.) (1996) *Children in Families. Research and Policy.* London: Falmer Press.

Bundesministerium für Familie, Senioren, Frauen und Jugend (1998) *Zehnter Kinder-und Jugendbericht. Bericht über die Lebenssituation von Kindern und die Leistungen der Kinder- und Jugendhilfe in Deutschland.* Bonn.

Dencik, L. (1989) Growing up in the Post-modern Age: On the Child's Situation in the Modern Family, and on the Position of the Family in the Modern Welfare State. *Acta Sociologica* 32(2): 155–80.

Donzelot, J. (1980) *Die Ordnung der Familie.* Frankfurt am Main: Suhrkamp.

Einasdottir, J. and Wagner, J. T. (eds.) (2006) *Nordic Childhoods and Early Education. Philosophy. Research, Policy, and Practice in Denmark, Finland, Iceland, Norway, and Sweden.* Greenwich, CT: Information Age Publishing.

Hengst, H. (1996) Kinder an die Macht! Der Rückzug des Marktes aus dem Kindheitsprojekt der Moderne. In Zeiher, H., Büchner, P. and Zinnecker, J. (eds.), *Kinder als Außenseiter? Umbrüche in der gesellschaftlichen Wahrnehmung von Kindern und Kindheit* (pp. 117–34). Weinheim und München: Juventa.

Herrmann, U. (1986) Die Pädagogisierung des Kinder- und Jugendlebens in Deutschland seit dem ausgehenden 18. Jahrhundert. In Martin, J. and Nitschke, A. (eds.), *Zur Sozialgeschichte der Kindheit,* (S.661–683). Freiburg im Breisgau/München: Karl Alber.

Honig, M.-S., Joos., M. and Schreiber, N. (2004) *Was ist ein guter Kindergarten? Theoretische und empirische Analysen zum Qualitätsbegriff in der Pädagogik.* Weinheim und München: Juventa

Honig, M.-S. and Ostner, I. (2001) Das Ende der fordistischen Kindheit. In Klocke, A. and Hurrelmann, K. (eds.), *Kinder und Jugendliche in Armut. Umfang, Auswirkungen und Konsequenzen. 2., vollst. überarb. Aufl.* (pp. 293–310). Opladen: Westdeutscher Verlag.

Huinink, J. (2002) Polarisierung der Familienentwicklung in europäischen Ländern im Vergleich. In Schneider, N.and Matthias-Bleck, H. (eds.), *Elternschaft heute. Gesellschaftliche Rahmenbedingungen und individuelle Gestaltungsaufgaben,* Zeitschrift für Familienforschung, Sonderheft 2 (pp. 49–73). Opladen: Leske & Budrich.

James, A. and James, A. L. (2004) *Constructing Childhood. Theory, Policy and Social Practice.* Basingstoke: Palgrave Macmillan.

Janssens, A. (1998) The Rise and Decline of the Male Breadwinner Family? An Overview of the Debate. *International Review of Social History* 42, Supplement. 1–23.

Joos, M. (2002) Childcare zwischen Dienstleistung und Bildungsanforderungen. *Zeitschrift für Soziologie der Erziehung und Sozialisation* 22(3): 229–46.

Joos, M. and Betz, T. (2004) Gleiche Qualität für alle? Ethnische Diversität als Determinante der Perspektivität von Qualitätsurteilen und -praktiken. In Honig, M.-S., Joos, M. and Schreiber N. (eds.), *Was ist ein guter Kindergarten? Theoretische und empirische Analysen zum Qualitätsbegriff in der Pädagogik* (pp. 69–118). Weinheim und München: Juventa.

Lamb, M. et al. (1992) *Child Care in Context: Cross-cultural Perspectives.* Hillsdale, NJ, Lawrence Erlbaum.

Lewis, J. (2001) The Decline of the Male Breadwinner Model: Implications for Work and Care. *Social Politics* 8(2): 152–69.

Michel, S. and Mahon, R. (eds.) (2002) *Child Care Policy at the Crossroads. Gender and Welfare State Restructuring.* New York and London, Routledge.

Nauck, B. (1996) Beitrag zur Reform des Kindschaftsrechts aus sozialwissenschaftlicher Sicht. In Evangelische Akademie .Bad Boll (ed.), *Kindheit in Deutschland. Interdisziplinäre Beiträge zur Reform des Kindschaftsrechts* (pp. 23–32). Bad Boll (Protokolldienst 21/96).

Ostner, I. (1998) Quadraturen im Wohlfahrtsdreieck. Die USA, Schweden und die Bundesrepublik im Vergleich. In Lessenisch, S. and Ostner, I. (eds.), *Welten des Wohlfahrtskapitalismus. Der Sozialstaat in vergleichender Perspektive,* (pp. 225–52). Frankfurt and New York: Campus.

Proksch, R. (1996) Die Rechte junger Menschen in ihren unterschiedlichen Lebensaltersstufen. *Recht der Jugend und des Bildungswesens* 44(4): 473–91.

Roßbach, H.-G. (2005) Vorschulische Erziehung. In Cortina, K. S., Baumert, J., Leschinsky, A., Mayer, K. U. and Trommer, L. (eds.), *Das Bildungswesen in der Bundesrepublik Deutschland. Strukturen und Entwicklungen im Überblick,* (pp. 252–84). Reinbek: Rowohlt.

Schreiber, N. (2004a) Jenseits pädagogischer Qualität? In Honig, M.-S., Joos, M. and Schreiber, N. (eds.), *Was ist ein guter Kindergarten? Theoretische und empirische Analysen zum Qualitätsbegriff in der Pädagogik* (pp. 101–18). Weinheim und München: Juventa.

Schreiber, N. (2004b) Private Betreuungsarrangements für Kinder – Entwicklung eines Betreuungsindexes mit Daten des DJI-Kinderpanels und Vorschlag eines Erhebungsinstruments für zukünftige Befragungen. Universität Trier, Zentrum für sozialpädagogische Forschung, Arbeitspapier II-17.

Tietze, W. and Roßbach, H. G. (1991) Die Betreuung von Kindern im vorschulischen Alter. *Zeitschrift für Pädagogik* 37(4): 555–80.

Walter, W. (1999) Die drei Ordnungen der Familie. Zur Institutionalisierung von Lebensformen. Unpublished paper. Universität Konstanz.

Wieners, T. (1999) *Familientypen und Formen außerfamilialer Kinderbetreuung heute. Vielfalt als Notwendigkeit und als Chance.* Opladen: Leske & Budrich.

Zinnecker, J. (2000) Kindheit und Jugend als pädagogische Moratorien. Zur Zivilisationsgeschichte der jüngeren Generation im 20. Jahrhundert. *Zeitschrift für Pädagogik* 42. Beiheft: 36–68.

11
Childhood in the Welfare State[1]
Jens Qvortrup

This chapter discusses the position of children in the modern European welfare state and children's legitimate access to cash and services made available by the welfare state. Whatever the welfare regime, following Esping-Andersen's (1990) typology, however, its historical context in Europe is invariably that of a capitalist economy, which was eventually tempered by welfare measures to alleviate the crude effects of the unfettered market. The reality of such a capitalist economy-cum-welfare state does not, however, tell us much about the ways in which children and childhood are constructed. For this reason this chapter will address the following questions:

- What is children's market status before state intervention?
- Are children, objectively speaking, in need of welfare state provisions?
- What is the place of children in welfare state theory and practice?
- Who, in terms of groups, institutions and agencies, is primarily responsible for children's welfare?

As we shall see, children and childhood are not necessarily part of the welfare state or of welfare state thinking, even if children are necessarily members of the welfare society and capitalist society, because the idea of 'a good childhood' was never an intrinsic part of the welfare state. I shall argue that this is still, in principle, the case. When ideas and impressions in Europe about the state as the main acknowledged agent of welfare were conceived, and the state was upheld in terms of its neutrality and impartiality in serving and protecting its members, in particular the weaker among them, it was far from obvious that children belonged to the state, let alone had any legitimate rights as claimants.

Whether one prefers to find the rationale for the welfare state in Bismarck's politics, and thus see it as an instrument for preventing the threat of unrest among the working class, or in Beveridge's, and thus understand it as a mechanism for ensuring fairness to losers in the market economy, it is possible to identify the redistributive effects of state interventions, in cash or in kind. It is also possible to establish that strong welfare state regimes are different from those regimes that believe that market forces overall are a blessing rather than a curse. What is demanded, basically, is patience on the part of those who are asked to believe that if they wait long enough, they too will enjoy the benefits. This is particularly true for children who, as rights-holders and claimants, are late-comers in a double sense.

First, and historically, children are arguably the only group who have not yet been recognized as claimants of current political and societal resources. The political and industrial revolutions of the West, according to Bendix, 'led to the eventual recognition of the rights of citizenship for *all adults*, including those in positions of economic dependence' (1977: 66; emphasis added) – but not for children who, as subjects, have not been able to benefit from these changes. In a sense, following Bendix, they are still – politically and economically – part of a feudal system, which accords no immediate rights '*to subjects* in positions of economic dependence such as tenants, journeymen, workers and servants: at best they are classified *under the household* of their master and represented through him and his estates' (Bendix 1977: 66–7; emphasis added).

It would, of course, be outrageous to suggest that there has been no change in the position of children over the last 500 years, but it is interesting to note that formally children remain, by and large, classified under the household – or perhaps more precisely the family – without individual rights as subjects; and despite the considerable progress made recently as a result of the UN Convention on the Rights of the Child, children still lack economic and political rights as autonomous citizens.

Second, children are also lagging behind from a life-phase perspective. Thus, it has been argued that it is not necessarily unfair if children experience differential treatment; viewed from a life-long perspective there is, it has been suggested, some justice in this since sooner or later they will reach adulthood and therefore, 'if we treat the young one way and the old another, then over time, each person is treated both ways. The advantages (or disadvantages) of consistent differential treatment by age will equalize over time' (Daniels 1988: 88). Children will, in other words, in due course, obtain the right and the opportunity to compete equally with adults in the market or become a target for redistributive measures if they fail.

According to this reasoning children as a social group are not seen as legitimate beneficiaries of resources and thus childhood remains a site in which rights and the ability to make claims are absent. Such an argument is, however, tantamount to proposing that it is the fate of children to be treated differently from adults and that the failure to acknowledge child poverty (or wealth for that matter) as a problem is inevitable. In effect, the logic of this position is that one should not be concerned if children are relatively more exposed to hazards than adults and elderly people: sooner or later they will get their rights as beneficiaries. In addition, denying children the right to access necessary resources will also delay any attempts to give them citizenship rights on an equal footing with other groups. Finally, as Sgritta (1994: 358) argues, it suggests that society is 'immutable, stable, ahistorical' and thus overlooks the reality of rapid change that may very well – and in fact does – leave persons born at different times exposed to varying conditions. In other words, the likelihood that conditions will not even out over time is overwhelming.

However, children's lack of access to claims and rights does not necessarily affect their material situation because resources are channelled to them in a welfare state and there is no doubt that some of the redistributive effects of welfare state measures do benefit children. Yet the question remains to what extent this is intentional as opposed to merely being an effect derived from resources being targeted at other groups, such as children's parents. It can therefore be argued that such benefits do not ensue from legitimate or constitutional claims made by children and that, as Bendix argues, such claims can only be made once they become adults.

This is the precarious status of childhood in a European context, irrespective of its welfare state design. It has indeed become increasingly unacceptable for them to be hurt, abused, deprived; yet the idea that they should be taken seriously as rights-holders is not yet rooted among the European populace. It may well be an empirical reality that children have access to the most relevant resources along with other groups, but their precarious situation is highlighted by the fact that their access to welfare measures is not guaranteed by law. Indeed, their current welfare status is the result of incidental amendments at the discretion of day-to-day policy-making. Therefore, children are, in principle, more exposed to market forces than other groups, a situation that is only exacerbated by their status as dependants under the (almost exclusive) guardianship of their parents. This makes children by and large a private matter, something that is reflected in the fact that interventions on their behalf by extra-familial bodies or agencies are frequently seen as unwarranted or illegitimate.

The market: children's inclusion and exclusion

All Europeans – children, youths, adults and the elderly – live in a capitalist market. For the sake of clarity, however, let me briefly consider children's role in this society before state intervention.

Basically, children are *included* in the market in two ways First, they – or at least some of them – occupy a waged job outside of school hours. This is allegedly their only acknowledged economic contribution and adult society looks on it with ambivalence. Although it may loom large for the children involved, for their families and for some niches in the economy it remains (as I have argued elsewhere; see Qvortrup 2000) too minuscule a part of a modern industrial society's production to be considered separately.

Second, children are included in the market as consumers by means of their own, but mainly their parents' (and sometimes their grandparents') money. As such, children are an important target for commercial advertising and a variable to be reckoned with in the budgets of many trades. However, since this is merely an effect derived from incomes available to them, I shall not follow this strand either (see Cook 2000; also Casas this volume). Much more important, I think, is that children, as individuals and as a group, are largely *excluded* from the market.

There are four principles according to which goods are distributed in our society (see Rubinstein, 1988):

1. the *fair exchange*, which means that 'the net rewards, or profit, of each man be proportional to his investments' (Homans 1961: 75);
2. the *meritocratic*, which in our society is established mainly in terms of educational achievements;
3. the *entitlement*, according to which assets are distributed due to for instance inheritance or seniority; and
4. the *need*, which has been introduced relatively recently in historical terms.

The first two principles pertain to the market in terms of *achievement*. This implies the *de facto* exclusion of children, who are seen neither as investors nor as contributors. They therefore have no basis for claims in terms of reciprocity, nor do they possess educational merits on the basis of which they might legitimately demand a share of societal resources. It is worthwhile in this context to note that children, in terms of the conventional definition of their situation, are also effectively prevented from having their school achievements assessed as a valuable input to the social fabric (see below).

As to entitlement, which is not strictly speaking a market principle, children may have a right to inheritance, but this will typically be administered on their behalf by their guardians. Only when it comes to need are children recognized, and this principle is the only one that is definitely beyond the realm of the market. Children do qualify as needy recipients due to their age, and thus this principle is formulated in terms of *ascription*, as is also, by and large, the entitlement principle. The question remains whether children really are the subject of the principle of need, or whether even this is delegated to someone else.

Whether the exclusion of children in their own right from a market-based distributive system is just or not is another matter. The fact that they are excluded from the market and destined to rely on a needs criterion, by implication, classifies them as dependants and therefore contributes significantly to portraying them as non-deserving members of the system. From this perspective, their needs are, accordingly, supposed to be met by other agents, among which the most important is their family, while the welfare state features only as a secondary agent, should this become necessary.

Since welfare state considerations and measures, in terms of both intentions and outcomes, must be assessed as expressions of distributive justice, let me briefly resume the discussion of justice alluded to above. As we saw, a philosopher like Daniels does not see a problem in discriminating against children since, he argues, they will catch up later in life. It is characteristic of discussions of social justice, as a legal or economic problem, that children are excluded from considerations, as pointed out by Bojer, who makes a meritorious effort to bring them into a Rawlsian chain of argument, although the word 'child' does not occur in the index of Rawls' famous work (1973).

It is Bojer's view that the Rawlsian contract 'implies concern also for children as subjects in themselves' (Bojer 2000: 24), which deals with children from a lifecycle perspective. Yet, as I understand it, her major argument is that overlooking children in terms of distributive justice may jeopardize the rational choices they make as adults, and since no one can choose their own childhood, a lack of consideration in providing for children to give them equality of opportunity severely hampers their ability to involve themselves in risk-taking in adult life on equal terms with others. One might add that the inequality this entails has implications for children whose fate is determined by parental choices that have, in turn, been determined in and by their own childhoods. This raises questions about social arrangements for children, even in the advanced welfare states of the Nordic countries.

> Everywhere, the workplace and production of material wealth command priority before the nurture and rearing of children. Economic incentives are certainly not geared towards making child care a materially rewarding profession. Parental leave is considered disruptive to the workplace.
>
> (Bojer 2000: 36)

Bojer is concerned with children's rights and conditions. Due to the interconnectedness of child and adult conditions from a lifecycle perspective, she has a point, even if her justification for making primary goods (love, security, material resources, opportunities to grow and develop) available to children is that they enhance adults' opportunities to make rational choices. It is indeed important to bring children explicitly into these significant debates, as Bojer does; however, the future of children remains the yardstick. One might therefore ask: what does distributive justice for children look like *without* the prospect of human capital-building, i.e. without a perspective on their adult future? (see Esping-Andersen et al. 2002; Lister 2003; Olk 2006).

In addition, in the Rawlsian scheme it remains difficult to include children as subjects, given that (a) the arguments are based on rational choices made by adults, and (b) that children are not considered able to make such choices. This is a discussion I shall not take up here, however (see Mortier 2000).

Children's objective needs for welfare measures

Although the needs criterion is not part of market vocabulary, the market does not completely ignore children. This is partly because it leaves its imprint in practically every corner and aspect of our life, including children's everyday lives. It is also, however – and most importantly in the context of our economic-political system – partly because children are ideologically regarded as belonging to their parents, which means that it is parents who are responsible for them, including economically. And since parents' capacity to care for their children is highly dependent on the market, children will inevitably also be affected by the market, albeit indirectly. It follows from this that children's well-being, short of state intervention, is basically dependent on their parents' class, which again is contingent on their ability to obtain a fair exchange for their investments or contributions on the one hand and their educational qualifications on the other.

Parents' market dependence has other implications. For example, the whole family benefits economically for it has two incomes rather than one; on the other hand, both parents working creates a problem to be solved, namely childcare during the working day. In addition, qualifications having a high market value, which lead to high net rewards, seem historically to be connected with individualism and secularization, which in turn is likely to be one reason for the rise in the divorce rate; this, in turn, creates a whole new set of needs in terms of children's well-being that consequently have to be covered. Many others issues could be identified.

There is ample evidence to document the outcome of the interaction of these factors for the material well-being of children. Most dramatically, this can be seen in the developing nations, as attempts are made by bodies such as the International Monetary Fund and the World Bank to solve economic problems by means of austerity measures, implying exposure to the market at the same time that cuts in health and educational programmes are deemed necessary. Evidence for developed countries is also clear (see UNICEF 2000). Before taxes and transfers – i.e. in a pure market situation – child poverty ranges from 15.8 per cent in Norway to 36.1 per cent in the UK; in Germany it is at 16.8 per cent, while in Sweden it is a surprising 23.4 per cent.[2] Unfortunately, there is no comparison with other age groups as far as these pre-tax and pre-transfer incomes are concerned.

Parents' labour market participation leaves them with little choice – their children, up to a certain age, are obliged to attend some kind of institutional arrangement, be it kindergarten, school, after-school clubs or the like (see the contributions to this volume for examples). This in turn implies a more or less rigid schedule for children and constraints on their mobility. At the same time, in countries where the demand for such arrangements is far from met, parents and children are faced with the no less severe problem of making parents' work fit in with children's need for care.

There are, in other words, a number of internally connected factors that provide a framework for children's life worlds even before the state intervenes to ameliorate their effects, and it is important to bear these in mind when we address the question of responsibility for children's welfare. As the Canadian economist Harry G. Johnson reminds us:

> since the society is founded on the belief that individual freedom to introduce change serves the social good, the society and not the individual member should assume the costs that this freedom may impose on other members when these costs become unreasonably high. Beyond a certain point, the society collectively should bear the economic risks imposed on the family by dependence on the sale of its services, because society itself creates those risks.
>
> (Johnson 1962: 191)

So far I have dealt with children's position as a result of the market and, by and large, one can conclude that children themselves are not thought of as market actors. Nonetheless, however good the intentions, children cannot escape the massive influence of the market particularly because of their dependence on their parents' market value. The family is often portrayed as a 'haven in a heartless world', as if the two were discrete, and one should certainly not overlook a family's protective importance for children; I wonder, however, if a greater danger does not lie in underestimating the impact of the 'heartless world' on the family? Therefore, in considering the extent to which society responds to the needs of children and their parents through the welfare state measures it adopts, one should not forget the interests of society as a whole in such interventions and indeed, its interests in both the family and children.

Children's place in welfare state theory and practice

Although children are often mentioned, the question of *how* they are represented in traditional welfare and citizenship theory remains unanswered. A preliminary search shows quite meagre and inconclusive results. Apart from cases where children are accounted for empirically (see Titmuss 1968; Townsend 1970; Ringen 1997), one has to say that to the extent children are considered at all, the literature reveals considerable inadequacy in dealing with them and they therefore remain difficult to incorporate into any all-embracing analysis (but see Kränzl-Nagl, Mierendorff and Olk 2003; Alanen 2007; Olk and Wintersberger 2007).

Thus Dahrendorf (1996: 35) talks about 'the vexing issue of children in the scheme of citizenship', but is apparently unable or unwilling to accept it as a serious issue. In *Welfare*, intended as an introduction to and overview of the field, Norman Barry (1999) does not mention children at all. For Marshall too children remain invisible, as Bulmer and Rees (1996) note in a book on Marshall's classic work, *Citizenship and Social Class*. They explicitly list children among the 'omissions from Marshall's schema', which identifies three main categories of citizenship:

1. *legal citizenship* or civil rights such as 'liberty of person, freedom of speech, thought and faith, the right to own property and to conclude valid contracts, and the right to justice';
2. *political citizenship* in terms of the franchise and right of access to public office; and
3. *social citizenship* in terms of social rights ranging from 'the right to a modicum of economic welfare and security to the right to share to the full in social heritage and to live the life of a civilised being according to the standards prevailing in society'.

These types of citizenship correspond to four sets of public institutions: the first two are the *courts* (for protection of civil rights) and the *representative bodies* (to secure access to participation in decision-making). The other two are the *social services*, which are there to ensure minimum protection against poverty, ill-health and other misfortunes, and *schools*, so that all members of the community to receive at least a basic education (Table 11.1).

Following the UN Convention on the Rights of the Child, there is more to say about the first two sets in the political and the legal realms; nevertheless, it is my contention that both continue to be largely marginal as far as children are concerned. I shall therefore concentrate on the other two institutions corresponding to Marshall's third category: social citizenship.

As mentioned above the market leaves children vulnerable financially as well as in terms of services. I do not intend to comment in any detail about the comparative situation of children in different countries, if for no other reason than because space does not allow more

Table 11.1 Marshall's basic scheme

Categories of citizenship	Corresponding institutions
Legal	Courts
Political	Representative bodies
Social	Social services
	Schools

than a superficial discussion of the tremendous complexities in these areas (see Rostgaard and Fridberg 1998). If, however, one looks at the rules and the realities of children's 'social citizenship', to use Marshall's term, there are at least three striking facts as far as Europe is concerned:

1. Everywhere there is a basic minimum below which children are unlikely to fall; as far as poverty and deprivation are concerned, for example, data on child mortality, nutrition and health care suggest that some protection is provided compared to a pure market situation (as can be found in the US but much more commonly and extremely in the Third World).
2. In terms of services, all European countries regard schooling as a social right, although it is not always clear who its main beneficiary is – the family, the child or society? On the other hand, nowhere are services such as crèches, kindergartens and after-school care seen as something that the community is obliged to provide free of charge.
3. There are such huge differences in financial and service provisions among European countries that a remarkably high level of political discretion must exist in terms of recognizing children's social citizenship as a legitimate claim.

Despite trends to privatization and deregulation since Reaganism, Thatcherism and the dismantling of the Soviet bloc, there remains some belief in the idea of the welfare state, not least in continental Europe and particularly in the Nordic countries. In most European nations, it is part of the programmes of most influential political parties to secure a decent standard of living for families with children, and nowhere is it regarded as acceptable to deny the existence of child poverty. In all these countries, therefore, there are measures to ease this burden. Public discourse about the reality of child poverty is vague, however: while on the one hand there are few institutionalized and obligatory means for eradicating it, public opinion regards it as a scandal – even more so than poverty in general. As the German political scientist Christoph Butterwege has observed: 'In the public debate, children eventually count as deserving poor while fit-for-work receivers of social assistance are perceived as undeserving poor, who can safely be harassed' (quoted in Niejahr 2001; my translation). The general attitude is thus expressed in clearly moralistic terms, while a moral standpoint would require institutional mechanisms for the eradication of child poverty.

Although there are huge differences among EU Member States, however, measures are taken in all of them to alleviate the burden of poverty.

In the league tables quoted above, the effects of policy measures were given: from a pre- to a post-tax and transfer situation (i.e. as a result of public intervention in a pure market situation) the poverty rate in Sweden was reduced by 89 per cent, in the UK by 45 per cent, in Norway by 75 per cent, and in Germany by 36 per cent. This varied picture reflects the fact that not only are there different and often quite efficient policies, but also, and most importantly, that nowhere do states have a clear obligation to eradicate child poverty. This becomes even clearer when we look at the differences in the incidence of poverty between children of lone-parent families and children of two-parent families (Table 11.2).

In each case, there are reasons for this dispersion. As is well known, in each country there are different administrative units responsible for implementing welfare measures and it may well be that what is granted at one level is clawed back at another. A well-intentioned decision at the national level – for example, to extend kindergarten coverage – may cause problems at the municipal level if they have not been granted sufficient means by central government. Thus parents may be asked to contribute to the cost, which in turn implies a reduction in their disposable income. This apparent conflict between administrative levels might be contained if families (or children) were given rights to certain services such as kindergartens, but children typically do not have such rights.

The most important example of what appears to be a right for children is education. Thus in all European welfare states, children's enrolment in schools is more or less 100 per cent and it is also, by and large, free. As far as schooling is concerned, however, there are some intriguing problems. First, it is often said that children have a right to attend school or, more precisely, to receive an education. In fact, not even this

Table 11.2 Child poverty: before tax and transfer for all children; after tax and transfer for all children, for children in lone-parent families and in other families

	Pre-tax and transfer, all children	Post-tax and transfer		
		All children	Children of lone parents	Children in other families
UK	36.1	19.8	45.6	13.3
Ireland	n.a.	16.8	46.4	14.2
Sweden	23.4	2.6	6.7	1.5
Germany	16.8	10.7	51.2	6.2
Norway	15.9	3.9	13.1	2.2

Source: UNICEF (2000).

is true in most countries: parents have an *obligation* to make sure that their children receive an education, and children are obliged to receive this education. What is interesting is that not even here are welfare measures targeting children; it is the *parents* who are targeted. To the extent that children have rights, it is a right they are forced to receive.

Second, it is questionable whether it is reasonable to regard schooling as a welfare measure for parents and/or children at all. As suggested by the German Fifth Family Report, the cost of schooling might better be regarded as a societal investment, in line with other measures to provide for societal infrastructure in general (Bundesministerium 1994: 291). From this perspective, schooling is seen not primarily as an individual's right but as a collective service for society as a whole. This has important implications.

It suggests that since investment in education is for the common good and thus of equal significance to all members and sectors of society, this investment must count as a contribution to maintaining and reproducing society as a whole. This must be the case, since educational investment is borne by the public purse. One should recall, however, that parents are also heavily involved in their child's education and therefore contribute to the reproduction of the labour force, and not merely to the child's becoming an adult. From the point of view of fairness, therefore, the implication of the German Family Report's proposition is that compensation to the family for parents' contributions would also be a payment to the common good. This was the Report's conclusion, but it was accepted with reluctance by the German government because of the tremendous costs that its implementation would incur. This is understandable from a political point of view, but is hardly consistent with the view that children's welfare and well-being are important to maintaining and reproducing society.

Nobody doubts that schools are indispensable; this being the case, it would only be logical if schools were regarded unequivocally as an inseparable part of what is understood to be 'a good childhood'. The paradox is that even if we all agree that schooling is a societal project, we fail to perceive that children are embedded as a part of this reciprocal equation at the contributors' end.

The argument about schooling as a prerequisite for societal reproduction, and not merely one of individual reproduction serving children in their quest for personal futures, has been raised by several writers including Margaret Wynn in her classic book on family policy (Wynn 1972). More recently Folbre has made a similar point, but in more general terms, arguing that 'parents should be compensated for their efforts ... for raising children' (1994: 89). Johnson goes even further, assuming that schooling (and thus a new relationship between children and adults) is not the responsibility of individual parents and therefore not one that should be shouldered by them alone, but by society in general. He suggests that 'society should be ready to assume the financial burden of maintaining school children as well as of paying the costs of teaching them' (1962: 190).

Johnson does not explain in detail what he means by 'maintaining school children', but links the point with children themselves as actors:

> it needs to be recognized that in the opulent society an increasing part of the real costs of education is the earnings forgone by going to school instead of to work, a cost which may put severe pressure on poor children to drop out of school even though the advantages to themselves and society of further education are great.
>
> (Johnson 1962: 190)

Written over four decades ago, this now may sound a bit old-fashioned. The principle, however, remains true and accords with Kaufmann's (1996) uncompromising dictum, that society has colonized children's labour and left the costs to the family.

The debate initiated by Johnson and Kaufmann brings into focus an argument in favour of compensating not just parents but also children themselves. As Johnson indicates, children are not only incurring opportunity costs, more importantly, they are doing useful work in school. As such they are performing as 'achievers' in a new societal division of labour and therefore, by implication, should be considered as members of society who deserve, as a right, a fair proportion of societal resources (see Qvortrup 1995, 2000).

From the point of view of children, it is a significant step forward in recognizing them as social citizens that their main activity – school work – should be acknowledged on a par with other endeavours that contribute to the social fabric. Most important is that, from this perspective, children's school work is regarded as being as much for the benefit of the collective as for the individual, a perspective that may influence discussions about who should bear the costs of investment in children and childhood.

Johnson mentions an additional principle of social policy in modern society – raising the 'standards of services and amenities provided collectively, and of the quality of the environment' (1962: 190). An opulent society can hardly claim 'to be employing its opulence wisely' (Johnson

1962: 191) if, among other things, 'the schools look like factories used to look and factories like schools ought to look' (1962: 190), i.e. that children's workplaces have deteriorated compared with those of adults. Schools are thus an example of institutions for children in which the buildings and equipment do not meet a reasonable standard. In many countries (Denmark, UK and Norway), complaints are voiced about run-down school buildings and the fact that politicians have allowed them to deteriorate. Calculations have been made of the costs for bringing them up to a standard commensurate not only with a decent standard of living, but also with the health needs of children. This serves to illustrate the argument outlined above that no *demands* can be made by children and parents in order to improve their living conditions; it remains a question of *political discretion*. In addition, it is an example that indicates a generational gap: only old people's homes compete with children's institutions in terms of poor standards, whereas such standards would never be tolerated in public buildings or corporate offices.

Agents of responsibility for the welfare of children

In terms of prevailing family ideology in Europe, there is no doubt that parents are considered responsible for children's welfare, morally as well as economically, whilst the state has a legal obligation to safeguard children's welfare only in cases where parents fail to fulfil their responsibilities. The question is not whether this state of affairs is morally defensible or not; it is more about the extent to which it is rational in view of the goals of society, such as the maintaining social order and balance, safeguarding short-term desires for the welfare of children and their families, and long-term aims of maintaining and reproducing the labour force and pension schemes. What we are currently seeing instead in all developed nations are unintended, undesired and even adverse trends, such as low fertility rates, ageing populations, child poverty and a failing ability to reproduce the labour market – to mention only the most conspicuous examples relevant to this discussion.

The family and the state do not always have interests in common; indeed, they often compete as far as children are concerned. Nevertheless, it is remarkable that it is only these two agents that seem to be recognized as responsible partners in addressing such questions of importance for society as a whole. It is my thesis that the major problem since the beginning of the twentieth century is that, for the first time in history, we have come to face a situation in which *those who are obliged to care for children do not benefit from doing so economically, while those who are profiting from children being raised, do not contribute.* It is this major paradox which arguably accounts for the imbalances we are presently facing, and this paradox is all the more astonishing since it runs counter to the very idea of the market principle of fair exchange, according to which each receives in proportion to his or her investment.

To restore an appropriate balance the re-establishment of the principle of fair exchange in investments and benefits is required. This implies that families with children are compensated for their outlay for reproducing the labour force (see Johnson 1962; Wynn 1972; Folbre 1994). The state is also a partner in making investments, but only in the sense that it is redistributing its income. The crux of the matter therefore is the need, through fiscal and other policies, to make other potential partners responsible – i.e. the current free-riders who are benefiting without making proportional investments.

Among the actors having an interest in the results of family and state investments is corporate society, or the world of business and trade in its many forms. Corporate society, which in the long run is dependent on a well-educated and healthy labour force, has by and large been eclipsed or managed to exclude itself from any responsibility for producing the labour force.

A third important group are people in households without children, in particular childless persons,[3] and others who have not been willing or able to reproduce themselves. They are eventually establishing themselves as free-riders – both in practice and as an interest group (cf. child-free zones, gated communities, and the like) – most of whom are men. As Folbre states:

> Increases in the private costs of raising children … are exerting tremendous economic pressure on parents, particularly mothers. Economists need to analyze the contributions of non-market labour to the development of human capital: as children become increasingly public goods, parenting becomes increasingly public service.
>
> (Folbre 1994: 86)

It is therefore important for any discussion of children's welfare to seek to identify potentially interested parties (whether these interests are recognized or not) as well as the nature of the interests they hold. In some countries, the conflict of interests between families with children and those without is already apparent: this is the basis for discussions in Germany about 'equalizing the family burden' (*Familienlastenausgleich*), supplemented by the complementary notion of 'equalizing family achievements' (*Familienleistungsausgleich*), meaning that 'achievers' in raising children have a right to be supported by relieving them of some of their burdens.

There are, however, other areas of conflict that need to be discussed. Any discussion about children seems to bring forward at least two interest groups: defenders of the family (e.g. Kaufmann) and advocates of gender equality (Folbre). In each camp 'the best interest of the child' will be postulated, as suggested by Wintersberger (2000: 186–7); but the question that needs to be addressed by childhood research is what is meant by this. Can we, in other words, take it for granted that the interests of families and the interests of women are identical with the interests of children or childhood, however these are defined?

Conclusion

The analysis of childhood in the welfare state has a long way to go and, as I have sought to demonstrate, children's claims on resources in society are weak. In a pure market, they have only their parents to rely on, who are not proportionally reimbursed for their investment in their children. Even under welfare state regimes, the status of children as rights-holders is doubtful since they are seldom targeted and are typically at the mercy of discretionary policies.

As has been the case in social science theory in general, children have also been neglected in the theory of welfare analysis (see Kränzl-Nagl, Mierendorff and Olk 2003) and, as used to be the case in the new social studies of childhood, there is again an urgency in establishing childhood in its own right, this time as a component of welfare state theory. The prevailing view that only a needs criterion is relevant for making welfare provisions available to children has a number of drawbacks. Not only does it lead to individualization of the problem, it also renders children as undeserving without legitimate claims in their own right. Only if a dialectic is established between children and their parents as deserving claimants and rights-holders on the one hand, and society on the other, as being critically in need of children, can a rational, inter-generational basis for welfare policies be imagined and made real.

Notes

1 This chapter is based on a previous publication: (2003) Kindheit im marktwirtschaftlich organisierten Wohlfahrtstaat. In Kränzl-Nagl, R., Mierendorf,

J. and Olk, T. (eds.), *Kindheit im Wohlfahrtstaat. Gesellschaftliche und politische Herausforderungen* (pp. 95–120). Frankfurt a.M.: Campus Verlag.

2   Poor in this context means people who have income below 50 per cent of the median; the equivalence scale is the modified OECD scale, which implies that the first person is given a value of 1, the second 0.5, while others – typically children – 0.3.

3   Involuntary childless couples constitute a particular problem in that they demonstrably wish to share both the burdens and joys of having children. It would therefore be inappropriate to include them among those shirking societal responsibility.

References

Alanen, L. (2007) Theorising Children's Welfare. In Wintersberger, H., Alanen, L., Olk, T. and Qvortrup, J. (eds.), *Childhood, Generational Order and the Welfare State: Exploring Children's Social and Economic Welfare*. Odense: University Press of Southern Denmark.

Barry, N. (1999) *Welfare*. 2nd edition. Buckingham: Open University Press.

Bendix, R. (1977) *Nation-building and Citizenship: Studies of Our Changing Social Order*. Berkeley, CA: University of California Press.

Bojer, H. (2000) Children and Theories of Social Justice. *Feminist Economics* 6(2): 23–39.

Bulmer, M. and Rees, A. M. (1996) Conclusions: Citizenship in the Twenty-first Century. In Bulmer, M. and Rees, A. M. (eds.), *Citizenship Today: The Contemporary Relevance of T. H. Marshall* (pp. 269–83). London: UCL Press.

Bundesministerium für Familie und Senioren (1994) *Familie und Familienpolitik im geeinten Deutschland – Zukunft des Humanvermögens*. Bonn: Fünfter Familienbericht.

Cook, D. T. (2000) The Other 'Child Study': Figuring Children as Consumers in Market Research, 1910s–1990s. *The Sociological Quarterly* 41(3): 487–507.

Dahrendorf, R.(1996) Citizenship and Social Class. In Bulmer, M. and Rees, A. M. (eds.), *Citizenship Today: The Contemporary Relevance of T. H. Marshall* (pp. 25–48). London: UCL Press.

Daniels, N. (1988) *Am I My Parents' Keeper? An Essay on Justice between Young and the Old*. New York and Oxford: Oxford University Press.

Esping-Andersen, G. (1990) *Three Worlds of Welfare Capitalism*. Cambridge: Polity Press.

Esping-Andersen, G. et al. (2002): *Why We Need a New Welfare State*. Oxford and New York: Oxford University Press.

Folbre, N. (1994) Children as Public Goods. *The American Economic Review* 84(2): 86–90.

Homans, G. C. (1961) *Social Behavior: Its Elementary Forms*. London: Routledge & Kegan Paul.

Johnson, H. G. (1962) *Money, Trade and Economic Growth*. Cambridge, MA: Harvard University Press.

Kaufmann, F.-X. (1996) *Modernisierungsschübe, Familie und Sozialstaat*. München: Oldenbourg Verlag.

Kränzl-Nagl, R., Mierendorff, J. and Olk, T. (2003) Die Kindheitsvergessenheit der Wohlfahrtsstaatsforschung und die Wohlfahrtsstaatsvergessenheit der Kindheitsforschung. In *Kindheit im Wohlfahrtsstatt: Gesellschaftliche und politische Herausforderungen* (pp. 9–55). Frankfurt and New York: Campus Verlag.

Lister, R. (2003) Investing in the Citizen-workers of the Future: Transformations in Citizenship and the State under New Labour. *Social Policy & Administration* 37(5): 427–43.

Mortier, F. (2000) Rationality and Competence to Decide in Children. In Verhellen, E. (ed.), *Understanding Children's Rights* (pp. 67–87). Ghent: Children's Rights Centre.

Niejahr, E. (2001) Die grosse Not der Kleinen. *Die Zeit* 51, 13 December.

Olk, T. (2006) Children in the 'Social Investment State'. Key note lecture at the concluding conference of COST A19 Children's Welfare, Roskilde, June.

Olk, T. and Wintersberger, H. (2007) Welfare State and Generational Order. In Wintersberger, H., Alanen, L., Olk, T. and Qvortrup, J. (eds.), *Childhood, Generational Order and the Welfare State: Exploring Children's Social and Economic Welfare*. Odense: University Press of Southern Denmark.

Qvortrup, J. (1995) From Useful to Useful: The Historical Continuity in Children's Constructive Participation. In A.-M. Ambert (ed.), *Sociological Studies of Children*. Greenwich, CT: JAI Press.

Qvortrup, J. (2000) Children's Schoolwork: Useful and Necessary. In Brood and Rozen, *Tijdsschrift voor de Geschiedenis van Sociale Bewegingen*, 4: 145–61.

Qvortrup, J. (2001) School-Work, Paid Work and the Changing Obligations of Childhood. In Mizen, P. and Pole, C., *Hidden Hands: International Perspectives on Children's Work and Labour* (pp. 91–107). London: Routledge and Falmer.

Rawls, J. (1973) *A Theory of Justice*. Oxford: Oxford University Press.

Ringen, S. (1997) *Citizens, Families and Reform*. Oxford: Clarendon Press.

Rostgaard, T. and Fridberg, T. (1998) *Caring for Children and Older People – A Comparison of European Policies and Practices*. Social Security in Europe 6. Copenhagen: The National Institute of Social Research.

Rubinstein, D. (1988) The Concept of Justice in Sociology. *Theory and Society* 17(4): 527–50.

Sgritta, G. B. (1994) The Generational Division of Welfare: Equity and Conflict. In Qvortrup, J., Bardy, M., Sgritta, G. B. and Wintersberger, H. (eds.), *Childhood Matters: Social Theory, Practice and Politics* (pp. 335–61). Aldershot: Avebury.

Titmuss, R. (1968) *Commitment to Welfare*. London: Unwin University Books.

Townsend, P. (ed.) (1970) *The Concept of Poverty*. London: Heinemann.

UNICEF (2000) *A League Table of Child Poverty in Rich Countries*. Florence: UNICEF.

Wintersberger, H. (2000) Family Citizenship or Citizenship for Children? Childhood Perspectives and Policies. In Cavanna, H. (ed.), *The New Citizenship of the Family. Comparative Perspectives* (pp. 174–88). Aldershot: Ashgate.

Wynn, M. (1972) *Family Policy*. Harmondsworth: Penguin Books.

Index

The index is in word-by-word order. Publication titles are indicated in italics eg: *Every Child Matters*

CPSIA information can be obtained at www.ICGtesting.com
Printed in the USA
237629LV00001B/37/P